'I'll See Myself Out, Thank You'

Books by Colin Brewer:

Psychiatric problems in women: some psychiatric aspects of abortion and contraception.

(With June Lait) Can social work survive?

(Editor). Treatment Options in Addiction: medical management of alcohol and opiate abuse.

'I'll See Myself Out, Thank You'

The arguments for medically-assisted rational suicide

Edited by
Colin Brewer and
Michael Irwin

SKYSCRAPER

Published by Skyscraper Publications Limited
Talton Edge, Newbold on Stour,
Warwickshire CV37 8TR

www.skyscraperpublications.com

First published 2015

A CIP catalogue record for this book is available
from the British Library.

ISBN-13: 978-0-9926270-9-6

Designed and typeset by
Chandler Book Design

Printed in the United Kingdom by
Latitude Press Ltd

CONTENTS

Preface   1

1. The story so far   9
   From King George V to Dignitas   9

2. The other end of the stethoscope   35
   Taking Control   35
   Death of a Campaigner   39
   An unfortunate way to die   44

3. Forgotten but not gone   49
   Voice from the Coalface   49
   Leave it to the patient   53

4. Dying with Dignitas   63
   An 'Emergency Exit'   63
   Fellow-travelling   69
   The balance of the mind   78
   An Instinct for Kindness   95

5. Four score years and then?   99
   Rational Old-Age Suicide.   99
   Labour and sorrow   106
   The noble act of suicide   108
   A ripe old age   113
   Death be my friend   120
   A right to autonomy   122
   Easeful death for the very elderly   130

6. Religion and Philosophy   135
   The Christian case   135
   Cancelling our captivity   139
   The ethics of assisted dying   144

A Basic Human Right …   150
Dementia, MARS and voluntary euthanasia   161
The 2014 House of Lords debate   174
The quality of death   183
Christian attitudes to suicide   185
Acts of suicide   192

7. A death in the family   197
Up the slippery slope   197
Laura and me   202
My mother the murderess.   206

8. The activist's tale   209
My Journey   209
'I'll see myself out thank you'   214

9. No laughing matter?   217
Mortality as fact   217
Ready for a good death   220
Vacation Parc   224
Glenn's last tape   229

10. Palliative care: The promise and the reality   249
Let's all be Friends At The End.   249
Assisted dying in Flanders: Summary   258
Putting people to sleep.   266

Appendix   267
Assisted dying – the current situation in Flanders:
euthanasia embedded in palliative care   267

Acknowledgments   285

Useful Contact Details   287

Index   293

Preface

Colin Brewer and Michael Irwin

This book is a collection of essays by people who want to have the same control over their deaths as they have had over their lives. It aims to guide readers through the medico-philosophical minefield that currently obstructs the road to freedom of choice for the inhabitants of our country in the closely related matters of assisted dying, assisted suicide, self-deliverance and voluntary euthanasia. The first two terms are often expanded to *medically*-assisted dying and *medically*-assisted suicide, though precisely who does the assisting seems less important to us than the arguments surrounding assistance. To help the debate, we propose a new term: Medically-Assisted Rational Suicide (MARS). It emphasises the typically calm, sober and unhurried decisions by at least averagely rational people to end their lives sooner than might otherwise happen 'naturally – i.e. without direct intervention. However, some deaths, though natural and inevitable, will only occur after several years of progressively more unpleasant and undignified physical and mental dissolution. Other cases involve the prospect of years of stable but intolerable disability. That is one reason why we are not so keen on the term 'assisted dying.'

We rather like 'deliverance' as a generic term to cover all the others. However people define them, they all involve individual citizens wishing, after long and careful consideration, to deliver themselves – or to be delivered – in a dignified way from varieties of unavoidable present or impending distress that they do not want to be forced to tolerate. This is not what most people immediately understand by the simple word 'suicide.' Another important feature of MARS is that it is always (and crucially) the individual patient himself or herself – *and nobody else* – who initiates the request and usually takes an active role in the deliverance process by swallowing all or part of the lethal medication, or by initiating a lethal infusion if swallowing is impossible. For convenience, we shall often use 'deliverance' and 'MARS' interchangeably in this and other chapters.

Whether a doctor injects some or all of the lethal medication (voluntary euthanasia) or whether he simply prescribes it for the patient to swallow (MARS) seems unimportant provided that death within a few minutes and without discomfort is what the patient wants. Both could reasonably be described as 'medically-assisted dying' but there may be some important stylistic and legal (or legalistic) differences between them. That is another reason why we dislike the term. Still, however the medication gets into the patient's bloodstream, it seems to us on a par with deciding whether to decorate a room yourself or to get an experienced artisan to do the job instead and perhaps rather better.

Anything else – including the common 'double effect' practice of giving terminally ill patients large doses of sedatives and analgesics, ostensibly for pain relief but in the usually unstated hope that they will quickly die – may be good medicine and not even unwelcome to the patient but in the absence of a specific and documented request, it is not, and cannot be, any of the things described above. It may, though, amount to involuntary euthanasia or something very close to it and it probably happens more often in Britain, where even voluntary euthanasia is illegal, than in the three Benelux countries, where it is not. However humane in its intention, this casuistic pharmaco-philosophical fudge deprives dying patients of the chance to say a formal farewell to their world. In an age of widely-dispersed families, it also minimises the opportunities for family members to arrange their commitments so that they too can be present at the death. We have regressed a long way from the traditional comforts and support of the death-bed scenes that were common until well into the 20th century. (Though as Quentin Crisp remarked about expiring in the presence of friends, 'We have then to die and be polite at the same time. It may not be easy'.)[1]

Historically, 'self-deliverance' was a term coined specifically to describe the bringing about of one's own death in this situation by taking responsibility for the whole procedure, including acquiring one or more of the means to do so. However, as with coming into the world, so in leaving it: people know that expertise is useful for a dignified exit and they increasingly want access to it. Some of them know that doctors – the most obvious source of this expertise – quite often use it when they themselves need deliverance. Why should doctors deny to their patients something that is a source of such comfort to that small, well-informed elite of which we are fortunate to be members? One of our medical contributors, retired surgeon Rodney Syme, positively rejoices in the peace of mind that this wonderful privilege gives him. Nevertheless, three physicians – Dr. Michael O'Donnell and Drs Ann and Klim McPherson – show how even being a doctor (or a doctor's spouse) does not necessarily prevent the terminally ill from experiencing the painful, undignified failures and limitations of palliative care. The experience is also very traumatic for family members who have to witness these failures.

Our own contributions cover the history of attempts to change the law in Britain, some practical and psychiatric aspects of medical documentation and travel to Switzerland for deliverance and the often rather neglected issue of people who want to die simply because they are getting steadily older and feebler and can see only further deterioration. The Society for Old Age Rational Suicide (SOARS) now exists for this large and growing constituency.

A chapter written by Dignitas staff-members gives the history of that organisation. (There are now two others that will also help non-residents of Switzerland.) Because we know that many doctors as well as actual or potential patients are interested in this topic, we include details (anonymised, of course) of the psychiatric assessment of some people who took the decision to obtain deliverance in Switzerland because it was not possible here. However, they are described in a fairly non-technical way that we hope will be easily understood by the unmedical. The playwright Chris Larner writes about taking his dying wife to Dignitas.

The contribution from the Rev. Prof. Paul Badham argues that Christianity, if it believes in a loving and compassionate god, is quite compatible with support for MARS. Unfortunately, St. Augustine's 4th century anathematisation of suicide as a worse sin even than murder is at least partly responsible, we suggest, for the frankly superstitious, irrational and punitive attitudes to suicide that were incorporated into English (though interestingly, not Scottish) law until well into the 19th and 20th centuries. We summarise the development of monotheistic and particularly Christian attitudes to suicide since Roman times and argue that they still exert a malign and atavistic influence on public debate, especially among our mainly religious opponents.

Our contributors are mainly people prominent in the public, political, academic, journalistic, medical and cultural life of Britain and (in two cases) of other countries – Belgium and Australia. Some (Jean Davies, Dr. Libby Wilson) are best known for their activism.

Melanie Reid gives us an insider's view – that of someone made paraplegic by a riding accident. At the very least, she demonstrates that by no means all disabled people deplore the prospect of having some choice. Chris Woodhead, a victim of motor neurone disease, represents another numerically important group for whom MARS is very much preferable to a slow death from creeping paralysis, often with choking and suffocation as the final terrors.

Others (Virginia Ironside, Angela Neustatter, Baroness Warnock, Peter Tatchell) write about their experiences of family members who managed – or more often failed – to obtain the dignified death that they hoped for.

Most contributors strongly invoke the principle of autonomy, even if they do not mention it by name. The more philosophically-focused contributions (Dr. Antony Lempert,

Prof. John Harris, Prof. Julian Savulescu, Prof. Anthony Grayling) examine it in some detail and add other important principles of medical ethics such as human rights, beneficence and non-maleficence.

Several contributors – Lord Avebury and the art critic Brian Sewell in particular – are well into old age. While currently getting more pleasure than pain from life, they would like to be able to make their exit when or even slightly before that positive balance becomes negative, rather than having to endure possibly several years of progressive and progressively more distressing bodily and mental decay. In short, they are typical of the sort of people who join SOARS. So are the journalist Minette Marrin and the writer Gillian Tindall. Like us, Gillian is a former committee member of the old Voluntary Euthanasia Society (VES) but feels that the rather restricted aim of the   Bill proposed by its successor, Dignity in Dying, which is being debated by the House of Lords in the 2014 – 2015 session, does not confront the central issue of personal choice.

People with advanced dementia or stroke may be unable to play any active role in their dying and may even be barely conscious but may have made it clear in Advance Decisions (formerly called Advance Directives) that in these situations, they would very much want their lives to be ended – actively if possible, passively if not. Baroness Warnock addresses this particularly knotty problem. Since surveys consistently show that many people worry even more about dying of dementia than they do about dying of cancer, we have included a chapter of our own about it. Unfortunately, dementia is a prospect for a steadily increasing proportion of our steadily ageing population.

The geneticist Steve Jones and the novelist Will Self provide characteristically quirky and humorous perspectives. Comedian Stewart Lee illustrates the issues involved in a short-story format.

Fortunately, only one contributor, the journalist Deborah Moggach, describes how someone was imprisoned for helping a fellow-human being, blind and suffering from cancer, complete a well-planned but technically inadequate attempt at self-deliverance. In sharp and rather touching contrast, Karl Sabbagh, in 'Glenn's Last Tape' tells the story of a Canadian art lecturer, Glenn Scott, disabled by motor neurone disease. Having sold his house, he hired a carer to take him in his wheelchair on a terminal Grand Tour of Europe, ending in his beloved Rome, where several of his friends joined him to make their farewells. He would have preferred not to die alone but did not want to put them at risk of prosecution. A video-camera recorded his successful overdose as evidence that nobody had assisted his self-deliverance.

In the last year or so, at least two British palliative care specialists have admitted that even the best hospices and palliative care cannot save a significant minority of the dying from unpleasant and undignified ends and now argue that palliative care should include the option of MARS. We have therefore reprinted a Belgian paper by Dr. Paul Vanden Berghe and other palliative care specialists, published originally in the *European Journal of Palliative Care,* that makes this case. It seems such an important matter that we have given it a separate introduction. Prof Badham's chapter on Christianity and MARS also notes the very significant fact that palliative care physicians in Oregon withdrew their opposition to that state's 'Death with Dignity Act', freely admitting that after eight years of its operation, none of the dire consequences they predicted had come to pass. This section – and the book – ends with the shortest contribution from veteran journalist Katharine Whitehorn. She makes the same point that unbiased researchers have reported as coming from the mouths of patients having decidedly bad deaths in hospices: that we wouldn't let this happen to the family dog or cat. Indeed, these days, we prosecute owners who do let it happen.

We think it cannot be long before a Benelux-style acceptance of deliverance happens here among palliative care clinicians and we cite research suggesting that the unusual over-representation of religious doctors and nurses in British palliative care is an important inhibiting factor. Those with strong and doctrinaire religious beliefs against deliverance are free to try to die as they prefer. We seek only the same freedom for those without such beliefs – who, as it happens, are the large majority in Britain.

Reference:

1.   Crisp Q. *Resident Alien*, London, Flamingo, 1997, p. 26

1

The story so far

From King George V to Dignitas

Colin Brewer

Some time in the early 1980s, I was invited to speak in a debate about voluntary euthanasia at the Medical Society of a Midlands city. My opponent, a classic bible-quoting fundamentalist, said the usual biblical things – only God can decide when someone is to die, voluntary euthanasia is just a euphemism for murder, suicide is a sin even if, regrettably, no longer a crime, diagnoses can be wrong, we mustn't play God, suffering and dying can be ennobling and spiritual experiences, hospices are the answer and anyway, nobody need suffer pain these days. I said the usual libertarian things – many people don't believe in a god, the comparison is not with murder but with assisted suicide (suicide being rarely mentioned and never specifically condemned in the bible), nobody should be forced to be ennobled or spiritualised if they don't want to be, hospice care often can't do much for loss of dignity and independence and even the best pain relief doesn't always work. During the subsequent audience discussion, an old, long-retired surgeon stood up. 'When I was a houseman', he said (and that must have been in the early 1930s) 'if we had any really terminal cancer patients, the consultant would usually say after the ward round 'I think those three should be dead by tomorrow, Perkins, don't you?' and they usually were.'

There must have been a lot of discussion in those days about euthanasia of both the voluntary kind and the involuntary-but-benevolent kind described by the old surgeon because in 1935, the Voluntary Euthanasia Society – the world's first such organization – was founded by several of the medical and social Great and Good, including the royal surgeon, Lord Moynihan. The royal physician, Lord Dawson of Penn, was not among them but we know what he thought about the matter because he told the House of Lords during a debate on legalizing voluntary euthanasia in 1936. There was no need for formal legalisation, he felt, because all good doctors did it anyway. In an era when most people died at home, that was probably true. We also know that he meant what he said because when his diaries surfaced in the 1980s, they recorded how he had dispatched the dying King-Emperor George V with a pharmacologically questionable but clearly effective mixture of morphine and cocaine injected straight into the Imperial jugular, in the presence of Queen Mary and the about-to-be King Edward VIII. Even better, the timing of the fatal infusion was chosen so that the announcement of his death would just make the next day's *Times* but be just too late for the lumpen-press. [1]

The education I received at my medical school was not a narrow one but I don't recall any specific instruction about the techniques of euthanasia. For that, I had to wait until my first house job in 1964 when Jake, the senior registrar, just happened to mention it when we were relaxing after a ward round. It was an orthopaedic unit, which in those days meant that the female ward was largely filled with old ladies with fractured hips. Most of them were still quite lively despite their age and made good recoveries but inevitably, some were well into senility and dementia. Equally inevitably, we used to ask ourselves whether it was a humane and sensible use of resources to operate on this sort of patient, most of whom were physically frail, but we operated all the same. Naturally, the post-operative mortality was quite high. A fairly recent paper suggests that it still is for this sort of patient and hasn't changed much over the last twenty-odd years. Even now, nearly a third of such patients aged over 90 die within the first month of admission.[2]

Jake said that there were two techniques you could use discreetly in hospital in situations where you felt that the kindest thing to do for an in-patient was to give them a quick and civilized death. (It was taken for granted that GPs, working in the privacy of the patient's bedroom, had a much wider range of techniques at their disposal.) One was to inject a quick syringeful of potassium chloride or calcium chloride into their drip to stop the heart but obviously, someone might notice you doing it and if the patient died soon after your visit, questions might be asked. So the alternative was to put nothing incriminating into the drip but just run it rather fast in the hope that it would overload the circulation and cause a fairly quick and humane death from cardiac failure or pneumonia. This conversation took place in the nursing office with nurses present and there was nothing furtive about it. It seemed entirely reasonable and nobody said that this was one oral tradition we could do without. I imagine that similar conversations took place in hundreds of other wards at that time. They probably still do, though perhaps more discreetly.

The first time that the question of using one of Jake's options arose was when we admitted a woman of 95 who had been bedbound and severely demented for the past five years. She had an epileptic fit in bed and her bones were so soft that the convulsion snapped a femur in mid-shaft. We could operate and hold the ends together with a metal plate or we could put her in traction for twelve weeks. Given her very frail state, the likely outcomes were a choice between a relatively quick death from surgery or a protracted one from bedsores and pneumonia. Both were probably quite painful ways to die and either way, her quality and appreciation of life would be rather minimal. The consultant opted for surgery. He was not the sort of man to discuss ethical issues but I suspect he thought that it would be the quickest way to end her almost vegetative existence. I think it was the ward sister who first wondered aloud whether there was any way we could save her from this pointless therapeutic suffering and we decided to try. We lacked the courage to use potassium chloride so we resorted to the rapid drip technique but she was restless and confused and the drips kept blocking. Because she was in pain, we could legitimately give her opiates but although we gave her a generous dose, it had little effect. She had her surgery and died three days later. Today, greatly improved anaesthesia and greatly reduced anaesthetic and surgical mortality would probably have kept her alive for longer but would not have improved her awareness – or made her grateful for the improvements.

A similar situation arose with a patient who was admitted after yet another stroke worsened her arteriosclerotic or 'multi-infarct' dementia. Again, nurses and junior doctors thought that an early release would be a mercy and again we tried and failed. Even in general practice, on the only occasion when I had to deal with a very terminal cancer patient who wanted me to end his sufferings, he merely slept well for a night after I injected what I hoped was a lethal dose of opiates and sedative anti-emetics. He gave me a rather hurt look when I visited the next day, though he died the day after without any further intervention. Do not make the unhistorical mistake of judging this style of paternalistic medical decision-making by the rather different standards of today's post-'Rights Revolution' era. Personally, I was always keen to involve patients and their families in discussions about their care but I was perhaps in a minority at the time and paternalism was both routine and not always resented. There are still plenty of patients who say, in effect: 'Doctor, I think you know best and certainly better than I do. I'm happy to leave it to you to decide.' As it happens, I tell my accountant much the same thing.

I wrote about these failures of will and technique in *World Medicine* in about 1978. It provoked a lot of letters, mostly from religious readers but it also led to a telephone call from Scotland Yard. A weird anti-abortion group – weird because they claimed to be non-religious – had written to the Director of Public Prosecutions saying that in my article,

I had clearly admitted to the attempted murder of three patients and what was he going to do about it. I expect the DPP groaned and rolled his eyes but he also asked the Yard to investigate. When they phoned and explained that they wanted to interview me, I was just about to go on holiday but the sergeant was very nice about it. No problem; it would wait until my return. This was reassuring – at least they didn't want to take away my passport – but only slightly. The interview, when it came, was very civilized. The Medical Defence Union (my professional insurers) provided an advisor who took the view that whatever I had done, it came under the heading of clinical discretion. (What would they say today?) I didn't deny anything and although after a decade I genuinely couldn't remember any of the patients' names, I gave the Yard enough information, including the name of a GP cousin for whom I had been working at the time, so that they could easily have tracked down the patient with terminal cancer. They don't appear to have tried very hard. My cousin confirmed that they never contacted him.

A few weeks later, the sergeant phoned me. They had made a decision and would I please come to the Yard so that they could tell me. His tone didn't suggest that I ought to pack a spongebag and a few good books. Sure enough, the DPP was going to take no action because there was 'insufficient evidence.' This little ritual over, we had a relaxed discussion during which the sergeant showed an intelligent interest in the subject. He said that if he ever got into such a state himself, he hoped that he would be treated by a doctor like me and he added a bit of friendly but superfluous advice (superfluous because my career in adult psychiatry and addiction medicine involved two specialties where

the question of voluntary euthanasia hardly ever arises).
'Don't use insulin or barbiturates, sir. It makes life very
difficult for the Director of Public Prosecutions.'

Soon after my encounter with Scotland Yard, the VES asked
if I would be willing to join their committee as a co-opted
member. The committee members were a mixed lot. Some of
the older ones seemed to have been there almost since 1935
but there was some comparatively young blood, including
Mary-Rose Barrington, an amusingly waspish solicitor, the
writer Gillian Tindall, the broadcaster and former Liberal
MP Ludovic Kennedy and Wilfred Brown, a life-peer and
former industry minister in the 1964 Wilson government, who
later became the chairman. When asked for my thoughts,
I said that I would be pleasantly surprised if we managed
to get the law changed in my lifetime, despite consistently
overwhelming support in public opinion surveys (how right
I was!) and that we ought therefore to consider publishing
a booklet telling people how to end their lives themselves if
they felt that there was no acceptable alternative. All doctors,
I pointed out, had this knowledge and it was a great comfort,
so what could be wrong with sharing it with our patients?

This idea was well-received by most of the committee
though some of the older ones were less happy. When it was
announced that the proposed booklet would be discussed
at the next Annual General Meeting – normally a sleepy
and poorly attended affair – there was great excitement.
Unprecedented numbers (about 250) attended and for
the first time, TV cameras filmed the AGM, concentrating
entirely on the voting for a motion to proceed with the
idea. It was carried by a large majority. During the next
few months, the membership, which had never been more

than about 2500, rose to around 10,000. I wrote most of the proposed booklet myself, assisted by a VES member who was a pharmacologist. The committee added a few general and cautionary paragraphs and the writer Arthur Koestler, one of our several distinguished vice-presidents, wrote the preface. This is part of what he wrote:

'The whole concept of death as a condition would be more acceptable if dying would be less horrendous and squalid. Thus euthanasia is more than the administration of a lethal analgesic. It is a means of reconciling individuals with their destiny. ... But as the progress toward legislation will be slow, a matter of years or even decades, the publication of a practical guide to 'auto-euthanasia' will, we hope, bring peace of mind to many who would otherwise despair. There is only one prospect worse than being chained to an intolerable existence: the nightmare of a botched attempt to end it. I know that I am speaking in the name of many (some of them personal friends) who tried and failed – or who don't dare to try for fear of failure.'

Within a few months, we were ready to go but some members of the society and the committee were so opposed to the idea that an extraordinary general meeting had to be called, under the VES constitution, to settle the issue. It was a wonderful demonstration of democracy in action. Every inch of floor and window-sill in the hall was occupied. The old guard were swept away and new committee members were elected who said that they would be prepared to face prison if the government tried to prevent publication. (Recognising that sacrifices of this kind are better deferred to the end of one's professional life rather than in the middle, as mine was, the committee graciously allowed me to step down until after publication.) However, all this democracy was causing delay. Scotland – more specifically, the Scottish legal system – came to the rescue.

The law under which we might have been prosecuted was a fairly new one. Until 1961, attempting suicide was a crime punishable – and frequently punished, right up to its decriminalisation – by imprisonment. When it was finally abolished, a new offence of aiding, abetting or counselling a suicide was introduced with penalties of up to 14 years imprisonment. There was a possibility that our proposed booklet might breach that law. However, in Scotland – which has a separate legal system – suicide had never been a crime and therefore there was no specific offence of aiding or abetting equivalent to the English one. The Scottish branch of the VES decided on a unilateral declaration of independence and with a lot of very willing collaboration from us, they were able to publish their own booklet – 'How to die with dignity' – just in time for our next AGM in 1980. It was the first such guide in the world. Enlarged and regularly updated, it remains in print as 'Five Last Acts' unprosecuted and available to members of the Scottish society, which anyone living outside Scotland can also join.[3] It can even be bought on Amazon.

Mary-Rose suggested using the term 'self-deliverance' instead of 'euthanasia' – voluntary or otherwise – which had acquired some undesirable connotations since the Nazi regime's decidedly involuntary programmes. It was used by the Scots in their publication and we called our own booklet, which came out a few months later, the 'Guide to Self-Deliverance.' It also had more positive connotations than 'suicide', as we noted. ' 'Self-deliverance' is not a euphemism.

...There is nothing soft-edged about 'self-deliverance': its overtones are as precisely delimited as those of the more familiar 'suicide.' It implies that the person dies by his or her own hand, with a peaceful mind and for reasons that those closest will endorse. They will know that they were not intended to feel guilt or grief, but rather to share sympathetically in a final display of courage and good sense.' We also quoted from the Stoic philosopher Epictetus, the poet and divine John Donne ('The keys of my prison are in mine own hands') and Nietzsche ('The thought of suicide is a great consolation: with the help of it one has got through many a bad night'). More memorably, Mary-Rose also suggested that we should change our name to 'EXIT', which we duly did. Several other societies had sprung up in various countries and several of them adopted the same title. It was changed back to VES a few years later but the society is still often referred to as EXIT. Such was – and still is – the level of public support for voluntary euthanasia that there were quite a few EXIT cartoons, none of them unfriendly. I think that being able to joke about death is a good sign and Private Eye's 'New last words' cartoon series keeps up the tradition.

VES Scotland, based in Edinburgh, kept its new EXIT title but in 2000, a split occurred. Scottish EXIT continued to provide self-deliverance information to a worldwide audience but many of its members in the Glasgow area established FATE (Friends At The End) which does not provide that sort of information but campaigns for a change in the law. In particular, it very actively supports the efforts of Margo MacDonald, a member of the Scottish parliament until her death from Parkinson's disease in April 2014, whose Assisted Suicide (Scotland) Bill is being discussed in that legislature (as of September 2014). Unlike Lord Falconer's bill, it would legalise MARS for both terminally-ill individuals and for those who are suffering unbearably from a progressive life-shortening illness.

The publication of the two Guides received mixed reviews but many of them were favourable. Both the *British Medical Journal* and the *Lancet* said nice things about them, as did several newspapers. Some people naturally worried that it would lead to a sharp increase in suicide using the recommended methods, especially by the young and impulsive. I thought that this was unlikely and predicted as much in an article I wrote for *World Medicine* at the time. First of all, nobody could buy a guide unless they had been a member of the society for at least three months. Secondly, I thought that the existence of the Guides might help to make doctors more cautious about prescribing the sort of sedatives and antidepressants that featured in so many overdoses and suicide attempts. My prediction subsequently turned out to be even more correct than I could have guessed, for rates of suicide by overdoses declined sharply from the early 1980s, as the epidemiologist Prof. Richard Farmer and I subsequently noted.[4] Nevertheless, we worried that some love-sick teenager would be found dead with, as it were, the Guide in one hand and a semi-literate but impassioned 'farewell cruel world' note in the other. However, we never heard of any such cases and certainly not in the first few high-profile months following publication. The best-known user of the 'Guide' was probably our vice-president, Arthur Koestler. When he wrote the preface, he was in reasonable health for someone pushing eighty but he was developing chronic lymphatic leukaemia and steadily

worsening Parkinsonism and decided to call it a day before
the illnesses took that option out of his hands. Numerous
polls confirm that most people in Britain can sympathise or
at least empathise with Koestler. Here is his suicide note

'To whom it may concern.

The purpose of this note is to make it unmistakably clear
that I intend to commit suicide by taking an overdose of
drugs without the knowledge or aid of any other person.
The drugs have been legally obtained and hoarded over a
considerable period. Trying to commit suicide is a gamble
the outcome of which will be known to the gambler only if
the attempt fails, but not if it succeeds. Should this attempt
fail and I survive it in a physically or mentally impaired
state, in which I can no longer control what is done to
me, or communicate my wishes, I hereby request that I
be allowed to die in my own home and not be resuscitated
or kept alive by artificial means. I further request that my
wife, or a physician, or any friend present, should invoke
habeas corpus against any attempt to remove me forcibly
from my house to hospital.

My reasons for deciding to put an end to my life are
simple and compelling: Parkinson's Disease and the slow-
killing variety of leukaemia. I kept the latter a secret even
from intimate friends to save them distress. After a more or
less steady physical decline over the last years, the process
has now reached an acute state with added complications
which make it advisable to seek self-deliverance now, before
I become incapable of making the necessary arrangements.
I wish my friends to know that I am leaving their company
in a peaceful frame of mind, with some timid hopes for a
de-personalised after-life beyond due confines of space, time

and matter and beyond the limits of our comprehension. This 'oceanic feeling' has often sustained me at difficult moments, and does so now, while I am writing this.

What makes it nevertheless hard to take this final step is the reflection of the pain it is bound to inflict on my surviving friends, above all my wife Cynthia. It is to her that I owe the relative peace and happiness that I enjoyed in the last period of my life – and never before.'

Koestler died in March 1983. The note was dated June 1982. Below it appeared the following:

'Since the above was written in June 1982, my wife decided that after thirty-four years of working together she could not face life after my death.'

Further down the page appeared Cynthia's own farewell note:

'I fear both death and the act of dying that lies ahead of us. I should have liked to finish my account of working for Arthur – a story which began when our paths happened to cross in 1949. However, I cannot live without Arthur, despite certain inner resources.

Double suicide has never appealed to me, but now Arthur's incurable diseases have reached a stage where there is nothing else to do.'

From what I saw of the Koestlers during our discussions about the 'Guide', Cynthia's decision to join him in death was not altogether surprising. She obviously worshipped him – treating Arthur rather as I imagine his servants treat the Pope – and evidently felt that nothing would compensate for him after he died. This sort of attitude is quite common among older married couples, who sometimes engage in 'double exit' suicide pacts when both (or even just one of them) are beginning to deteriorate, even though well short of dementia or immobility. It can hardly be ruled out just because one partner is younger and fitter. To those who say that 'she shouldn't have done it' because she would probably have adapted given time, there are at least two answers. One is that people *don't* always adapt and may not want to take the risk of spending a year or two in purgatory only to find that they still feel very unhappy. The second is that the concept of freedom includes the freedom to make mistakes about your own life and death.

The first edition of the 'Guide' sold out in a few months and we planned a second, updated edition. The government hadn't intervened or threatened prosecution thus far but they eventually asked a judge if he could give a 'declaratory judgment' as to its legality. The judge refused to do so and said that if the government wanted to know if it was illegal, they would have to prosecute us and take their chances in court, as would we. He was kind enough to say that if a book of this sort had to exist, it was difficult to think of one that could be better written but for various reasons, the society decided not to go ahead with the plan. The main reason was that people could always get hold of the Scottish version if they wanted information and a few similar guides had become available in other countries. The former *Sunday Times* journalist Derek Humphry was planning to publish 'Final Exit', describing how he had helped his wife to end her life when she was becoming terminally ill with cancer, and also how other people had done similar things. It included much of the information that was in the 'Guide' but would paradoxically be available at any bookshop. When it appeared, it topped the non-fiction best-seller list for several weeks. Mary-Rose, Ludovic and

I wrote to the *Times*, asking whether the government was going to be consistent and either sue Derek or confirm that it wouldn't sue us if we republished. Not surprisingly, they declined to respond: but they didn't sue him.

Despite the welcome growth in hospice and palliative care facilities, the VES – which changed its name in 2005 to Dignity in Dying, with the narrower aim of securing MARS for terminally ill people expected to die within six months – gets more and more requests for help and advice. One day, I had an urgent phone call from them to ask if I could help a woman who had been 'sectioned' under the Mental Health Act and was being threatened with ECT (Electro-Convulsive Treatment) against her will because she was trying to starve herself to death. I went to see her straight away. Susan was a divorcée in her early fifties and had enjoyed being a teacher until two strokes, caused by hypertension, ended both her work and her sporting hobbies, which included scuba diving. The second stroke also left her largely confined to bed and after a year or so, she decided that enough was enough. There were no financial problems, she was well looked-after in a good care home and her grown-up children visited regularly but even they could understand that life for this strong-minded and still articulate woman wasn't much fun. They didn't want her to die but they were prepared to support her if that was what she wanted to do. A few months previously, a psychiatrist had concluded that she wasn't suffering from a depressive illness, just understandably fed up with life and the high probability of further strokes.

Accepting that most of the standard methods of self-deliverance – overdoses, hanging, car exhausts, shooting, drowning, even defenestration – wouldn't be possible for her, she decided to use the only remaining method: starvation. This requires real determination and is clearly not for the ambivalent. At first, the care-home matron and the GP were sympathetic. So, initially, was the psychiatrist summoned by the GP to rule out once more a treatable depression but at some point, everyone started to get frightened. When Susan hadn't eaten or drunk anything for a few days, they forced her to be admitted to an NHS psychiatric ward and since she refused antidepressant drugs, they were indeed proposing to give her ECT within a day or two. I examined her in the hospital and got the family round as well. Realising that this case might become very public and that I would have to be particularly sure of my facts, I searched diligently for signs of depression but really couldn't find any. Neither was there any evidence of a significant personality change, as sometimes happens after brain damage from strokes or other causes. Supported by the family, I said that if the hospital went ahead with ECT, the Society would use every legal and journalistic option to frustrate them. With Susan's and the family's permission, I told the story to John Illman, a leading medical journalist and one of my former editors, who wrote about it in the next issue of the *Observer*. Faced with this two-pronged attack, the hospital backed down. Provided that she took fluids and vitamins, they would allow her to starve to death on one of the medical wards. This was a rather odd compromise but better than forcing her to have ECT. Susan gained her self-deliverance eventually. Because of her acceptance of fluids under duress, it took her two months to die. Without fluids, death would have released her in a week or two at most.

People like Susan with severe physical handicaps may

obviously find it difficult to end their lives without assistance
but even those who retain their mobility can find that
carefully laid plans for a civilized do-it-yourself death at the
right time are frustrated by the messy unpredictabilities of
life itself. One of my neighbours in London, Hugh, was an
amiable old bachelor in his late seventies. During the war,
he had apparently done brave and exciting things in enemy
territory and when he retired, he was employed for many
years as the secretary of one of the smarter London clubs.
Perhaps a military background, with its traditional concern
for tidiness and good organization, makes people particularly
attuned to the idea of not lingering on in an undignified and
malodorous state. Hugh was hospitable and a good cook
despite increasing weight and declining health. He knew
of my involvement with the VES and when he invited me
round to dinner, he often referred to his hope that when he
died, it would be at home and not a protracted business. A
couple of times, he showed me his fine collection of vintage
barbiturates and sought reassurance that the quantity was
sufficient and that they had not deteriorated. Hugh had
several bottles of pills and capsules, mostly with hand-written
labels dating from the 1960s. I told him that he had enough
to poison half of St John's Wood and that old tablets, like
old cartridges, usually worked well enough if they were kept
dry and cool.

Sadly, his soldierly plan to swallow the whole lot when the
time was right (doubtless washed down with his best claret
after giving a really good party) turned into a civilian debacle.
He started to become mildly demented and intermittently
confused. After some hospital admissions, he went into a
rather classy and expensive old peoples' home. His furniture

went into store but he had not been able to retrieve his colourful stash of blue-and-red Tuinal and bright orange Seconal capsules before it did so. He wasn't mobile enough to go to the depository to collect them himself and he couldn't really ask anyone else to get them for him. In any case, he was increasingly vague about where exactly he had last hidden them. When I visited him in the home, he sometimes lamented the loss of his exit strategy, but as he became more demented, he mentioned it less and less. Eventually, and after several strokes, he had the sort of sad and gradual dying that many people have and that most people hope to avoid. With any luck, at least he wouldn't have been able to recall much of it.

Although legalisation may still be some way off in Britain, there have been several useful developments. The judgment in the case of Tony Bland, a boy who was in a persistent vegetative state for several years after suffering massive anoxic brain damage in the Hillsborough football crowd disaster, established some very important principles, which was why it was so fiercely opposed by the anti-MARS brigade. It was accepted, for example, that if your brain has ceased to function apart from a few physiological brain-stem reflexes maintaining only blood pressure and respiration, you cease to be a human being for most practical purposes. If someone has previously expressed a wish not to remain physiologically alive when they are psychologically and socially dead, their wishes may and even must be respected. It is not yet legal to end such an existence quickly and cleanly by giving a lethal injection but it is acceptable to end it by cutting off the supply of food and water, thus causing a slow and, for onlookers, distressing death by starvation or dehydration.

It is also legal to sedate the patient heavily while waiting for death, provided that there is a decent interval between the start of sedation and the last pathetic heartbeat. This is, of course, a bit of medical and judicial casuistry, as Lord Browne-Wilkinson, one of the High Court judges who made the decision, accepted. '...the conclusion I have reached will appear to some to be almost irrational. How can it be lawful to allow a patient to die slowly, though painlessly, over a period of weeks from lack of food but unlawful to produce his immediate death by a lethal injection, thereby saving his family from yet another ordeal to add to the tragedy that has already struck them? I find it difficult to find a moral answer to that question. But it is undoubtedly the law and nothing I have said casts doubt on the proposition that the doing of a positive act with the intention of ending life is and remains murder.'[5]

His fellow appeal judge Lord Mustill wrote: 'The acute unease which I feel about adopting this way through the legal and ethical maze is I believe due in an important part to the sensation that however much the terminologies may differ, the ethical status of the two courses of action is for all relevant purposes indistinguishable. By dismissing this appeal [against allowing him to die] I fear that your Lordships' House may only emphasise the distortions of a legal structure which is already both morally and intellectually misshapen. Still, the law is there and we must take it as it stands.' He also conceded that: '...when the intellectual part of the [appeal process] is complete and the decision-maker has to choose the factors which he will take into account, attach relevant weights to them and then strike a balance, the judge is no better equipped, though no worse, than anyone else. In the end it is a matter of personal choice, dictated by his or her background, upbringing, education, convictions and temperament. Legal expertise gives no special advantage here.'

The case of 'Miss B'[6] set further precedents. This former social worker suffered a haemorrhage into the spinal cord in her neck, which left her paralysed, helpless and dependent on tube-feeding. Since her brain was unaffected, she was cognitively intact and able to express an opinion. Her opinion was that the doctors should stop administering the food and fluids that were maintaining her entirely uncongenial existence and should allow her to die passively if they could not legally or in practice end her life actively. No doubt she would have welcomed a generous dose of something to ease her passing but if not, then she was willing to do it the hard way. Despite this clear indication of her views and a psychiatric opinion that she was not suffering from a mental illness, let alone a treatable one, her consultant physician continued to treat her, and thus to keep her alive, against her will and for this he was specifically censured by the court when Miss B sought legal protection from his serious failure of empathy. Miss B was transferred to another hospital with a consultant less in thrall to his own ideology, where her tubes were duly disconnected and she died in a few days. This legal outcome greatly strengthens the standing of Advance Decisions and although doctors still often ignore them or deliberately interpret them to suit their own philosophy rather than the presumed or stated philosophy of the patient, the criticism of Miss B's doctor should be a salutary reminder of whose life it is anyway.

Meanwhile, in The Netherlands, the legislation permitting

voluntary euthanasia was confirmed and formalized in 2002. In many cases, Dutch voluntary euthanasia is virtually the same as MARS because the patient often starts the process by swallowing a lethal or near-lethal dose of sedatives. The main difference is that once the patient is unconscious, the doctor then usually administers a coup de grace by injection that stops the breathing quickly and thus minimizes distress for watching relatives. It has shown itself to be highly acceptable to most of the Dutch electorate in a number of elections and to successive Dutch governments of various political persuasions. Repeated allegations by the Leviticus Lobby that such legislation undermines the public's trust in doctors is contradicted by the fact that Dutch GPs have a higher approval rating than those of almost any other country. Similarly, although the local and national US hospice movement initially tried very hard to block or overturn the law that permitted medically-assisted suicide in the state of Oregon, after about eight years, they dropped all their objections (as described in Chapter 6 by Prof. Badham) because none of their dire predictions had come to pass.

In Australia's Northern Territory during 1995-6, voluntary euthanasia was made fully and explicitly legal even before it achieved that status in The Netherlands, and several terminally ill patients (including a nurse) seized the opportunity, one of them even travelling there from her hospice bed in another state. However, although the Federal system allows Australian states a lot of legislative autonomy, Northern Territory was not a full state and its anomalous constitutional status allowed the Leviticus Lobby in the Federal Parliament to organize and to overturn the democratically expressed and clear majority will of NT's legislature. Every standard trick in the book was used in their campaign and one or two new and imaginative ones, such as the suggestion that the legislation was aimed at exterminating the NT's substantial Aboriginal population.

Now that Dame Cicely Saunders, the iron-willed doyenne of the Hospice movement, has gone to her eternal rest, some of her pupils may come out of their closets, in the sense of being more honest about what they actually do. 'Terminal sedation' is the current phrase but what it boils down to is that even if you are in great pain and distress despite the best that palliative care can do, the hospices will still not arrange things so that your friends and relations can come and say a last goodbye on a convenient date and then attend your funeral a day or two later. However, they will sometimes now consent to administer a generous cocktail of sedatives designed to keep you unconscious while your respiration gets gradually weaker and – with luck – your lungs fill with secretions leading to death in a few days. Terminal sedation may also be incorporated into the curiously-named (and currently being reformed) Liverpool Care Pathway for patients thought to be near death anyway. Religiously-inclined physicians, who are over-represented in British palliative care, are more likely to be unhappy about using terminal sedation – and also about discussing end-of-life decisions with patients themselves.[7]

However, even an abbreviated dying process can still be difficult and distressing for family members. It was for trying to relieve their distress that Dr. Nigel Cox found himself facing a charge of attempted murder and being convicted of it by a tearful and clearly troubled jury. In 1993, Dr. Cox was a consultant rheumatologist at a hospital in Winchester. People do not usually die of arthritis – even the rheumatoid variety – and therefore rheumatologists typically have little need to consider MARS, or other 'end of life decisions', as a clinical issue. However, the rheumatoid process can sometimes affect other organs and Dr. Cox had one patient whose liver was badly affected and who had severe anaemia – necessitating numerous blood transfusions – in addition to crippling, painful and treatment-resistant arthritis. She and Dr. Cox had a good and lengthy clinical relationship. Eventually, with the support of her family, she decided that enough was enough. The family gathered round her hospital bed and Dr. Cox administered – or caused to be administered – a large dose of heroin. She did not stop breathing so he administered some more. The breathing became slower but did not stop altogether and did not look as if it would do so soon. Everyone – including Dr. Cox – was getting rather distressed by this time. If Dr. Cox had been better informed about opiates, he would simply have given even larger doses, following the protocol recommended by my nice sergeant at Scotland Yard and the generally hypocritical and casuistical doctrine of 'double effect.' ('I know this dose may kill her but that's not what I intend.') Heroin will always stop the respiration if you give enough of it but some people are amazingly tolerant, especially if they have been taking opiates regularly.

Perhaps Dr. Cox had also been taught by someone like Jake. At any rate, he eventually took a syringe, filled it with potassium chloride solution and injected it into the nearly-dead body of his patient. Her heart quickly stopped beating and the family relaxed. Like the good doctor that he was, Dr. Cox then recorded in her notes exactly what he had done. All the ward staff knew what was going on. History does not record how many of them agreed totally with his actions that day, how many agreed partially and how many disagreed totally but evidently none of them thought that a crime had been committed of such seriousness that it had to be reported to the police. Except for one nurse, a Roman Catholic. Not surprisingly, the local version of my nice Scotland Yard policeman found Dr. Cox's successful coup de grace harder to ignore than my own failed attempts. Or perhaps he shared the views of the Catholic nurse – who was soon reviled and ostracized by her colleagues. The dead woman's family were furious and further distressed when Dr. Cox was arrested and charged.

At his trial, Dr. Cox was found guilty of attempted murder but he did not go to prison for this very serious offence. The judge put him on probation. The General Medical Council administered a barely audible slap to his wrists. His hospital, which had suspended him on full pay, quickly unsuspended him and allowed him to return to his grateful and doubtless mostly admiring patients. Such outcomes reflect the inconsistent and illogical attitudes that are the inevitable consequence of too much religion and too little philosophy. This point was nicely made in the *British Medical Journal* by Carl Elliott, a professor of medicine, ethics, and law, who wrote a short paper called 'Philosopher-assisted suicide'.[8] 'Philosophers have...argued...that it is difficult to make rational moral distinctions between withdrawal of life sustaining treatment, which doctors have come to believe is ethically acceptable, and active euthanasia, which many doctors apparently believe is not. Philosophers rather than doctors reflect the views of the public, which in many countries seem sympathetic to the idea of physician-assisted death.' Prof Elliott's suggestion, perhaps slightly tongue-in-cheek, was that if doctors were unable to master the relevant philosophical principles, perhaps the problem should be handed over to philosophers, who could soon master the relatively simple principles and techniques of medically-assisted rational suicide and voluntary euthanasia, up to and including lethal injection.

MARS is now legal in Colombia, Luxembourg and Belgium as well as the Netherlands and physician-supported accompanied suicide is legal in Switzerland. MARS, in the sense of allowing doctors to give a prescription for lethal medication to terminally ill patients, was legalized in Oregon in 1996 and has since been legalized in the states of Washington and Vermont. Case law probably supports it in Montana. A well-financed religious campaign narrowly defeated it recently in Massachusetts. In almost all western countries, majority public opinion consistently supports at least some relaxation in laws that fail to make a distinction between benevolent and malevolent assistance. When the Suicide Bill of 1961 was debated in the House of Lords, Lord Denning argued that 'you cannot aid and abet a crime when it is no longer a crime. Indeed, it is illogical to have this clause.' For most crimes, motive and intent are crucial. Mary-Rose suggested a useful analogy. If you are walking in the country and you see a couple having energetic alfresco sex two hundred yards away, you can't be sure whether what you are seeing is rape or consensual sex. From a distance, they can look very similar but if you were to ask the participants, you would soon discover the difference. Selling insurance isn't a crime but selling insurance that people don't need is very definitely a crime with serious penalties, as several banks have recently discovered. The same principle should apply to MARS, which is why the law in Switzerland and other countries specifically distinguishes between benevolent and malevolent assistance. It's malevolence that is bad and potentially criminal; not assistance.

References:

1. Ramsay, J. H. R. A king, a doctor, and a convenient death. *British Medical Journal*, 1994,308:1445

2. Roberts S, Goldacre M. Time trends and demography of mortality after fractured neck of femur in an English population 1968-98: database study. *British Medical Journal* 2003;327: 771-4

3. See website: www.euthanasia.cc

4. Brewer C, Farmer R. Self poisoning in 1984: a prediction that didn't come true. *British Medical Journal* 1985 Feb 2;290(6465):391.

5. www.bailii.org/uk/cases/UKHL/1992/5.html Also *Airedale NHS Trust v. Bland*, [1993] 1 All ER 858 (H.L.)

6. Slowther A. The case of Ms B and the 'right to die' J Med Ethics. 2002 August; 28(4): 243.

7. Seale C. J Med Ethics. 2010 Nov;36(11):677-82.

8. Elliott C. Philosopher-assisted suicide and euthanasia BMJ, 1996; 313: 1088-9

2

The other end of the stethoscope

Taking Control

Ann McPherson,
founder of 'Healthcare Professionals for Assisted Dying.'

At a cancer check-up in early June 2009, I got the news I most dreaded. The tumour doctors had discovered in my pancreas three years earlier, and from which I'd been free for two wonderful years, had returned and spread to my lung. 'We can't say for sure how long you will live, but you know as well as I do the prospects of living for more than a few months are not great,' my oncologist — a friend as well as a colleague — told me. I was dumbstruck, unable to think beyond the horror of sharing the news with my family. Telling Klim, my medical scientist husband of forty years, was the easy part.

'Bad news,' I told him, catching him on his mobile. 'The scan results have shown that it's come back.' I didn't need to say anything else. We knew the statistics: only three per cent of people with pancreatic cancer are alive five years after the initial diagnosis. The latest news strongly suggested I was not going to be one of those three per cent. Indeed, we knew I'd be lucky if I survived long enough to spend the summer with my family. And it was the thought of them — my three children and their families — that was breaking my heart. I could only think of the milestones I'd miss in the lives of my kids, now in their 30s, and my five grandchildren. My children were home for a family celebration that weekend, so I was able to talk to them alone, passing on this saddest of news — and finding comfort in their loving responses.

It was then I confronted my feelings about dying. I was, I realised, as frightened as anyone else at the thought of my impending death. For the past four decades, as a GP in Oxford, I'd looked after scores of people with terminal illness. So I understood the risk of spending my last hours in pain, perhaps unable to breathe properly or bereft of dignity. I vividly recall one patient dying of cancer, enduring a slow death in a hospice. I've also seen how a patient's painful or uncomfortable death can lead to the family falling out or feeling that they themselves failed their loved one. Too often, a bad death blights the memory of a parent or spouse for years afterwards. Faced with a painful death, I wanted to take control of my final hours. More importantly, I wanted to be able to protect my family from seeing me suffer.

But since 1962, the law has threatened doctors who assist patients to die — though until recently, it's been widely assumed that doctors have the option to help terminally ill patients on their way, if that's what is wanted. If that sometimes happened before the Harold Shipman scandal, it's now a rare occurrence. The fallout of his wickedness was a tightening up of the regulations surrounding doctors prescribing patients drugs, making it hard for them to provide help in the timing of their patients' dying. I remember feeling helpless as the patient died that slow death in a hospice; she'd stockpiled some drugs she hoped would let her take control over the time of her passing, but had developed a blockage in her bowel, which meant she couldn't take the pills. Consequently, she had to endure a lingering death — against her will.

Let me be clear, assisted dying is about supporting a normal process — it is not assisted 'suicide', with its connotations of despair, weakness and failure. When I was told my cancer had returned eighteen months ago, multiple sclerosis sufferer Debbie Purdy was fighting a legal battle to be allowed to be accompanied by her husband to the Swiss clinic, Dignitas, to die, without fear that he would be prosecuted. When she won that right, I was only too pleased for her victory. Yet for me, such a journey was not an option. I certainly wanted to die surrounded by family — but in Britain, preferably in my own bed, in my own home. I decided to do whatever I could to ensure that, should the need arise, a doctor would be able to give me medication to end my agony — rather than me having secretly to stockpile drugs that might not even work properly.

It seemed — and still does seem — unjust that such a choice is not available to the 70 to 80 per cent of the public who say in surveys that they want such a choice. Even more unfair is that assisted dying is forbidden largely because those making the legal and political decisions tend to have a vested interest professionally against assisted dying or have particular religious views. I felt incensed that the British Medical Association, which claims to represent doctors, opposes physician-assisted suicide without having canvassed its members.

When I went public with my bad news in the *British Medical Journal*, the response to my article was wonderful, with hundreds of doctors emailing me to support the stand I'd taken on assisted dying. But there was also hostility from palliative care specialists who felt a campaign for assisted death was an accusation that their branch of medicine has failed. Such a view is absurd to me, as a grateful recipient of palliative care. I'd be in considerable pain if my GP didn't prescribe the morphine I take almost every day. Far from being opposed to palliative care, I see assisted dying as one part of this important speciality.

There is also the 'slippery slope' argument, the view that legalising assisted dying could put pressure on vulnerable people whose death might be convenient for their relatives. I agree this is a critical challenge for legislators. But it has been done. In the U.S. state of Oregon, physician-assisted suicide is permitted when a patient has been declared terminally ill by two doctors and requested lethal drugs three times.

The changes I want will mean doctors must get better at engaging in hard conversations with their terminally ill patients. That isn't always easy. Doctors want to tell people everything will be OK and some people want reassurance until the end. But for those who want the chance to take control of their death, the choice must be there.

To those who say this will encourage patients to throw in the towel, that is not my experience. Last December, I was in severe pain and was convinced I'd have to find a way to die. But I was also desperate to stay alive. So when my doctors told me they were doing all they could to find ways to relieve the pain, I was prepared to give anything a go. Eventually, they adjusted my drugs so my symptoms became manageable and I've lived the past year in surprisingly good health. Indeed, as the months have gone by, I've got over the shock of being told I am going to die and I've started to plan for next week.

Most of my effort goes into the website I helped to set up to let ordinary people share their stories about their experience of illness. Something close to my heart is a new part of the website where we are talking to carers of people with a terminal illness; I'm even wondering if I might be alive for the website's tenth birthday next year. Later this month, I hope to be at the launch of an independent commission on assisted dying, chaired by Lord Falconer.

Whatever happens, I know my children are behind my campaign. Not because I've told them about how awful it can be for patients and their families, as they face the fall-out of a protracted death. I have spared them that. But they do understand that it's my love for them that makes me care so passionately. And who has the right to deny me this?

Reprinted from Daily Mail, 23 Nov 2010

Death of a Campaigner

Klim McPherson,
Professor of Public Health Epidemiology at Oxford University.

There is a tragic irony about the death of my wife, Ann, who died after battling pancreatic cancer for four years. The many obituaries published since her death paid tribute to her professional life as a GP, writer, researcher and patient advocate — and most recently, as founder of Healthcare Professionals for Assisted Dying, which she formed two years ago, and as an active patron of the pro-choice charity, Dignity in Dying. In her final days, far from seeing the dignity in dying she wanted so desperately for herself and others, I watched my wife of 43 years suffering as she was forced to live in unbearable discomfort.

It was Ann's experience of caring for terminally ill patients that convinced her that the law should be changed, with appropriate safeguards, to allow doctors to end the lives of terminally ill people at a time of their choosing. She had to stand by as her patients were forced to endure a slow, uncomfortable death — and saw the pain such suffering caused their families. She became a vocal campaigner to end 'the cruelty', as she put it, imposed by those who resist the call for new legislation, thereby allowing the dying to suffer so horribly. Yet she found herself fighting a medical establishment that continues to insist that good palliative care and effective pain relief are all that is needed for a good death.

But instead of offering a compassionate exit to suffering as Ann and many others have called for, most palliative care charters aim to guarantee the 'highest quality care and support' to ensure that the terminally ill are able 'to live as well as possible for as long as possible.' But Ann's final days reveal such charters as largely empty words. As a much-loved and highly-valued GP, Ann was cared for by two fellow GPs and her own doctor, as well as a leading cancer specialist. As such, she had probably the highest quality care and support that it is possible to receive as a dying patient. Now, there is no doubt that she thoroughly appreciated this care during the four years after her diagnosis in 2007, when she was 61. But the cancer returned and spread to her lungs in July 2009. So she embarked on a palliative care regime involving large doses of morphine and other drugs to control her worsening symptoms.

Ann had retired from general practice the previous year, but with the pain and nausea controlled, she was able to continue working virtually full-time on her other projects. Memorably, she spoke alongside the actor Hugh Grant whose mother had died of pancreatic cancer and who had become a patron of the website and Ann's fervent admirer. In those final months, her symptoms were controlled sufficiently to allow us to go on holiday as a family, enabling Ann to have long conversations with our three children and five grandchildren, and I know she appreciated this with all her heart. Yet as she knew only too well, there is a limit to how far doctors can ensure the quality of life in a dying person.

Ann's medical team did everything within the law to allow her to live as well as possible right up to the end. But pain and nausea are only a part of the discomfort of the last days of terminal illness, particularly following the spread of cancer. Many times in her last months, Ann complained about the current legislation and the way it had to be interpreted so rigidly. She had no confidence, she said, that she could organise the dignified death that she felt was her right.

She was furious that she would be forced to live for as long as it took for her to die. At first we expressed sympathy while longing for her to go on living, helpless to understand the inner torment that was tearing her apart. She was, after all, a very brave woman, always smiling to hide her suffering. And there were good moments even as she was dying. I remember with pleasure a morning just a couple of days before she died when she was able to relax and enjoy being bathed, seeing her eight-year-old grandson and even able to eat a few spoonfuls of milky Weetabix.

But such moments do not justify forcing my wife to endure the relentless suffering of her final days that she described, with typical understatement, as 'pretty bloody awful.' In the last few weeks of her life, her needs were completely dominant and she was entirely dependent on others. There was little quality of life, only suffering — made worse by the knowledge that her loving family would not easily erase the memory of seeing her so helpless. Unable to eat solids and barely able to move, she developed an abscess on the incision in her chest where tubes drained her lungs of fluid that would otherwise have killed her, something that went untreated because antibiotics would have made her sick.

Above all, despite the powerful medication, she felt ill, exhausted and uncomfortable in a way that I imagine is only experienced by the terminally ill and can therefore never be fully understood by others. Ten days before she died, Ann dictated how she felt. 'It is nice to see people but if I had the choice there is no question that I would prefer to be dead. I feel so ill...'

The death itself was chaotic. The GP warned us on the Friday that Ann might be near death but we'd been told that a number of times before. So my son who was due to fly out on holiday the next morning with his family, decided to go ahead with his plans, having said his goodbyes. The next day around noon, I was downstairs while the GP was checking Ann's medication and my two daughters were helping the district nurse to change her dressing. The nurse said quietly that Ann was 'on her way' — but somehow we weren't at all ready for her to be going.

In her last moments, we were panicking — I was racing upstairs to her room while my daughters were running around to find towels that seemed to be needed. True, she wasn't in pain and her final days were as comfortable as possible, as promised by the new End Of Life Charter. But her medical team didn't — couldn't — ensure that her dignity and independence were preserved, another of the Charter's promises. Nor did they listen to her dying wishes or act on them — another promise. To fulfil either of these promises is illegal under current legislation. And so there was nothing peaceful about her death. Instead, we, her loving family, were in shock, racing around urgently attending to her needs while she was alone.

I believe that Ann, as far as she was aware of anything, was sad and angry that she'd had to endure so much and in the end was unable to prepare for her final moments. When Ann explained in the Mail why she had launched the assisted dying campaign, she said she was frightened of a death bereft of dignity partly because it might mean that her family would have to live with the memory of seeing her suffering and perhaps have their lives blighted by it.

'In my practice I have seen this happen and I felt I had let down these patients and their families,' she said. Now, I, too, have seen it happen and I share Ann's anger that the organisations that represent Britain's doctors still oppose assisted dying.

There is nothing humane about forcing people with terminal illness to stay alive for as long as they can — no matter how good the care they receive from a profession forced into cruelty by an inadequate law.

Reprinted from Daily Mail 14 June 2011

An unfortunate way to die

Dr. Michael O'Donnell,
former GP and former editor of World Medicine.

In journalism, as in medicine, research into one subject often throws light upon another. Five years ago, while researching the BBC Radio 4 series *The Age Old Dilemma*, I talked to old people who were preparing themselves to die in hospices and hospitals. I also sat in on meetings where doctors discussed the 'care of the dying.' I learned much about medical and non-medical attitudes to death but was also struck by the disparity between the way patients perceive events and the way doctors describe the same events when discussing them with their peers.

Two years later the disparity was neatly illustrated in a BMJ article[1] that told the story of a 62 year old woman 'bed bound with severe arthritis and in constant pain despite strong opioid treatment.' After writing an advance directive and a detailed suicide note that 'clearly expressed [her] distress at her longstanding pain and severe restriction of function and independence,' she swallowed a potent concoction of sedatives and sank into what she assumed would be oblivion.

I can only guess at her assumption, because, as is traditional in our journals, her story is written by the doctors. We read in detail the arguments they considered and the agonies they endured reaching their decisions. We hear nothing directly from the woman or her family about the agonies they endured. Their emotions and attitudes are described not by them but as they were perceived by the doctors.

The first medical decision was to deny the woman the oblivion she sought. She received 'lifesaving treatment' and awoke in hospital with paralysis of the left side of her body. Her doctors were, however, able to provide 'excellent symptomatic relief from her arthritis' before she was 'diagnosed with depression and started on fluoxetine.' Three months later she went home. Six months after that, the doctors who saw her described her as 'cheerful.' She 'acknowledged' that her quality of life had improved but 'considered' that it was still poor. She 'maintained' that she would have preferred to have had her wishes respected, to have retained her independence and dignity, and not to have survived. 'This position,' we are told, 'was confirmed in a subsequent letter.' We don't see the letter, or even a quotation from it, so we can't read what she thought, only what her doctors thought she thought. Indeed we hear nothing about what happened to her and her family during those six months.

The story ends with a chilling sentence: 'She lived almost pain-free for another 18 months with some reservations but no resentment over her management and *unfortunately* [my italics] subsequently died in hospital in a manner which she had tried to avoid.'

'Served her right,' the Devil whispered in my ear, 'for placing her trust in irrelevant fripperies like advance directives that fly in the face of one of medicine's traditional precepts: Mummy and Daddy know best.' Even worse than the euphemism (that use of 'unfortunately') is the casuistry that infects much medical discussion of death and dying. When I was a medical student in the late 1940s the moral stance favoured by my teachers was that of Lord Dawson of Penn who in 1936 'eased the death' of King George V by injecting a lethal mixture of drugs into his jugular vein. Later that year the second reading of a Bill enabling euthanasia was defeated in the House of Lords. By then Dawson had been created a Viscount — establishing, as Richard Gordon wrote, 'the going rate for regicide' — and, during the debate was one of the Bill's most vigorous opponents, arguing that legislation was unnecessary because 'good doctors' already helped their patients to die.

Today, Dawson's paternalistic attitude is unacceptable. Strict observance of the law is enforced in hospitals and reinforced by the presence of potential whistle-blowers. My wife, whom I loved dearly, was but one of many who had the mode of dying they most feared forced upon them. During the 60 years we shared our lives she often made me promise to do all I could to protect her from it. She hoped I could persuade some compassionate doctor to intervene 'in the way they used to.' Like me she found it difficult to see the moral distinction between starving and dehydrating people to death and ending life with one painless intervention. I tried to reassure her with talk of palliative care but, at the moment of truth, all I could do was pass on her wishes to hospital doctors who had no legal way to implement them.

Having witnessed her cruel undignified death, I will never lose the feeling that I betrayed her, though I remain grateful to the nurses — doctors were conspicuous by their absence — who cared for her with skill and kindness during the three days she took to die an undignified death. They tried hard to keep her at peace but the moments that dominate my memory are her spells of lucidity when her physical and audible signals were those of someone being tortured rather than comforted.

Too many medical debates about assisted dying degenerate into adversarial combat between groups defending strongly held beliefs. And, while well-meaning folk in High Places agonise over evidence-lite concepts such as the 'slippery slope', and intellectual cop-outs such as the 'double effect,' families like mine have to endure the reality served up in 21st century general wards unfrequented by specialists in palliative care.

It's no secret that some compassionate GPs still break the law to honour their patients' wishes, if they can do so surreptitiously. The decision should not be theirs. It's time we allowed people to make their own decisions, and offered them more choices, about the ending of their own lives.

This is an expanded version of an article first published in the BMJ on 23 October, 2010.

Reference:

1. *British Medical Journal* 2009;339:b4667

3

Forgotten but not gone

Voice from the Coalface

Melanie Reid,
*journalist, severely disabled as a result of
falling off a horse*

W hen asked about assisted suicide, I tend to pause and take a deep breath. You really want to know what I think? From the vantage point of a severely crippled body? Honestly? You want the voice from the coalface? You don't just want an opinion from some able-bodied moralist who presumes to know what's best for me? I find it ridiculous that an educated society, facing an unaffordable explosion in dementia and age-related illness, is prevaricating over this issue. It is, for me, almost inconceivable that the law lags so many decades behind modern realities; and is so out of step with the feelings of the vast majority of the population.

Where is the democracy surrounding death? The fact is simply this. Because of a religious minority, a few antediluvian pressure groups, and the might of modern medicine, we are condemning growing numbers of elderly, terminally ill or disabled people to a terrible lingering twilight rather than a good death in the circumstances of their choosing. And we are condemning the people who want to assist them to the threat of criminal prosecution. This is a scandal.

For the first time in nearly 40 years, MPs are to vote on assisted suicide (in 2006 a change in the law on assisted dying was defeated in the House of Lords by 148 votes to 100). The Conservative MP Richard Ottaway has secured a debate about the guidelines by the Director of Public Prosecutions on the issue, which have been in place since February 2010. The guidelines make it clear that prosecution is unlikely in cases of compassionate amateur assistance to die.

We must hope our MPs are bold enough to represent the nation's views and support this stance. A recent poll found that 82 per cent of people believe that the DPP's approach to prosecution is 'sensible and humane.' Every single person I know is of the same general opinion: that there is no point keeping humans alive just for the sake of it, when they don't want to be, in circumstances which we and they regard as intolerable. And if they need help to achieve a good death, in the comfort and peace of their own home, we should be able to give it to them. Yet we are being held back by a tiny number, not even 18 per cent I bet, who either believe the Bible rules it out or are so blinded by the doctrine of palliative care (or perhaps both), that they remove choice from the majority.

Ironic, isn't it, that we can buy 50 different types of pasta or ice cream? We can choose a million styles of hair, or clothes, holiday destination or car. Tidal waves of consumer choice lap against us every waking minute. Yet when we need help to effect a simple, primary decision to ease out of life; when we want to avoid becoming a living shell, stuck in bed, in pain, staring at the wall for months on end, and thereby condemning our relatives to a similar suffering, we are denied that choice. Or, if we are able, we must leave the country and go to a Swiss suburb to find it. In an age wedded to the gospel of human rights, in other words, we are denied the most basic human right of all.

I will be very blunt. Most mornings I contemplate suicide, briefly examining the concept in a detached, intellectual way. It's always during the hour when I am sitting on my shower chair over the loo, leaning forward over my purple, paralysed feet, fighting nausea and light-headedness, sore bones and paralysed bowels. This, without intending to sound self-pitying, is the worst bit in the day of a life as a tetraplegic — a cruel Japanese game show, full of repeated tortures.

And every day I stare at my toes and say to myself: 'Nope, got to keep going, got to keep fighting.' Because I choose, fiercely, to live for the people who love me; and will continue to do so until such point as they understand I cannot carry on. I hope that moment, if or when it comes, is many years away.

But you know sometimes, just sometimes, I get angry enough to wish that a few bishops, palliative care specialists and those dedicated campaigners from Care Not Killing — ah! what amazing arrogance lurks in a name — were in my skin, sitting in my shower chair, facing my future.

Knowing that I have a choice is a huge comfort to me; it sustains me on the days when I make the mistake of looking too far in the future. But the point is, I am blessed precisely because I have a choice. I can talk, use my hands to a limited degree. I could, if I sought to, take my own life without implicating anyone else. There are many other people who, because of their illness or their disability, do not have this possibility of self-determination. Their right to choose is denied to them. They need help to escape from their imprisonment; and they want to know that their family or friends will not be punished for assisting them to die.

The debate in Parliament is narrow in scope and only the beginning. It covers the terminally ill, which rules out spinal injuries and a host of other forms of chronic suffering. But it is an important start. Humanity and economics demand that, eventually — and yes, yes, yes, with all proper safeguards — assisted dying is extended to become legally available to all those who seek it, and not just cancer patients. People like me, living with the consequences of an accident, who dread growing old and lonely. People like my mother, who in the early stages of dementia expressed a clear wish to end her life and not be a burden on us.

There will be a whole generation of ageing baby-boomers, in fact, who will seek to go out of life in the same way they have successfully run it: in control, not in incontinence pads in a care home. This debate is not about other people. It is about every single one of us.

Originally published in The Times,
Tuesday, March 27, 2012

Leave it to the patient

Chris Woodhead,
former head of Ofsted

My father stirred suddenly on the sofa. 'Why can't we lie down together', he said, 'hold hands, and die?' My mother nodded quietly in agreement. I had thought they were both asleep and had been wondering when to go and make a cup of tea. As it was, I sat there, not knowing what to say, tears filling my eyes.

What is there to say when you have watched your parents decline physically and mentally to the point where they cannot cope? When they have sunk so deep into their individual desperation that they have begun to blame each other for the pain of their situation? When they know, and you know, that things are only going to get worse?

A couple of months later, it became impossible to look after my father at home and he went into the local cottage hospital. Every time I visited, a man in the bed opposite, who had, as a clergyman, spent his life comforting the sick in such places, would call out to me. 'There isn't a God, is there? No God would allow us to suffer like this, would He?'

I would go and sit with him, hold his hand, try to reassure him that his God was still with him. Then I would move across the ward to my father. He never said much. He hated being there and wanted more than anything in the world to go home. I had to tell him that he could not, and I think he began to hate me, too.

The night he died, I sat until 10 o'clock, listening to his erratic breathing, and wondered what to do. My mother was at home and she could not cope properly on her own.

I bent over, whispered 'goodnight' and told him, though I knew I would not, that I would see him in the morning. The phone went in the early hours and a nurse told me he had died. When my mother woke I wondered how she would take the news. She did not break down in tears. She didn't do anything for several minutes. Then she turned her poor face, twisted since the last stroke, to me and said 'Well, he's got what he wanted, hasn't he? I wonder how long I will have to wait'.

She died three weeks later. I was in Wales and had called to see how she was. We had talked about how, when the weather got better, I was going to bring her up to stay with me. Then, half an hour later, the phone went again. It was her carer, who told me that my mother had said she didn't feel well and, twenty seconds later, had collapsed in her chair.

Christine and I walked round Llyn Gwynant that afternoon. The winter sun lit up the black waters of the lake. I felt an enormous sense of relief. For her and for me. The anguish of the last few years was over. They did not have to suffer any more. I did not have to know that, whatever I did, it was not enough.

Eight years on, it is I who cannot cope. I was diagnosed with Motor Neurone Disease in 2006. My days of walking and mountain biking in the Welsh hills are over. It is a wheelchair, now, for me, and the most important object in my life is the slide board which makes it possible for Christine to lift me in and out of it.

Nobody understands anything about MND. Something goes wrong in the brain or the nervous system and messages are no longer sent to your muscles. As a result, you lose the ability to move. My legs went first, and then my arms. I am waiting for the next stage, when you can no longer swallow or breathe. I spend quite a lot of time thinking about what I ought to do.

There is no cure for MND. The best they can do is prescribe a drug which is meant to prolong life by a couple of months. Fifty per cent of patients die within fourteen months of the diagnosis; ninety per cent are dead within five years. Professor Stephen Hawking, who celebrates his 70th birthday as I write, has had the disease for the best part of fifty years. Anything seems possible when MND decides in its mysterious and insidious way that it is going to take over your life.

I am into my sixth year, and I am certain that I had the illness for several years before I finally bothered to visit the doctor. So, in a sense, I am one of the lucky ones. That does not mean I am going to escape. You think, for a month or two, that the decline has stopped, and then suddenly you know it hasn't. You know that something else has given up.

Last night was not good. I have only myself to blame for the indigestion that followed a takeaway curry. I can live with indigestion. What kept me awake was my fingers. They have begun to twist themselves over into a fixed claw shape. My toes, actually, are doing the same, but they are not making so much fuss about it. When my fingers lock over they cramp up, and it is painful. I lay in bed trying to straighten them and managed to mesh my hands together as though I were praying. This helped to relax them, but I then found I could not unmesh them.

I lay there in the dark, trying to resist a rising feeling of panic. I could have woken Christine, of course, who would have rescued me as she always does. But she was fast asleep and she is at my beck and call throughout the day. So I forced myself to lie there and wait for the cramps to unlock and dawn to come. I lay there thinking about the fact that my parents had left it too late. What, I asked myself, over and over again, was I going to do?

When you have MND, there are only three options. You kill yourself while you still have the physical ability to do it. You hang on for as long as you can and you end up in a hospice. Or you and your loved ones decide that you are going to find a way out, whatever the law might say, when the time is right.

If I had been on my own, I would have killed myself three years ago. I cannot remember the exact date, but the moment when I realised that time was running out for me as an independent human being is crystal clear.

A couple of steps lead down from the back garden into the courtyard of our house in Wales. I suddenly found myself flat on my face in that courtyard. I lay there for a moment or two, turned myself over and contemplated the canopy of trees above me. I remembered my father saying to me on his last visit that he was frightened of falling down those very steps. I had said to him: 'Don't worry, Dad. You're not going to go anywhere.' Now, it was me that was frightened. I knew exactly where I was going to go.

But I was not on my own. I had my wife to look after me and to think about. I had my daughter and grandchildren. I had my conviction that, if you are thinking of killing yourself, you need to think very hard. My basic attitude has always been that one should soldier on, stoic and insouciant in the face of life's tribulations. I have not always managed to live up to this precept, but I have tried. Too often, suicide is at best a selfish and at worst an aggressive act. I did not and I do not want my suicide, if it comes to that, to be selfish or aggressive.

What, though, do you do? Do you all sit down round the kitchen table and discuss whether the time is right? How can anyone expect one's wife or daughter to tell them that the moment has come? You cannot, of course. It is a nonsense. But decisions do not always have to be made explicit. I believe that when the time is right there will be a tacit understanding which will not need to be talked through in some farcical family conference.

I am glad that I did not tuck the hosepipe into the exhaust and start the engine. As I dictate this and Christine types, a purple, yellowish bruise has spread across the sky. There are good things as well as bad when you know that you are living on borrowed time, and the beauty of the world becomes ever more poignant.

So, too, do the trivial occurrences of daily domestic life. 'Let's have a cup of tea', she says. I manage to drink it without spilling most of it down me. I push a chocolate finger biscuit round my mouth without dislodging my dodgy bridge. There is fish and chips for dinner and a couple of episodes of *Sons of Anarchy* to watch afterwards. What more can a man want?

In my case the answer to this question is simple. I want our noble Parliamentarians, our bishops and archbishops, the great and the good of the medical profession, to shut up. I want them to stop poking their vainglorious fingers into something they cannot possibly understand. I want the right to die at a time of my choice, assisted, if necessary, by those who love me enough to help.

Let's park the argument that any change to the assisted dying law is going to expose hundreds and thousands of vulnerable people to the wicked machinations of relatives who want to bump them off. Let's stick with me. I have MND. I do not want to die before I am ready, but, equally, I do not want to end up in the living hell that was my parents' last years.

Some members of the National Union of Teachers might possibly disagree, but I think I am in possession of my mental faculties. I am happy to appear before any panel of psychiatrists or to be quizzed by any lawyer. The fact that I have a terminal illness, which will, sooner or later, make it impossible for me to swallow or breathe, is public knowledge. Why should the law dictate the timing and circumstance of my death? What possible damage to the public good could that death do?

I will ignore the puerile response some readers may be tempted to make to this question. The obvious truth is that it would do no harm at all. It is what, when the time is right, I want. In the last years of their lives it was what my parents wanted for themselves. It is what, I suspect, thousands of people want this Sunday and millions more will want when they, too, find themselves facing the questions I am facing.

Imagine. Just for a moment. Stop what you are doing. Shut your eyes and pretend you are in a wheelchair. You want to clean your teeth. Your husband or wife has given you the toothbrush. They are trying to help you raise the brush to your mouth. Your hands cramp round the handle and the brush misses its target. You let it go. You try again. The same thing happens. On the third or fourth go you manage, sort of, to clean your teeth. Then the toothpaste has to be mopped up off your clothes. That was this morning's indignity.

If you had asked me five years ago whether I would be able to put up with such nonsense, I would have laughed. My impatience was legendary. Now, every day I amaze myself. My inability to turn the pages of a book, or to answer an email, frustrates me enormously. There is the odd expletive, of course, but I have come to accept the tightening constraints of my everyday experience. The one thing that continues really to try my patience is the grandstanding of those who oppose any form of assisted suicide.

It cannot be beyond the bounds of human ingenuity to construct a system in which somebody suffering from a terminal illness, who wants to die, but who is unable to kill themselves unaided, could apply to the state for permission. Independent medical and legal expertise could be brought to bear, and a judgement reached. As a thoroughgoing libertarian, the whole idea makes me snort, but, if people are worried about the potential abuse of any change in the law then I could accept the checks and balances which might allow common sense to prevail.

If there are no practical impediments, then it boils down to one group of people imposing their values on another. I can respect the religious conviction of the churchman who believes that life is God-given and must be endured until God decides otherwise. Indeed, I have considerable sympathy with this position. Taking one's own life should, in my opinion, be, in every possible sense of the phrase, an act of last resort. But, if I have come to the point where that act is what I want, I do not think that anybody else's convictions should stop me doing what I have decided to do.

Neither do I think that somebody who is terminally ill should have to dig deep into their savings and travel to

Switzerland. You have, in fact, to be able to swallow the glass of sodium pentobarbital unaided, and I have probably passed that point.* I can still swallow, but, unless I am lying down, the odds against me being able to raise the glass and hold it to my lips are now too high. In any case, even if I had the physical capacity, I do not want to travel to a foreign country to have a poison ministered to me by strangers. I want to die in my own home.

I went through a phase when I thought that I should campaign to get the assisted dying laws changed. I decided against. The sad truth is that today's politicians do not have the courage to confront an issue that is this contentious. I do not think my decision about my death has anything to do with any Member of Parliament. I know, moreover, that the publicity which would surround any such campaign would make it even more difficult for doctors to exercise their professional judgement when they are caring for the terminally ill.

Prior to Shipman, one GP said to me recently, doctors would do what was necessary to minimise suffering. Now, the prospect of an enquiry into the circumstances surrounding any death makes most reluctant to do anything other than prolong life. It may not be what the patient wants. It may not be what the doctor wants either. But that is where we are and because I would rather rely upon the professional discretion of my GP than the pusillanimity of a Parliament fearful of rocking the media boat, I do not think that a campaign is going to do anybody in my position any good.

---

* Editors' note: at least one of the Swiss organisations uses a patient-initiated intravenous infusion instead of oral medication.

Actually, I am hopeful. 'Beam us up Asrael', as my friend, Geoffrey Hill, once, rather pithily, put it. Come the day, I am confident that Asrael, assisted, perhaps, by a couple of my friends, will beam me up to everybody's satisfaction. The debate about the ethics and dangers of assisted dying will no doubt rage on, long after I have disappeared. Good luck to them all, I say. Samuel Smiles had it right. I have a copy of *Self-Help* by my bedside table.

PS. To maintain domestic harmony, I should point out that the Woodhead household does not live on takeaways alone.

4

Dying with Dignitas

An 'Emergency Exit'

Silvan Luley, Ludwig A. Minelli
and Sandra Martino,
Dignitas

Dignitas, a Swiss not-for-profit members' society, was founded on May 17, 1998 in Forch, near Zurich, by Ludwig A. Minelli, a human rights lawyer. Today, with its sister association Dignitas-Germany in Hanover, which was established September 26, 2005, it has some 6,600 members in 70 countries around the world. Of this number, 810 live in the United Kingdom. We have an office in Forch, and we have a house in Pfäffikon-Zurich where accompanied suicides for members from abroad may take place. It is most important that Dignitas does not restrict its services to Swiss residents or citizens. The Good Samaritan did not request to see a passport before he helped the suffering man on the road – Dignitas ignores borders as far as possible. There are 20 people working for Dignitas – almost all of them are part-time, comprising board members, an office team, and companions who visit patients and assist with accompanied suicides.

We all want to live. However, we do not just want to barely live. We have very personal views which determine whether our life still holds some value for us. When someone is suffering greatly, the healthy cannot judge what that individual's life is worth.

But, it is Dignitas' first and most important task to look for solutions which lead towards re-establishing quality of life so that the person in question can carry on living. In 2002, the Swiss government concluded, from scientific research, that for every actual suicide there are as many as 49 attempted suicides which fail, with dire consequences. Dignitas' experience, derived from sixteen years of taking care of people who wish to end their lives for all sorts of reasons, is that Society should focus much more on the prevention of suicide attempts. Receiving access to an accompanied suicide is an important part in this. And, most interestingly, only some 14% of those Dignitas-members who receive access to an assisted suicide actually make use of this option. Regaining control over the last stretch of life, having an 'emergency exit', is sufficient relief for many and they do not need to take to ghastly methods with the high risk of failure. One third of our daily counselling work, by telephone, is with non-members. First and foremost, Dignitas is a suicide-attempt prevention organization, and therefore a help-to-live organization.

At the same time, if solutions towards life are impossible, the option of a dignified death must then be considered. However, the goal of Dignitas is to disappear, to vanish, to close down. But, as long as the governments, and legal systems, in most countries disgracefully disrespect their citizens' basic human right to a self-chosen dignified end of life and force them either to turn to risky suicide attempts or to travel abroad instead, Dignitas will serve as an 'emergency exit.'

People are not the property of the State. They are the bearers of human dignity, and this is characterized most strongly when a person decides his or her own fate. The freedom to shape one's life includes the freedom to shape the end of one's life. However, departing on such a 'long journey' entails responsibility. All individuals are part of society. Therefore, one should not set out on this journey without careful preparation, nor without having said appropriate goodbyes to loved ones.

Over the sixteen years of its existence, Dignitas has been involved in many legal cases. In particular, this led on January 20, 2011, to the following European Court of Human Rights decision in the case of Haas vs. Switzerland: 'In the light of this jurisdiction, the Court finds that the right of an individual how and when to end his life, provided that said individual was in a position to make up his own mind in that respect and to take the appropriate action, was one aspect of the right to respect for private life under Article 8 of the Convention.' Many opponents of assisted dying will claim that there is no right to die. They are wrong – certainly within the jurisdiction of the European Convention on Human Rights.

Dignitas also gets involved in legislative proceedings. Thinking only of the UK, we had a visit from members of the House of Lords Select Committee on Assisted Dying for the Terminally Ill Bill, led by Lord Joffe, in 2005. Then, members of the Commission on Assisted Dying, chaired by Lord Falconer, came to Zurich in 2010. For both, we provided detailed reports giving various facts and providing legal arguments. Also, we submitted extensive data for the consultation process on the draft Assisted Suicide (Scotland) Bill presented by Margo MacDonald to the Scottish Parliament.

In the cases of medically diagnosed severe or terminal illnesses, and unendurable disabilities, Dignitas can arrange the option of an accompanied suicide for anyone who joins our organization. But, there are many prerequisites linked to the arrangement of such an assisted suicide – for example, the person must be mentally competent, has to be able to carry out the final action which brings about death by him or herself, and has to send a written request to Dignitas with comprehensive historical and up-to-date medical records. In due course, various official documents (a birth certificate, proof of residence, etc.) must be provided. A Swiss physician – independent of Dignitas – assesses the request, and, if the information provided is sufficient, grants a 'provisional green light' (without this physician's and Dignitas' consent, there will not be an accompanied suicide). Upon arriving in Switzerland, a person has to have at least two face-to-face consultations, on different days, with this Swiss physician. It is very important to realize that this whole procedure can take several months.

Only if all the requirements are fulfilled can a Swiss physician legally write the prescription which allows Dignitas to procure the necessary medication for an accompanied suicide. This is a large dose of a fast-acting barbiturate which is dissolved in drinking water. After taking it, sleep occurs within a few minutes and one quickly drifts into a deep coma. After some time, death occurs peacefully and painlessly.

On October 25, 2002, the first British national, accompanied by his son and daughter, ended his life with the assistance of Dignitas. Aged 77, he was suffering from cancer of the oesophagus which had spread elsewhere in his body. Since then, until the end of 2013, a further 243 Britons choose to have their way and made an arduous journey to Dignitas. Indeed, the current legal status of assisted dying is inadequate and incoherent, as the Commission on Assisted Dying has stated in its final report. In total, Dignitas has helped more than 1,700 individuals from around the world, to reach their self-determined ending of suffering, generally in the presence of their loved ones.

There are three groups of individuals, suffering from various medical situations, who can generally be identified as eligible for an accompaniment at Dignitas, based on the present factual and legal situation in Switzerland: Those suffering from a terminal and/or severely painful condition; those suffering due to a severe disability (for example, young Daniel James who was almost entirely paralysed after a rugby accident); and those elderly people whose life has become too arduous as a result of a multitude of ailments related to old age (such as the conductor Sir Edward Downes who, aged 84, suffered from cardiac problems, arthritis in the back and knees, and was almost completely deaf and blind).

Nowadays, people are living longer, much longer. Of the many reasons for this development, one is the progress in medical science which leads to a significant prolonging of life expectancy. Obviously, this progress is a blessing for the majority of people. However, it can also lead to a situation in which death, as a natural result of illness, can be postponed to a point which is much longer than some individuals would want to bear. More and more people wish to add life to their years – not years to their life.

In the light of this development, limiting access to accompanied self-deliverance to certain people, such as those who are terminally ill, cannot be justified (although the current proposal for legislation on assisted dying in Britain, focusing on the terminally ill, is a step in the right direction). But, this discriminates against people like Tony Nicklinson, and also those few of the approximately 1.5 million people in the UK, over 85 who, due to their ailments, might rationally wish to end their long lives in a self-determined, peaceful manner.

On May 15, 2011, the voters of the Canton of Zurich strongly rejected two initiatives (by 84.5% to 15.5%, and by 78.4% to 21.6%) by conservative-religious political parties, one aimed at prohibiting access to assisted dying for people from outside Switzerland and the other aimed at prohibiting assisted suicide altogether. For many years, polling results show similar support for freedom of choice in 'last matters.' However, the opponents have not yet given up; therefore, this freedom has to be guarded and defended again and again.

Most of the difficulties that Dignitas deals with have their origin in the fact that we have always been convinced that the right to die is, in fact, the very last human right, and thus there should not be any discrimination just because of the place of residence of a person. We, in Dignitas, together with our friends of similar organizations around the world, are the real pro-life people because our work is about options and choices, about respect for humans.

Fellow-travelling

Michael Irwin

Between August 2005 and March 2011, I have accompanied four individuals from the UK to Switzerland to witness their assisted suicides in that country, where this possibility has existed for several decades.

It usually takes at least four months from the day that someone, in the UK, first contacts one of the three organizations in Switzerland (the well-known Dignitas, near Zurich; and two much smaller bodies – EX International, in Bern, and Lifecircle, near Basle), which are willing to help non-Swiss nationals in this way, until the day that they can actually end their life. It is a lengthy process as much documentation is required by these organizations and the independent Swiss doctors cooperating with them (such as a formal written request and very detailed past and recent medical reports), as well as by the Swiss authorities (who need various personal items like a full birth certificate and proof of residence – not just a gas bill, but an affidavit, sworn in front of a public notary – and, if one is married, a marriage certificate, and even a spouse's birth certificate).

Then, it is necessary to be able to cover various expenses. This includes payments to the organization involved; further fees to the Swiss doctor who has reviewed the medical records and now sees the individual concerned, on two different days, when that person has arrived in Switzerland; travel costs (everybody who goes to Switzerland, to die, should be accompanied by a relative or friend), including last-minute air fares and hotel expenses for three or four nights (Swiss hotels can be among the most expensive in Europe); and, afterwards, the cremation. On average, in 2014, the total cost can be up to £10,000: however, as Dignitas is a charity, some reductions are possible in deserving situations.

If there were two things that the four individuals, who I accompanied to Switzerland, had in common, it was a great determination to end their difficult and painful lives, and a very strong wish that they could have been given the same doctor-supported assisted suicide in the UK, in their own homes.

The first person I helped to make this final journey was May, a 75-year old widow living in Glasgow, who was terminally ill, and suffering greatly, due to multiple systems atrophy, a condition which is similar in many ways to Parkinsonism, but without the tremor. She was bedridden, and was looked after at home by day and night carers. When I saw her, in August 2005, she was deteriorating rapidly and was expected to go into a care home, or even a hospital, within a few weeks. She told me then that she did not want her two sons to see her suffer any more, especially after their father had died following a prolonged illness.

Suicide had never been a crime in Scotland – the 1961 Suicide Act only applied to England and Wales. So, although there was apparently no obvious crime in helping someone in Scotland to end their life, various individual members of Friends At The End (FATE, a help-to-live and right-to-die society, based in Scotland) became involved in assisting May to travel to Zurich, so that this 'crime' was a shared responsibility – for example, one person made the necessary arrangements with Dignitas, another obtained her air ticket, and a further friend handled the financial arrangements.

I was asked to accompany her on the KLM flight we took to Amsterdam from Glasgow, for a connecting flight to Zurich – and, one son saw us into the taxi from her home to the airport, while the other son (with May's best friend) met us in Zurich.

May had had a colourful life – from a comfortable time in Scotland to travelling a great deal (even, gambling in Las Vegas). Although determined to die in Switzerland, she was completely relaxed on the two flights. At one point, as we ate KLM sandwiches, she turned to me and said 'This is my last supper, but I only have one disciple with me.' Then, as we landed at Zurich airport, after all the passengers were thanked for flying on KLM and wished a 'safe, onward journey', May said, in a loud voice, 'If only you knew where I am going.'

Between getting off the plane (and May had to travel everywhere in a wheelchair) and going to see the Swiss doctor, for his final examination and official approval, granting her request for a suicide, and the signing of the prescription for the lethal medication she would soon swallow, the four of us (May, her son, her friend and I) drove around Zurich, in a large taxi, like relaxed tourists.

When we were in the simple, but attractive flat, then maintained by Dignitas in Zurich, various legalistic forms had to be signed before May drank a substance to 'settle her stomach', which is taken about 30 minutes before the lethal barbiturate is swallowed. May's friend did not stay with us. But, during this period, May spoke frankly with her son and myself about highlights in her life and her gratitude to us for being with her. She was so relaxed. As she raised the small glass, containing her final drink, she toasted both her son and myself. We were sitting around a table. Her son was next to her. As she quickly became drowsy, he leant over and supported her in her chair. Then, he picked her up and carried her over to a bed, where she died about twenty minutes later. It was a dignified death, which May desperately wanted – it was her final choice in life.

News of May's death did not appear in the media until January 2006. It was a front-page story in many national newspapers. But, one comment remains clearly in my mind – Minette Marrin, writing in the *Sunday Times* on January 29th, noted, 'It should not need brave trips to Switzerland or the courage of campaigners who break the law to restore us our freedom to choose our own death.'

The second time that I travelled to Switzerland, to see someone die, was in November 2006. Earlier that year, I had met Dave in his home on the Isle of Wight. A geologist, aged 61, he had progressively suffered from Huntington's Disease for four years, and was now confined to a wheelchair. He dreaded the possibility of going into a nursing home, and having to be fed through a tube. With the approval of his wife and children, he had been accepted by Dignitas, and one of their cooperating doctors, for an assisted suicide. His best friend had agreed to accompany him, but, a fortnight before the planned trip, this friend had to have urgent surgery for an aortic aneurysm, and so I was asked to make the journey with Dave. Interestingly, his GP, his neurologist, his psychologist and his main care worker were well aware of his intention to die in Zurich, and had all wished him well.

Dave and I spent the night before flying to Zurich at the Hilton Hotel at Gatwick. For his last dinner in England, he had invited the Health Editor of the *Sunday Times*, Sarah-Kate Templeton, to join us as he hoped that any publicity might encourage a change in the law – and, a detailed report appeared in that newspaper on November 19th, together with a large photograph of me pushing Dave in his wheelchair towards our plane.

Between seeing the Swiss doctor in Zurich and waiting to go to the Dignitas flat, Dave and I were alone together in our hotel. What do you talk about with someone who is scheduled to die by his own hands within forty-eight hours? With CNN News regularly on in the background of his hotel room (which allowed us to discuss some of the news items we heard), our conversation ranged from Formula One motor-racing to the nature of the universe, and from British politics to family life. Dave had a large breakfast on the morning of his death – two soft-boiled eggs, fruit salad, sweet semolina pudding, rolls, and English breakfast tea. As we waited for a taxi, in the hotel lobby, I remarked that the floor was 'nice granite.' Dave corrected me and said that it was marble, and proceeded to give me a five-minute explanation of the differences between the two substances (he was to die about two hours later). Just before Dave drank the lethal barbiturate, he calmly removed his wristwatch, and asked me to give it to his wife upon my return to England.

Again, I had witnessed someone who was determined to travel overseas to die, with the agreement of a doctor; who was completely at ease with his decision, and who ended his life in a peaceful, dignified manner, rather than exposing himself to a slow, unplanned, and possibly most unpleasant death, in the UK.

In February 2007, I travelled with Raymond, his long-term partner of twenty-eight years, Alan, and his adult niece, Simone, to Zurich. Raymond was terminally ill, suffering increasingly from pancreatic cancer. He had become quite religious, converting to Buddhism. Before Raymond and Alan left London, they were interviewed by a reporter from the *Guardian* as they felt that the first known Dignitas death, involving a gay couple from the UK, might be newsworthy, and both of them supported a change in the law to legalize doctor-assisted suicide.

Alan and Raymond lived in a Council flat in Hackney, in London. Because they were unable to pay all the necessary fees for going to Dignitas, I donated £1,500 – as, apart from helping Raymond, I wanted to highlight the fact that, if someone can afford all the costs involved, it is possible for that person to have an assisted suicide in Switzerland (nowadays, without any real risk to the relatives or friends who afterwards return to the UK); but, if someone is not so well off financially, then that person has to remain in the UK, without such an option, even if sometimes a reduction in some costs by Dignitas might be possible.

When we all left our Zurich hotel to travel to the Dignitas flat, it was raining hard. I sat in the front of the taxi. Suddenly, I noticed that, on the dashboard, there was a small Buddha figure – the Swiss driver then told me that his wife, from Thailand, was a Buddhist. As I turned around to tell Raymond about this, the sun suddenly came out. At once, the whole atmosphere in the taxi became cheerful and remained so for the rest of the journey. In the Dignitas flat, it is possible for those who die there to play their favourite music in the background – once, Raymond had been involved with Motown music – so, until after his death, Diana Ross sang quietly to him. Just a few minutes before he drank the barbiturate, Raymond, weak and quite jaundiced, asked

Simone to dance with him, which they did for a couple of minutes. Then, with a Buddhist gesture of farewell to each of us in the room, he swallowed his final drink, and soon died very peacefully – his final wish.

When Alan returned to London, the *Guardian*, and, also, the *Sunday Times*, refused to report on Raymond's death because, as one source told Alan, Raymond 'was not a celebrity', and going to Switzerland to die was 'now not very newsworthy.' Alan wanted to tell his story, and did so in *Gay Times* and the *Hackney Gazette*. Also, he 'wanted to challenge the law.' There had been a Home Office statement, in early 2007, that 'in our view, though the point is untested in the courts, an offence ... is committed even where the suicide occurs abroad ... if aiding, abetting etc. takes place in this country.' He kept on 'wanting closure' until, on July 17, 2009, he was suddenly arrested by four Hackney policemen who came to his flat. When I heard about this, I wrote an 'open letter' to the Hackney CID, stating that surely I should be arrested as well as I had 'given advice, moral support and financial assistance' to Raymond? In fact, this happened to me on July 31st. Both Alan and I were placed on bail after our arrests – this was renewed repeatedly until June the following year, when the Director of Public Prosecutions decided that no further action should be taken against either Alan or myself. One reason given by the DPP, for myself, was that I was 'aged 79 and that is highly likely to influence any sentence that might be imposed on him' (this led to the *Daily Telegraph*, on June 26, 2010, having a one-inch high headline saying 'Dr. Death ruled too old to face trial').

Nan was a close friend of mine for about fourteen years as we were both right-to-die activists – together, we attended several right-to-die conferences around the world, such as Tokyo (in 2004), Strasbourg (2007), and Melbourne (2010). Going to this last one was very difficult for her as she was increasingly suffering from severe and extensive osteoarthritis.

Nan had been a trained occupational therapist. She lived in central London, and, for many years, had had an active social life, often going to the theatre and political events, but her London activities became more and more restricted due to her progressive osteoarthritis. And, in her 85th year, she travelled to Bern, at the end of February 2011, with another close friend, Liz, and myself, to end her life there with the assistance of EX International.. She made her last trip in style. The three of us flew to Zurich from London's City Airport. There, we were met by a large, chauffeur-driven car, which drove us to Bern, where we all stayed in the Bellevue Palace Hotel, the best hotel in that city (incidentally, although Nan kindly offered to cover my expenses, I have always felt it important to pay for my travel costs whenever I have accompanied anyone on their final journey to Switzerland). On our first night in this hotel, we had a lengthy dinner, with the discussion ranging from personal stories about our families – Nan had been married to a RAF officer, and had three children – to right-to-die experiences we had had (Nan had also helped various people to travel to Switzerland, and knew very well what was involved, and Liz had also been on previous trips to Zurich and Bern). It was a very relaxed evening.

The next day, again with our chauffeured car, we all went for the final visit to the Swiss doctor who had reviewed Nan's medical records, earlier in the year, and now examined her and gave his approval for her assisted suicide. He himself was also beginning to suffer from osteoarthritis, and so could fully understand her situation.

Later, the same car took us to the flat, then used by EX International, in a most pleasant village outside Bern. Nan was beautifully dressed, and wearing some of her favourite jewellery. The usual bureaucratic Swiss procedures, that I had seen when someone had died in Zurich, were followed in this canton.

When it came to the thirty-minute period, between swallowing something 'to settle the stomach' and drinking the lethal dose of barbiturate, Nan, Liz and I sat quietly outside the bedroom where she would soon die. What does one talk about, in this situation? But Nan was the most relaxed person. Initially, she asked me about my oldest grandchild, who she had met in London, who was now studying in China. Then, about midway in this waiting period, Nan asked Liz, 'Do you have a nail file? – the corner of this nail is too sharp.' Fortunately, Liz quickly produced one, and the annoying nail was filed. Ten minutes later, still very calm, Nan walked into the bedroom and sat on the bed. She had asked me to hold a piece of Lindt chocolate for her in case she needed this after drinking the barbiturate solution which can taste bitter to many people. She quickly swallowed her last drink. I offered her the chocolate. But, her last words were, 'No thanks – it is not too bad.'

When she had died, as instructed by Nan, I telephoned her son, in the UK, to tell him about his mother's final day. She had strongly expressed her wish that none of her children should be present. In a note which Nan had asked to be sent to many of her friends, after her death, she wrote, 'For some time, my life has consisted of more pain than pleasure and, over the next months and years, the pain will be more and the pleasure less. I have a great feeling of relief that I have no further need to struggle through each day in dread of what further horrors may lie in wait. For many years, I have feared the long period of decline, sometimes called 'prolonged dwindling', that so many people unfortunately experience before they die.' Nan died in the way that she had long planned – a chosen and dignified death that she so wished could be an available option for many mentally competent, terminally ill, severely disabled, or elderly persons suffering with medical problems in the UK.

Each of the four persons I have accompanied to Switzerland were fortunate – they died with dignity. I remember each of their deaths as if they had occurred only a few days ago. Each of them impressed me so greatly. I can only end by repeating their shared strongly expressed wish: when will the possibility of a legalized doctor-supported assisted suicide happen in the UK?

The balance of the mind

Colin Brewer

In the last year or two, I have carried out psychiatric assessments for a few people who were planning to go to Switzerland for a medically-assisted rational suicide (MARS). In all cases, this followed a request to the patient by one or other of the three Swiss organisations who currently provide MARS. In some patients, the issue was whether a significant degree of brain damage existed – due, for example, to early dementia. In others, the issue was whether the patient was suffering from anything that could be called 'clinical depression' and if so, whether it was treatable. For all of them, the ultimate question was whether they had what relatively recent legislation defines as the 'mental capacity' to make decisions about their care and treatment, including decisions to refuse treatment and to seek MARS for intolerable and unrelievable distress. Mental capacity is also relevant to whether or not people are able to deal with financial and legal matters, such as signing a will, though that was never something that I was required to address.

The concept of 'mental capacity' is not a difficult one to understand, even for the layman. The Mental Capacity Act of 2005 has five basic principles. First, there is a *presumption* of capacity. That is, every adult has the right to make his or her own decisions and must be assumed to have the capacity to do so unless it is proved otherwise. Secondly, individuals have a right to be supported in making their own decisions and must be given all appropriate help before any conclusion that they are unable to do so. Thirdly – and particularly important in this context – they must have the right to make decisions even if the decisions seem eccentric or unwise. The two remaining principles are only relevant if someone does not appear to have capacity. They are that anything done for or on behalf of such people must be in their best interests and, finally, that whatever is done should be the least restrictive of their basic rights and freedoms. An important legal consideration is that 'capacity' is function-specific. In other words, a patient can have capacity for one function (such as making decisions about treatment or non-treatment) without necessarily having capacity for other functions (such as making complex financial decisions).

In order to demonstrate mental capacity in terms of the Act, the patient must show that he or she is able to receive and retain relevant information, show sufficient ability to understand and weigh the information (including any information derived from advice) and demonstrate the ability to communicate their decision. What this means in practice is that even patients with significant impairment of brain function may still have mental capacity provided that they pass the three basic tests. Thus, a moderate degree of dementia does not automatically equal a lack of mental capacity. Even relatively severe brain damage may still be compatible with having mental capacity.

Compared with brain damage, the concept of depression is more complicated and involves questions of judgement and philosophy as well as clinical skills and experience. Arguments about the differences between 'depression' and 'understandable misery' have kept psychiatrists busy and divided for several generations and are not likely to run out of steam any time soon. The medicalisation of misery (and of Life) is now quite often discussed in the media, particularly when a new edition of DSM (the Diagnostic and Statistical Manual of the American Psychiatric Association) appears. What used to be regarded as relatively ordinary quirks and variations in human behaviour (and fortune) increasingly have a diagnosis attached to them rather than an ordinary descriptive term. Thus children who would at one time have been regarded as stubborn, disobedient or merely tiresome may now be labelled as having Oppositional Defiant Disorder. Admittedly, the definition includes a requirement that the problem must go beyond the bounds of normal childhood misbehaviour, but that still leaves a large grey or subjective area and the same applies to several other DSM disorders.

Clearly, depression and suicide are closely related, if only in the sense that nobody seeks death because of an excess of happiness, whereas many people do so because they experience too much unhappiness or misfortune. Much of this reactive or understandable unhappiness is surely not most appropriately viewed as a 'disease.' That is not the same as saying that people who want help to deal with their unhappiness should be ignored but the record of suicide prevention programmes directed at those who have already demonstrated their vulnerability by making an attempt is not very encouraging. Some studies in the 1960s caused the Samaritans to claim that their establishment and growth around that time had been responsible for the sharp fall in suicides that was unparalleled in other comparable countries. The real explanation soon became apparent. It was due to the progressive replacement of toxic coal gas – the preferred British method of suicide – by non-toxic North Sea gas.

It has been widely recognised for several hundred years that merely wanting to die is not of itself evidence of mental illness. Not everybody accepts this and the Catholic Church in particular has a problem with the idea that wishing to die can be anything except a major sin – questioning the mercy and goodness of God – or a sign of madness. Canon law still ordains that suicides cannot be buried in consecrated ground, unless they were insane. The law is rarely enforced these days but it influenced subsequent European attitudes to suicide for well over a thousand years and I think that it still does.

The validity of historical Christian attitudes to suicide is discussed in the Rev. Prof. Paul Badham's contribution to this volume and more thoroughly in his book *Is there a Christian Case for Assisted Dying?*[1] In Section 6, I summarise the development of those early views. (For those who want an even wider historical view, I recommend Georges Minois's *History of Suicide: Voluntary Death in Western Culture*.[2] He notes, among many other things, that no fewer than 52 of Shakespeare's characters commit suicide.)

The readers for whom this book is written could hardly be more different from the tens of thousands of impulsive and often intoxicated people in the grip of strong but mostly transient passions and emotions, who make successful or unsuccessful suicide attempts every year in Britain. Typically, these attempts are linked to sudden and unexpected changes in their lives; the sort of changes that more mature and experienced people would generally expect to accommodate, perhaps with some help. Many in this large group (though there are quite a few exceptions) are relieved to have survived their attempts. That is emphatically not the case with MARS and deliverance.

The Swiss organisations are willing to consider MARS purely on the grounds of intractable mental illness. However, it involves some separate considerations which I will not address here, not least because none of my cases involved severe depression, let alone depression on its own. Indeed, all of them had severe and progressive medical/physical conditions that could not be relieved by any management that was acceptable to them. In most cases, 'depression' was not an important issue because despite much expert and comprehensive medical treatment and assessment, the patient had never received a diagnosis of depression or a prescription for antidepressants. In some cases, antidepressants had been prescribed in a low dose (well below the usual antidepressant dose) not for depression but for their occasional usefulness as an adjunct to pain relief. Nevertheless, the Swiss flagged it up and requested an assessment for depression.

Some patients had received antidepressant prescriptions from their GPs or specialists because these doctors wondered, not entirely unreasonably, whether the patient's desire to go to Switzerland for MARS might be a 'depressive' symptom that might respond to antidepressants. I say 'not entirely' because most GPs and many psychiatrists have an unreasonable faith in the effectiveness of antidepressant drugs. Good randomised clinical trials of antidepressants generally show that as many as 40-50% of patients will respond to placebo and other non-specific effects and that about 30% will not respond significantly or at all. That leaves no more than about 20% of patients who may have a specific and beneficial effect from antidepressants. Furthermore, no study has convincingly shown that antidepressants (with the possible exception of lithium in manic-depressive or 'bipolar' illness) have significantly reduced suicide rates. Indeed, early tricyclic antidepressants were so toxic that far more people died from taking overdoses of them than might conceivably have been diverted from making a suicide attempt. With these considerations in mind, let me now introduce a few real people. I have pseudonymised and/or slightly disguised all of them but the important clinical details are true.

JACQUES

Jacques has a degree in psychology, among other disciplines. He was born abroad (a fact that has caused some difficulties in getting the necessary documents for the punctilious Swiss authorities) but has had a successful and fulfilling academic career. Now in his late 70s, he remains in touch with some of his former students. Although antidepressants have been prescribed (see above) psychiatric assessments suggest that he has never been significantly depressed and it is not difficult to see why. He has a lively sense of humour, including the black variety and there is often much laughter during our meetings which, because he lives near some friends whom I often visit, were much more frequent than was required for purely bureaucratic reasons. I shall miss him when he makes his final journey. His reasons for requesting MARS are a mixture of the physical and the cerebral. Crippled by severe, painful and obvious arthritis, which makes him housebound, he also has long-standing heart disease and high blood pressure. Several years ago, he travelled to the Netherlands in the hope that he could obtain MARS there but was told that this was possible only for permanent – or at any rate, long-term – Dutch residents. Now he has additional worries about his eyesight and says his memory is not what it was. It sounds no worse than in most people of his age but he dreads the possibility of a sudden deterioration in brain function that would deprive him of the mental capacity to decide on the manner of his death. Given his history of heart disease and hypertension, his fear of a stroke is not unreasonable. He has long been divorced. His children have mixed feelings about his proposal but seem to accept his right to make this decision. Tests of brain function show no serious impairment. Evidence of depression was entirely lacking, as judged both by the standard rating scales and by my quite considerable experience of assessing and treating depression in both private and NHS practice, especially if we discount the two questions in the widely-used Beck

Depression Inventory that ask whether the patient feels suicidal and whether they are optimistic about the future. Jacques has had a good life. It is not good now and will not get any better. He wants to go before the very real chance that it will get much worse.

NICK

Nick has motor neurone disease – MND. (Americans call it 'Lou Gehrig's disease' after a US baseball player who died from it.) Until it struck him in his late 70s a few years ago, he had led a happy and privileged life. His house, in one of England's most beautiful villages, is full of good furniture, paintings and porcelain. Naturally, he does not want to leave it for the inevitably more utilitarian and less elegant surroundings of even the best care home, which he and Alice, his wife, could easily afford if they wished. He knows that death from MND can be particularly cruel and distressing for both patient and onlookers, involving as it does a progressive inability to swallow or breathe properly and an increasing tendency for food to get stuck in the windpipe or lungs.

Alice cooked a delicious lunch on my first visit, which all three of us enjoyed. Nick hoped to survive for at least a year because of various milestones he wanted to celebrate and was merely, at that stage, reserving his place in the queue for Dignitas. A few months later, after a sharp deterioration, he realised that he would have to miss out on the milestones and prepared for an early journey to Zurich. Reports have to be no more than three months old, so I made a further visit. As usual in MND, cerebral function was unimpaired. There was no sign of depression. Just a determination to have a quick, timely and civilised death rather than a protracted and unpleasant one.

In the event, further rapid deterioration occurred that made travel to Switzerland even more difficult. Fortunately, the GP – rather than a hospice consultant – was in charge of the terminal care arrangements. He knew and sympathised with Nick's wishes about death but in the normal course of MND, death could have been weeks away. MND is not usually a painful condition but the GP kept asking Alice if Nick was in pain. 'He wasn't, really, but eventually, I twigged.' Alice told me later. 'The GP was looking for an excuse to start him on morphine.' The nursing team evidently went along with this common variety of deception and/or self-deception. Nick's breathing, already compromised by MND, got slower, his lungs got congested and he couldn't cough up the secretions. It wasn't quite the quick death he wanted, untroubled by respiratory problems and after saying a proper goodbye to his family but it could easily have been much worse. Even if most hospice consultants probably don't believe that suffering is ennobling, they tend not to like using morphine when there is no conventional indication for it, as in Nick's case. Care is often shared with other hospice doctors. Questions may be asked. Ideological feathers may be ruffled. The GP, though not quite in the privileged and unquestioned position of Lord Dawson in George V's sickroom, found it easier to do what the hospice doctors might have wanted to do but probably wouldn't have done.

A further – religious – detail is worth mentioning. Their local (Anglican) vicar knew of Nick's plan to die in Switzerland but was very willing to hold a funeral service afterwards. Other clergy in the parish agreed. It seems strange that ordinary clerics and theologians can evidently hold very different views about MARS but bishops, who often disagree strongly with each other about major church doctrines, have always voted in the House of Lords as a monolithic block on this issue so far.[3]

HENRY

Henry is in his early eighties. A long-time supporter of voluntary euthanasia, he has developed early Alzheimer's disease and the busy social life that he and his wife used to enjoy is no longer possible, because he loses the thread of conversations. Retaining enough insight to realise that things can only get steadily worse and that he may soon not have the mental capacity to decide the manner of his death, he activates his Swiss connections. He meets me at the door and clearly understands why I have come and what we have to discuss. Mental testing shows definite short-term memory impairment but he never loses track of the purpose of our conversation, remains clear and consistent in his desire to go to Switzerland and recognises the consequences of this decision. He is not depressed and not even gloomy. In short, he has mental capacity. After a very good life, he wants a good death. He also tells me very clearly that he wants his far from insignificant estate to go to his family and not to the staff and shareholders of care homes.

MARJORY

Marjory was a nonagenarian living in some style in a large, airy apartment, overlooking one of London's parks with 24-hour care provided by two young and attentive people from a land where the elderly are still generally valued or at least respected. Marjory's case was complicated because she had a well-documented history of manic-depressive illness, for which she had been admitted to psychiatric clinics several times. However, it was significant that nearly all of these admissions had been to private rather than NHS asylums (as they were then called) because Marjory had been a very successful businesswoman. Indeed, like quite a few manic-depressives, her success was partly due to her manic swings because provided they were not too marked, they gave her the energy, drive, imagination and lack of need for sleep that enabled her to out-smart her competitors and to rest on her laurels during any subsequent depressive phases.

Long retired, she had developed a progressive disease that was likely to give her an unpleasant death within a few years. By itself, this would not have caused her to seek an early exit at this stage, even though she first became a member of Dignitas (to which she had given a generous donation) a decade earlier. However, she had also developed an intractable pain that was making her previously enjoyable retirement increasingly distressing and lacking in pleasure. None of her numerous specialists could come up with a clear diagnosis, let alone an effective treatment. However, an antidepressant had been prescribed for pain and this, together with the manic-depressive history and a suggestion – later discounted – of early Alzheimer's disease, naturally led the Swiss to ask her to arrange an assessment.

Several recent medical reports confirmed the absence of both dementia and depression but they were not recent enough for the Swiss. Her pain consultant was particularly reluctant to accept that MARS was not an unreasonable idea for a nonagenarian with intractable pain and doubly-limited life-expectancy. As with Jacques, my assessment of Marjory was punctuated by many laughs and interesting accounts of a busy and well-spent life. Of depression or of brain impairment beyond what one might reasonably expect to find in anyone of her age, there was no sign. No sign, either, of depression's non-identical twin – mania.

CHARLOTTE

I include Charlotte's case because although, like Henry, she had Alzheimer's disease and was in some respects more severely affected, her story has some positive features. It shows that Alzheimer patients who are arranging for MARS when the time seems appropriate can still get pleasure and fulfilment out of life. There are also some important diagnostic issues. Charlotte's dementia was quite slowly progressive and I first saw her four years after the initial diagnosis. By that time, it had reached the point where an alarm system had been installed in her house because she occasionally got confused and wandered the streets. However, she lived on her own, not far from her very supportive family, and had recently been re-elected to the chair of her local Women's Institute, whose members knew the diagnosis. The tipping point would come when she could no longer live in her own home. That point was approaching but she wanted to hang on until it was very near. Charlotte knew more than most patients about the realities of cerebral impairment because when her husband was still in his sixties, he got very severe pneumonia and the resultant lack of oxygen in his blood caused catastrophic brain damage. She had to share in the eventual decision to switch off his life support.

Apart from assessing whether her mental capacity was impaired by the dementia, I was also asked to decide whether or not she was 'psychotic.' This label had been attached to her following a couple of nocturnal episodes where she was not just confused but believed, during one of them, that some local youths had been banging on her front door. True or not (her daughter thought it was most likely a hallucination or the misinterpretation of an innocent noise) that belief developed into a fear that her daughter had been kidnapped and Charlotte went out to look for her. She was examined at home by a locum (i.e. temporary) psychiatrist who had never seen her before and, according to her daughter, stayed for barely ten minutes. He not only gave her a 'psychotic' label but also prescribed an anti-psychotic drug to go with it. This caused unpleasant side-effects, so Charlotte stopped it after a week.

Now, delusions and hallucinations are certainly common features of psychoses but in Charlotte's case, they had not lasted for more than an hour or so. We do not generally think of that kind of short-lived problem as a psychosis, especially if the patient already has a diagnosis of dementia. 'Psychosis' in this context implies a condition lasting for at least some days and often for weeks or months, during which time medication may be indicated. I thought it significant that all these isolated delusional episodes occurred in the middle of the night. Even young and healthy people sometimes wake in a confused state and hear imaginary sounds and it must be a lot easier if the brain is beginning to fail. There are even special names for hallucinations that occur when people are falling asleep (hypnogogic) or waking up (hypnopompic). They can be frightening but don't normally need any treatment.

In any case, there were no signs of any psychotic thought processes when Charlotte came to see me. Indeed, it wasn't immediately obvious that she had any cognitive impairment, since she could follow a conversation and correctly recalled a holiday with her daughter two weeks previously. However, more precise tests of memory showed definite impairments, consistent with her very detailed assessment at the local hospital the previous year. She wasn't at all depressed and said 'I want to make the most of everything I can while I can.' Nevertheless, within less than three months, she decided to activate her long-planned journey to Switzerland, where she had a peaceful death in the presence of her close family. Charlotte took the risk of losing her mental capacity before deciding to go to Switzerland but in her case, it paid off. Of course, the Swiss doctors involved make their own separate examinations, including psychiatric assessment, before prescribing the lethal medication.

Charlotte was a clergyman's daughter. Her religious faith was probably the strongest of this group and she had a firm belief in an afterlife

EDDIE.

Of all the people in this collection of case histories, Eddie is the one I shall miss the most. From a purely selfish viewpoint, I even wish he would delay or abandon his planned journey to Switzerland. First of all, he is the youngest of the group, only in his sixties. From a modest background, he reached senior positions in his profession and he also held a short-service commission in the army. Later, after a serious sporting accident forced his retirement, he became a magistrate and served on the board of several charities. He is a truly charismatic person, witty, well-informed and very articulate. Unfortunately, after losing much of his sight in the accident, he is now losing the rest.

You might think that a man with such obvious personal resources would adapt to this latest disaster with the same grit and determination that he showed earlier. You, however, are not Eddie. Clearly, he is no wimp but he says that he wishes he had not survived the accident. His particular dread is of losing his minimal residual vision and having to live in a world of total blackness. He experienced this for several weeks after the accident (aggravated briefly by terrifying visual hallucinations from the morphine he was given) and he does not want to go through it again. The decision to seek MARS if he were to lose all visual sensation is not a recent or transient one: he joined Dignitas ten years ago.

Like me, his family would prefer him to stay around but they accept that this impressive and strong-willed man is entitled to his own definition of intolerable suffering. There has never been any suggestion of mental illness in his many contacts with doctors and there is no sign of it now. Even if I thought that a trial of antidepressants might change his mind (and it seems vanishingly unlikely) he would refuse them, partly because his experience with morphine has made him wary of any drugs that affect the mind. He still has a lot of pain from his injuries but takes nothing stronger than paracetamol.

SANDOR

Finally, to the case of Sandor, a Hungarian-born Jewish refugee from the Nazis and thus someone who might be expected to place a particularly high value on his existence. (And also to know, better than most people, the crucial difference between voluntary and involuntary euthanasia.) Now approaching his centenary, he still played bridge regularly, devoured books and had eagerly embraced the internet. The most prominent item in his living-room was a computer that was as switched-on as he himself soon proved to be. Sandor suffered from no illness that was likely to carry him off within a year, let alone the six months envisaged in Lord Falconer's bill. His raised blood pressure and a few other circulatory problems that might have done so were well controlled with drug treatment. His father, who had also escaped the Holocaust, had lived to be 103 but this apparent genetic sturdiness was a source of worry rather than reassurance, for his father had developed dementia by the time he died. Sandor very much wanted to avoid a similar fate but what made him feel that he should exit sooner rather than later was the progressive deterioration in his quality of life. This was caused by a number of complaints that might have been individually tolerable but were collectively making for much more pain than pleasure. They included digestive troubles, dizzy spells, pain from crumbling bones and being unable to leave his house without assistance. All these problems become progressively more common in the very old and they often do not respond well to treatment, as was unfortunately the case with Sandor. He knew, with something approaching certainty, that these things would only get worse and he was worried that if he started to get demented, like his father, he would be unable to retain control of his death and dying.

Sandor had outlived his wife and one of his children. Because war and the Nazis had interrupted his education, his employment had involved positions that were less distinguished and perhaps less satisfying than those of most of the previous examples. However, he had always enjoyed his hobbies and a good social life and unlike many people in their 90s, he still did. He knew that he had, in many ways, been lucky and he did not want his luck to run out.

It was obvious that someone who still played bridge was unlikely to have any problems with his memory and the

Mini Mental State test confirmed that with a full score. His score on the Beck Depression Inventory was well below the cut-off point and he had never seen his doctors for any psychiatric reason, or received antidepressants.   Indeed, during our conversation, it became evident that 'depression' just wasn't one of the things that Sandor had ever done. His was a classic desire for Old-Age Rational Suicide. Apart from the barbiturate cocktail, he died in Switzerland in classic Victorian style, surrounded by family and friends.

Nearly all these people had led lives that marked them out as exemplary and high-achieving citizens of our country. They had mostly held responsible positions, their finances seemed generally better than those of the average citizen and all could afford at least some private care at home or in hospital, so that they had more choices than many people. Those who were divorced or widowed could usually have sold their houses and had months or years of the best care available but they rejected this choice. All seemed to have mostly enjoyed life and with good reason.   They wanted deaths that matched their lives – with a minimum of pain, of course, but also well-organised, civilised, considerate of others, not too long and above all, dignified.

References:

1. Badham P. *Is there a Christian case for assisted dying?*, London SPCK 2009

2. Minois G. (Transl. Cochrane L) History of Suicide: Voluntary Death in Western Culture. Baltimore, Johns Hopkins. 1999

3. An account of Nick's illness and death was written pseudonymously by his daughter in the Financial Times of 14th March 2014 under the title: 'Helping Dad die: a daughter's story'.

An Instinct for Kindness

Chris Larner,
playwright

It's Tuesday the ninth of November, 2010. Seven in the morning and I'm in a hotel in Switzerland, drinking espresso, smoking roll-ups and my head spinning cartwheels of anxiety. The thought occurs to me that I must make this into a play, and at once I am repulsed by my own crassness. But three months later, back in England, I'm sitting in the *Raj Poot,* Streatham, telling producer James Seabright, that the story is burning a hole in my heart and won't keep quiet, and asking him if he'd produce *An Instinct For Kindness.*

I had gone to Switzerland to help my ex-wife Allyson get to Dignitas, where she would end her life. We stayed in Switzerland for three days: me and Allyson and her sister Vivienne. On the Tuesday morning, we wheeled Allyson into a portakabin building on an industrial estate, around the corner from the hotel, and Allyson knocked back 25ml of the foulest-tasting stuff you ever put in your mouth.

Back at the Swiss hotel, Vivienne and I are on our own. Everyone is looking at us, either that or pointedly not doing so. I don't know which is worse. We smell of Death. We smell of taboo. We are disgusting. The following morning, in Allyson's room, we are packed and ready to go back home, stunned as cattle. A chambermaid is at the open door. We have bin-liners full of redundant medicines and nappies, we have bulging suitcases and an electric wheelchair, dismantled and gaffer-taped for transportation. We are weighed down with the clutter of grief and guilt, and the chambermaid sees it all. I have seen her around, these last three days, not to speak to but they've worked around us: coming back to change the sheets when we're downstairs for cups of tea. I wave her away, signalling, *do next door first,* but she stays there. I say, in bad German, *the other room, thank you.* She stays there, sheepish but stubborn, looking at Vivienne. *Deine Schwester,* she says eventually – and it's a question – your sister? I translate for Vivienne, who starts like a guilty thing as if the police have called. Yes, I say, her sister.

Ist besser fur Sie, says the maid, impelled to continue no matter what. In a soft tone she says, *ist besser fur Sie, jetzt. Ich denke so. Ist besser fur Sie.* Again I translate but now the tears are thick lumps in my throat and Vivienne's eyes are not her own, either. Thank you, I say, yes, it's better. She was in a lot of pain. *My mother* says the chambermaid, softly, touching her own heart, *my mother. The same.* And so it goes. The first of many who will touch her own heart, to touch ours, to show that we are not alone. In a shitty world, full of Lies and Adverts, incurable diseases and curable cruelty, the human instinct for kindness, for empathy, shines through stubborn. And there rests some kind of Hope. At least for those still living.

It might perhaps seem mawkish, perverse, even to consider writing and performing such an experience, but I have long since got over my squeamishness. During rehearsals, Hannah Eidinow (my brilliant director) and I would have to stop, often, to cry or walk around the block, cursing ourselves for being so weird as to seek immersion in such upsetting material. But as we worked, I found, too, anger welling up inside me, and I knew that there was a reason beyond personal catharsis, to be making this show.

For Allyson had suffered twice. Firstly, as the MS took hold; year by year stripping her body of function, of mobility, of dignity, of stamina; shrinking her life and her horizons inexorably to turn the confident, vibrant woman who I had met in 1982 into a frightened, emaciated and helpless figure in a wheelchair; for whom medical science could do nothing and for whose future held only further deterioration and pain. Tragic, sure, but no one's fault: MS is a cruel disease for which – although advances have been made – there is no cure.

But secondly, as if her health was not enough, to be dragged through the maze of needless stress which getting to Dignitas entails, was simply cruel. People think that getting to Dignitas is easy: it ain't. It's an expensive, stressful, secrecy-shrouded, semi-legal, bureaucratic and logistical nightmare.

Once she had decided that enough was enough – a decision which she put off as long as Hope shone bright in her optimistic heart – it would have been kind to have let Allyson die in her own bed, surrounded by friends and family and love. Instead, we struggled a thousand miles from home, speaking in a foreign language, amongst strangers. Saying goodbye in a cold and clinical apartment, and the ashes arriving back by DHL, a fortnight later.

There are many ethical, moral, legal and practical matters to be considered in changing our law on assisted dying. There are concerned voices which must be heard and accommodated. It is not an easy matter. And, of course, we should fight tooth and nail for palliative care and hospices to be available to all, with those services funded better than their current pitiful levels. This is unarguable. We should help people to live as long and as happily as is possible.

But equally, when someone is suffering like Allyson suffered, has suffered enough and is suffering still: when someone can say in the clarity of her mind: I want now to die, please let me die, surely we should be civilized enough to allow her that release. Otherwise, we are a cruel land.

When the BBC announced they were to air Terry Pratchett's documentary, in which he followed two individuals who ended their lives at Dignitas, the BBC received twelve hundred complaints: *how dare you spend licence-payers' money on promulgating this monstrous point of view* – you get the picture. But – and here's the thing – seventy percent of those complaints arrived *before* the documentary was aired. In other words, the objection was to debate itself, not any conclusion. Personally, I rail against the silence, and I know Allyson would agree with me, and that is why I shall continue to perform *An Instinct For Kindness* so long as it might be necessary.

5

Four score years and then?

Rational Old-Age Suicide.

Michael Irwin

Being born in 1931, and still alive, means that I am now past my sell-by date. Calling an elderly person 'old' is generally discouraged in both the UK and the USA. Therefore, it was rather surprising when, in 2009, the 8th edition of *Mosby's Medical Dictionary*, published in Missouri, defined someone '85 years of age and older' as being 'old-old.' Today, in the UK, there are about 1.3 million people who are old-old. By 2040, one person in twenty will be in this group.

Of everything that someone can ever experience, nothing is really more overwhelming than the thought of one's death. Most people naturally try to keep this event out of their minds for as long as possible but while we should not have a morbid preoccupation with death, I believe we should all plan ahead, carefully considering, in the hope that we have a choice, how we might want to die. We should also be willing to talk about it (especially when we are relatively healthy) with family and close friends. After all, it is a collective destiny for all living creatures on Earth.

Society gives copious advice on how to bring a baby into this world. Why do we not provide equal guidance, and even greater assistance, about how we can safely leave this existence? While we generally have a good palliative care system in the UK (which provides one form of 'assisted dying'), which will be adequate for many people, there are many other individuals, like myself, who do not want to live 'to the bitter end.' Surely most intelligent people would prefer to die relatively comfortably of their final medical conditions rather than die from the often unpleasant side-effects or complications of futile treatments? From my own knowledge, very few doctors themselves 'cling to life against all the odds', undergoing such unrealistic care. I do not want my relatives and friends to remember me as an increasingly decrepit person, especially if I become more and more dependent on others, even those who love me, for my basic needs.

There is no recovery from being old-old. When one is young, living to a ripe old age would always seem to be a cause for celebration. But, many very elderly people live in fear of how they will endure it as the extra years will often become more of a curse than a blessing. It is a harsh reality that, once most people reach their mid-eighties today, their futures will be relatively short. Dying soon after this point in time, while still in fair control of my life and faculties, may mean sacrificing a very modest period of simple existence, but at least I will be spared the humiliation of a progressively deteriorating body. Above all, I want my three daughters and my partner, Angela, to remember me as someone as close to my normal self as possible. And, now thinking economically, I would not want to waste my somewhat limited financial resources on ending my life in an expensive nursing home. I want to leave adequate legacies to my family – a much better way to help Angela and my children.

Nowadays, many of us die slowly, with different parts of our bodies breaking down at varying rates. For many elderly individuals, our final death is often preceded by years of chronic ill-health. My main medical problems, at present, are some difficulty in walking (due to a lower spine injury sustained in a major car accident in 2007), controlled hypertension, gout, and a gradual dwindling energy. Fortunately, at present, none of these conditions essentially limits my desired activities. But, ageing is beginning to diminish me slowly. In fact, when my death does come, it will take away only part of my original adult self (of course, the 'original me' fortunately lives on in the genes existing in my three children and eight grandchildren – my evolutionary legacy).

During the 1980s, when I was the Medical Director of the United Nations, in New York, I became aware of 'living wills', and I have had such a document (regularly revised) for myself since those days. Thus, if I lose my mental faculties, my relatives will know the degree of medical care I wish to receive (essentially, none!). Soon after I retired back to London in 1993, I became active in the Voluntary Euthanasia Society, becoming its Chairman in 1996 (until 1999) and again in 2001 (until 2003). Then, I began campaigning to change the law in the UK to legalize medically-assisted rational suicide (MARS) for the 'terminally ill.' Unfortunately, mainly because of strong opposition from religious organizations (and, to a lesser extent, from disability groups and the 'medical establishment'), I do not expect this to happen soon.

But, in addition to providing, one day, some choice for the terminally ill, I believe that equal attention should now be given to the eventual possibility of legalized doctor-assisted suicide for those mentally competent individuals who are severely disabled (who can forget Tony Nicklinson, 'locked-in' for over seven years?), who suffer much longer than those likely to die within months, and also for those who become old-old and suffer from various medical problems.

Surely the decision (and, now, I am being very personal) to decide, at an advanced age, that enough is enough and avoiding further suffering to have a dignified death is the ultimate human right for all very elderly, mentally competent individuals. Unfortunately, today, death for the old-old is rarely dignified – many will die in hospitals or care homes where their lives are often depersonalized, shaped by rules and regulations. Therefore, on December 10, 2009 (a date annually observed globally as Human Rights Day), assisted by Angela Farmer, Nan Maitland and Liz Nichols, I founded the Society for Old Age Rational Suicide (SOARS)[1]. Our logo is the derelict West Pier in Brighton and Hove, once a place of great excitement and pleasure (like so many elderly people!).

Supporting the rationale for SOARS was a 2002 statement from the European Court of Human Rights which stated that, 'In an era of growing medical sophistication, combined with longer life expectancies, many people are concerned that they should not be forced to linger on in old age or in states of advanced physical or mental decrepitude which conflict with strongly-held ideas of self and personal identity.'

Of course, the opponents of MARS, even for the terminally ill, and perhaps for those severely disabled, will say that old age rational suicide (it is vital to stress the word 'rational') is an example of a 'slippery slope.' But, some 'slopes' can be beneficial – an excellent example is to remember how people, in the UK, obtained the vote in national elections. Years ago, only rich, male landowners could vote. Then, more men became voters. Then, women over the age of thirty. Then, all adults who were over twenty-one. And, finally, in 1969, all those over eighteen could vote. The law was gradually changed after parliamentary decision, backed by great support in the general population.

Today, MARS and/or voluntary euthanasia for the terminally ill is possible in Belgium, Luxembourg, the Netherlands, Switzerland, and the U.S. States of Oregon, Vermont and Washington. And, Belgium, the Netherlands and Switzerland also provide such assistance for both the severely disabled and the very elderly with medical problems. Are we so different to the Dutch or the Swiss? Of course, we are not. And, fortunately, the Swiss are willing to help foreigners.

Public opinion, in the UK today, generally agrees with the possibility of old age rational suicide. In July 2010, an ICM national poll, commissioned by SOARS, showed that 67%, of the 1,009 adults surveyed, supported this. In March 2011, another national ICM poll of 1,008 adults revealed that 66 per cent were in agreement. And, in March 2013, a further ICM poll showed that 70% of those interviewed agreed with the idea of old age rational suicide.

For old age rational suicide to become legalized, it will be essential to have very strict safeguards, such as:

Two doctors (one a consultant geriatrician) agreeing

that the individual is mentally competent and has carefully considered all the possible options.

An interview with an independent legal expert, experienced in family matters, to ensure that there is no pressure being applied by relatives.

A waiting period of at least two months between a request being made and the necessary medication being provided (which must be taken in the presence of an experienced healthcare professional),

A report being provided to a central government office.

Unfortunately, the possibility of legalized old age rational suicide in the UK may not happen for many decades. But, I hope that there can be an open public discussion now with many, especially parliamentarians, considering what they might possibly want for themselves when they become old-old.

I anticipate that my death will happen in one of three ways – very suddenly (such as from a massive heart attack or stroke, without any obvious warning – this is possible because of my extensive hypertensive history); fairly quickly (when I would expect that the 'instructions' written in my advance decision – the present term for a 'living will' – would be respected); or gradually, as the necessary detailed steps are taken for a 'Swiss option' when I am suffering due to being obviously old-old. It is impossible to prepare for the very sudden exit except to live each remaining day to the full because it might be my last one. And, it would be wonderful for me (but, not initially for her) if this happened when I was next to Angela.

If I become completely mentally incompetent – from, perhaps, a major stroke or a severe car accident, and remain in this state for at least two weeks – I expect then that the 'instructions' expressed in detail in my present advance decision will be followed. Most British doctors today have no difficulty in respecting what is written in these documents, but, if this should not happen in my case, I am confident that my two health care proxies, named in this advance decision, will successfully 'go into battle' on my behalf.

Because I have been so impressed, from very personal experiences, by the 'Swiss option', this is the avenue that I will follow (if I have not died suddenly or had need to rely upon my advance decision) when I am old-old and burdened with various medical problems. I have been a member of Dignitas since 2003 when I first met Ludwig Minelli, its founder, at his home in Forch, a suburb of Zurich. In addition, I also joined EX International (based in Bern) in 2007. When a friend heard that I was now a member of these two Swiss organizations, willing to help foreigners with a doctor-assisted suicide, he joked that I was like a man who wears both braces and a belt to hold up his trousers – a form of double insurance. Finally, soon after a third Swiss group, able to assist foreigners, was established in early 2012 – Lifecircle, in Biel-Benken, near Basle – I also joined them, essentially to show my support for their work, and to have still a third possibility for myself.

Personally, at the right moment in the future, I hope that I'll See Myself Out, Thank You, with a rational doctor-assisted suicide, with the help of some of my Swiss friends – surely an appropriate finale for the founder of SOARS. If only this possibility was available today in the UK – that would really be paradise on Earth!

Reference:

1. www.soars.org.uk

Labour and sorrow

Lord Avebury,
former Liberal MP, human rights campaigner

Over the last 20 years I have had a few close shaves that made me think about death, including a quadruple bypass, a burst colon, lung cancer and an aortic aneurysm. None of these were conditions that involved more than temporary pain and a fairly low risk, though

All that lives must die
Passing through nature to eternity.

But then in August 2011 I was diagnosed with myelofibrosis, an incurable form of blood cancer, that ultimately leads to various unpleasant and painful symptoms, needing frequent blood transfusions to prevent the arteries seizing up with fibres. Would I then want to carry on with a Golgotha of suffering, affecting the family and carers, or would I sooner forego the last few weeks of misery?

More and more people are going to confront that dilemma, as medical science enables them to live fairly normal lives well beyond Psalm 90's expectation that

'the days of our years are three score years and ten....'.

But the verse continues:

'....and if by reason of strength they be fourscore years, yet is their strength labour and sorrow'.

The final stages may be a crescendo of pain and suffering, from which death is the only release. How can we say that the law should deny people in this situation access to the exit door? Terminally ill patients who are mentally competent ought surely to be able to get medical help to end their lives. Unless they are absolutely desperate, refusing medication or ceasing to eat or drink are not to be contemplated. A relative of mine who died in a care home not long ago did neither but used to say every time I visited her that she wished she could die.

It is estimated that one in ten suicides in England are by people with a terminal or chronic condition, which implies that some 500 suicides a year are by people with a serious physical illness. The true number is probably higher because coroners are aware of the social stigma of a suicide verdict and so try to avoid it. If those people had been able to consult their doctor about assisted dying, they could have been referred for expert counselling and might have decided to soldier on with life.

Ultimately, though, a patient should have the right to make this decision, and to be helped to carry it out, relying on J. S. Mill's principle that an individual's freedom should only be restricted to prevent harm to others. This is the bedrock of Liberal thinking on personal liberty. I reach this conclusion even though as a Buddhist I recognise the precept against the taking of life. But the Buddha taught the virtue of *karuna*, an active form of compassion which involves the alleviation of suffering, an intrinsic characteristic of the human condition. This suffering may be not only the patient's, but his immediate family's as well. They may be physically, mentally or financially exhausted by the duty of care.

The practical difficulty of deciding whether an illness is terminal is not insuperable. When I was first diagnosed with myelofibrosis, a consultant estimated that I had one year left of useful life. I'm still in reasonable shape 18 months later and clearly not yet terminal but I think it will not be difficult to recognise when it does eventually reach that stage.

Finally, is it not wrong to force a person who is determined to end his life to travel to Switzerland, with his carers, for the purpose? This is surely a matter on which the whole of Europe should adopt the same law, so that terminally ill patients do not have to undertake long journeys across international frontiers as they approach death.

The noble act of suicide

Brian Sewell,
art critic, journalist.

Every night I swallow a handful of pills. In the morning and during the day I swallow others, haphazardly, for I am not always in the right place at the right time, but at night there is a ritual. I undress. I clean my teeth. I wipe the mirror clear of splashes and see with some distaste the reflection of my decaying body, wondering that it ever had the impertinence to indulge in the pleasures of the flesh.

And then I take the pills. Some are for a heart that too often makes me feel that I have a misfiring single-cylinder diesel engine in my rib-cage. Others are for the ordinary afflictions of age and still others ease the aches of old bones that creak and crunch. All in their way are poisons – that they do no harm is only a matter of dosage.

I intend, one day, to take an overdose. Not yet, for the experts at that friendly and understanding hospital, the Brompton in Kensington, manage my heart condition very well. But the bone-rot will reach a point – not beyond endurance but beyond my willingness to endure it – when drugs prescribed to numb the pain so affect the functions of my brain that all the pleasures of music, art and books are dulled, and I merely exist. An old buffer in a chair, sleeping and waking, sleeping and waking.

The thought of suicide is a great comfort, for it is what I shall employ if mere existence is ever all that I have. The difficulty will be that I must have the wit to identify the time, the weeks, the days, even the critical moment (for it will not be long) between my recognising the need to end my life and the loss of my physical ability to carry out the plan.

There is a plan. I know exactly what I want to do and where I want to do it – not at home, not in my own bed. I shall write a note addressed 'To whom it may concern' explaining that I am committing suicide, that I am in sound mind, that no one else has been involved and, if I am discovered before my heart has stopped, I do not want to be resuscitated. With this note in my pocket, I shall leave the house and totter off to a bench – foolishly installed by the local authority on a road so heavy with traffic that no one ever sits there – make myself comfortable and down as many pills as I can with a bottle of Bombay Gin, the only spirit that I like, to send them on their way.

With luck, no one will notice me for hours – and if they do, will think me an old drunk. Some unfortunate athlete will find me, stiff with rigor, on his morning jog. I have left my cadaver to a teaching hospital for the use and abuse of medical students – and my sole misgiving is that, having filled it with poisons, I may have rendered it useless.

There are those who damn the suicide for invading the prerogative of the Almighty. Many years, however, have passed since I abandoned the beliefs, observances and irrational prejudices of Christianity, and I have no moral or religious inhibitions against suicide.

I cherish the notion of dying easily and with my wits about me. I am 82 and do not want to die a dribbling dotard waiting for the Queen's congratulatory greeting in 2031. Nor do I wish to cling to an increasingly wretched life made unconscionable misery by acute or chronic pain and the humiliations of nursing. What virtue can there be in suffering, in impotent wretchedness, in the bedpans and pisspots, the feeding with a spoon, the baby talk, the dwindling mind and the senses slipping in and out of consciousness? For those so affected, dying is a prolonged and degrading misadventure. 'We can ease the pain,' says another of this interregnum between life and death. But what of those who want to hurry on?

Then the theologian argues that a man must not play God and determine his own end and prates of the purification of the soul through suffering and pain. But what if the dying man is atheist or agnostic or has lost his faith – must he suffer life longer because of the prejudice of a Christian theologian? And has it occurred to no theologian that God himself might inspire the thought of suicide – or is that too great a heresy?

Suicide may even be a noble act. During the Battle of the Atlantic in the Second World War, there were many examples of suicidal heroism when men relinquished hold on dinghies or flotsam for the sake of other men, and swam away to die. I have no doubt that in Afghanistan now some soldiers have taken suicidal risks for their peers in the platoon. Self-sacrifice may in such circumstances be a response more powerfully instinctive than self-preservation. These are suicides whom we do not hesitate to honour. Surely self-sacrifice and suicide are different only in degree? Why then do so many of us deplore the calculated suicides of those who see no point in the endurance of pain or the emptiness of a life maintained and conditioned by drugs, or a life simply not worth living?

My mother had an extraordinary will to live and, when the demons of dementia stormed her brain, she retreated into her girlhood and lived her early life again, while nurses attended to the functions of the shrivelled bag of bones that her body had become. She was, in some wonderful way, content with what she had and determined to continue with it. But other women in my life offer very different examples.

Frances, told that chemotherapy might give her six more months and that without it she would die in three, kept her joyful wits and glossy hair and lapsed into unconsciousness at home, content to know that she was still beautiful. Mary, swept into hospital with pancreatic cancer with only weeks to live, was given morphine, but contrived to increase the dose so that it killed her overnight. Lillian, on the other hand, a sometime ballet dancer, dying of old age, her frail body littered with the tubes and wires of medical salvation, woke from near-death to ask: 'Oh God, am I still here?' A cry for pity, yet she was compelled to endure another month before death naturally supervened.

It was Mary who introduced me to the idea of assisted dying, the euphemism for an act of suicide of which the subject was incapable without help. She talked often of her wish to go quickly and easily when the time came, but had discovered that if she could not manage it herself, she could not rely on her doctor to do the deed. The Zurich solution she found too complicated, cold and alien. 'Will you give me the push?' she asked. I gave her the answer she wished to hear, but had not the foggiest notion of how it could be done. I asked a doctor friend, but he adamantly refused to answer.

It is not fair to ask one's doctor, for his oaths oblige him to do the very opposite. It is the doctor, indeed, who may save the life of the despairing suicide – the victim not of age, but of broken marriage or love affair, of failed career or bankrupt business, or the adolescent who feels disgraced by academic failure or sexual direction.

It was the 16th century Spanish mystic St. John of the Cross who in 'the dark night of the soul' conjured the perfect picture of despair as the point of stifling hopelessness beyond which nothing lies. This is suicide of a very different kind, from which, if discovered in time with understanding, sympathy and love, there may well be a dawn to the dark night.

But I speak for those of sound mind who have considered what is to be done with them if their bodies let them down in ways that are beyond endurance and who have left it too late to inflict death on themselves. To ask close members of the family is not only to cast them into the deep, dark and ancient anguishes explored by the dramatists of classical Greece, but to put them in legal jeopardy. To ask a friend is to require of him the greatest act of love, for he too is vulnerable to the law.

In December 1997, Parliament debated the 'Doctor Assisted Dying Bill.' This was to give those who suffer incurable illness, terminal illness or dire physical impairment the right to commit suicide when they are physically incapable of the act, calling on doctors to provide the means to pursue the execution. Much talk was the immediate consequence, but no action followed. It is time to try again.

Could Parliament not at least pass a Bill that allows doctors to assist the dying of patients who, unquestionably lucid and articulate, have expressed an unequivocal and determined choice? It is so simple – it is a living will, a witnessed legal document clearly expressing the wish to be put into the arms of Morpheus if we are stricken mute and motionless.

Reprinted from The Mail on Sunday. 14 July 2013

A ripe old age

Rodney Syme,
retired surgeon, Australia

A ripe old age. A glimpse at my Oxford English Dictionary reveals 'ripe' defined first as '(of fruit or grain) ready for harvesting and eating' and second '(of a cheese or wine) full-flavoured and mature.' That sounds good to me, I'll have a piece of that. I guess a ripe old age would be what most of us would opt for if we had a choice. But wait: 'ripe' is not defined in human terms.

Then the dictionary does go on to define the phrase 'ripe old age', being 'a person's age that is very old.' Pondering this, two things concern me. A fruit that is ready for eating will, if not picked when ready, soften on the tree, become oxidized and lose its sweetness, fall to the ground and decay. Wine and cheese will, similarly, have a 'use by' date, followed by deterioration and disappointment. So, we need to be careful what we wish for.

Ay, there's the rub, as Hamlet would have said, and Hamlet was good at asking questions.

Do humans have a 'use by' date? An inevitable programme leading past maturity to decay? Does a 'ripe old age' carry a burden of decay, deterioration and disappointment?

The answer is very likely to be yes, unless you are either very lucky, or very careful.

We now know that we are governed by our genes. A serving of bad genes means we might not live past 40 (muscular dystrophy, haemophilia or Huntington's chorea), or mean we will be likely to develop cancer. A serving of good genes means we might live to 100-110 (if no other factor intervenes), but hardly anyone lives beyond this time. Our batteries are genetically determined to run out by then. And just as well: we need to move on to make room for new generations.

Along our path to a ripe old age, we may be struck down by external environmental influences – principally accident or disease. Prior to the mid 19th century, very few people lived to a 'ripe old age', this singular rarity undoubtedly leading to the development of the phrase. Infant mortality, and maternal mortality in childbirth were enormous. Only ten of J. S. Bach's twenty children lived to adulthood. In the 14th century, plague wiped out a quarter of Europe's population. Even in the 18th century, smallpox caused epidemics of grievous proportions. People died very quickly of these infectious diseases. Syphilis and tuberculosis were more chronic infections brought to Europe from the New World. Due to dramatic changes in public health and medicine, these scourges are either unknown or exceedingly rare now in the Western World.

At the beginning of the 20th century, average life expectancy was around 40, but now, a little over 100 years later, it is at 82 and rising. This is the modern miracle of public health and medicine, but it means that many more of us will live to a 'ripe old age.' What are the implications of this for humans genetically predetermined to run out of gas at 100-110, given that we have managed to avoid any serious disease that prematurely cuts us off from a ripe old age?

Unfortunately, it means that we will inhabit a slowly degenerating body for a number of years. For some time I have been in the habit of describing the Five Horsemen of the Apocalypse of Ageing (apologies to Revelation), but as I write this, as a 78 year old, I feel I must expand it to Seven. My initial five were blindness, deafness, immobility, incontinence and loss of cognition, but personal experience means I must add muscular weakness and loss of balance. They may all, either individually or collectively, add up to a loss of independence and its disastrous consequence – sequestration in institutional care.

Irrespective of whether we suffer from any diagnosable disease in any organ of the body, organ function will decline with age. This is obvious in our skin, which we can observe but also affects our heart, lungs, kidneys, liver and brain and yet the medical profession does not recognize 'ripe old age' as a diagnosis. You may live to be 100 and not be considered 'terminally ill'.

All of these Seven Horsemen can seriously affect our quality of life. Incontinence is a tremendous affront to one's dignity, and can cause serious social isolation. Immobility, muscular weakness and loss of balance may cause falls, limit physical ability, and again lead to social isolation. For some time, as I grow older, I have pondered whether I would prefer to be blind or deaf. Being a lover of music and conversation, I have come down on the side of being blind rather than deaf but I'm not sure I could tolerate a severe degree of either. Loss of cognition would be the ultimate insult; that, of course, means dementia, which is now the third most common cause of death in Australia.

Dementia is not confined to the aged, but does become increasingly common with age, affecting 25% of those in their nineties. Of all the medical conditions known to me, I cannot select any that I fear more than Alzheimer's disease.

The end stage of dementia is characterized by what I have described as the 'infantile triad' – incontinence of bowel and bladder, inability to communicate, and being spoonfed – to which I now realize I should add immobility and total dependence. Shakespeare described this as the seventh age of man – 'a second childishness and mere oblivion, sans teeth, sans eyes, sans taste, sans everything.' This is not how I want to end my life. I am sure I am not alone.

The end result of this loss of independence, with or without dementia, is an aged care home. Previously called 'nursing homes' (an oxymoron if ever there was one – not in the least like home and very little nursing) it is not necessarily the quality of care in them which is the problem, although Professor of Neuropsychology, John Bradshaw, when seeking a haven for his multi-stroked wife, found that the available places ranged from 'the splendid to the execrable.' It is a conceptual problem, an existential problem, that all too often turns out to be a practical problem. I have been rude – or bold – enough to describe these as 'our second prison system.' The likenesses are compelling – one usually enters against one's will by someone else's decision, one's life becomes regimented, one's freedom is constrained, one is confined with others one does not choose to live with and with whom one may have nothing in common, and it is a life sentence. Ay, a life sentence, and for what crime? For reaching a ripe old age.

These places are an invention of the 20th century, a result of increasing life span and changing social circumstances, whereby children cannot, or occasionally will not, look after their ageing parents. Described by some as 'God's waiting room', by others as warehouses for the old, they seem to be regarded by governments, the medical profession and most of society as an admirable solution to the problem of ripe old age. This may be a harsh judgment, but I make it because I do not hear any voices raised in society that question this solution to the ageing problem. I do hear politicians and economists lamenting the future tsunami of increasing numbers of the aged and diminishing numbers of the young to look after the aged in care homes, and the frightening cost of this. However, what frightens me is the appalling assumption that this increasing multitude of dependent people actually want to accept this great boon that society offers as a (?final) solution. Has anybody actually bothered to ask our ageing population if they want this solution? Choice or default?

For the last 20 years, I have been giving many public lectures and conducting many workshops on end-of-life issues. I am left in no doubt, from questions and discussion, that older people overwhelmingly do not want to end their lives in an institution. Yet that is where about 30% of people die. Professor John McCallum found that 'few regard this as their preferred option.' Palliative care expert Roger Hunt found that such an institution was the preferred place of death for only 0.8% of his study group of more than 2000. Many more die in hospital, after being transferred from their nursing home, for some final attempt at futile treatment to prolong their lives, which they don't want, and haven't been asked about but haven't taken the care to indicate that they don't want it. The vast majority of frail elderly enter these places by default, not by their own voluntary decision but because someone else says it is a good idea or a necessity. They have no alternative.

For the last twenty years I have also been counselling people about end-of-life options. There has been a fascinating change over these twenty years in the people with whom I talk. Initially they were mostly people with terminal cancer or neurological conditions but as my notoriety through my writing and public speaking increased, I began to see more and more people of ripe old age who were determined to avoid institutionalization and who were determined to gain some measure of control over the end of their lives. Would these people have taken medication to avoid entering a nursing home? They certainly would and that is what they were seeking.

Most of them are 'ready to die' in the sense that if they were to go to sleep and not wake up they would be content. They have had what I call a 'completed life' (a more accurate and kinder term than 'tired of life'). They have nothing more to achieve in life; in fact they are now incapable of any achievement. There is little if any purpose or enjoyment in their life; they are simply waiting to die, and of course, they are often riding with the Seven Horsemen. They suffer the social death of slow dying in an institution. This space between being ready to die and actually dying is a time of great suffering.

How common is this feeling in society? I have no idea, since no one has been bold enough to ask this question. There are, however, a number of excellent qualitative studies which reveal that these attitudes are prevalent in the small numbers of frail older persons or institutionalized persons interviewed. One was Marion Miller, interviewed for *Seven Dying Australians*. She said: 'Every day I hope I don't wake up in the morning, I want to die … the fact is that when it comes to institutional living, there is no good place.' Another was writer Nikki Gemmel's 99-year-old grandmother who had become unable to look after herself. The day before she was due to go into a nursing home, 'She dug in her heels. Snapped that she didn't want it, we weren't listening. The hospital called a family conference; all the way through she covered her ears, crying 'Stop talking, too loud, all of you.' She lost.' Dr. Mari Lloyd-Williams wrote of her qualitative study: 'It appears that a good death for this population would be death that involves the minimum amount of physical or mental dependence or disability, minimum burden to others, and one that involved staying in their own homes'.

Yet these people have no voice. They are marginalized and patronized, even by their own families who will not listen to them or take them seriously. And so they just fade away to an ignominious end that is complete anathema to them, an insult to all that their previous lives and values have stood for.

Michael Irwin, Colin Brewer and I are privileged as medical graduates to have a knowledge and understanding of these matters – based on study and personal experience – that most others do not have. We all only die once; it is a unique experience that we are not trained for. Dying can be difficult and gruesome, accompanied by immense physical, psychological and existential suffering, if we do not consider it as a possibility (we should, we can't avoid it) and prepare by thought, communication and documentation how we want our lives to end.

I am particularly privileged, since I have my medication that will allow me to choose when, where, how, and with whom, I will die. I will not have to go to Zurich and seek help from other humane people. As such, I have no fear of death or of dying. I have no fear of a ripe old age simply because I will be able to avoid an 'overripe old age.' I will be able to say 'I'll see myself out, thank you.'

Death be my friend

Minette Marrin,
journalist

Sentimentalists, readers of light novels and John Buchan lovers must share my regret that for quite some time, the famous West Highland Sleeper from Euston to Fort William has ceased to run its leisurely journey. I have always felt a particular affection for the romance of the night train to the North, with the much eulogised rhythm of the wheels and the glamour of dawn in a cold Scotch mist. It isn't actually necessary to take the train to feel elevated by the mere idea of the journey – I have taken it only once – and I suppose that several million pounds of subsidy annually was rather a lot for the taxpayer to fork out, just to stimulate the imagination of a few armchair travellers.

All the same, it was sad to say goodbye to all that, and for another reason too. I had always thought of the West Highland Sleeper as a lifeline, or rather as a death line, after a very touching news story several years ago. An elderly husband and wife, after a happy and interesting life together, were both stricken in early old age by painful and debilitating illnesses. After writing affectionate letters to their children and an apology to the guard, they boarded the night train at Fort William, took a suitable dose of pills together, locked their sleeper door and arrived without fuss at Euston, both dead. This, they felt, was the least troublesome way of shuffling off this mortal coil.

I have always felt that theirs was a heroic death, noble in its courage and generous in its unselfishness. They didn't want to be a burden to the world, to their children or to each other. Yet in our culture suicide is still considered a shameful thing, and euthanasia even more horrible. A television documentary in the 1990s about a Dutchman who asked his doctor to kill him caused a terrible fuss – there were even questions in the House of Commons, and more than 100 MPs signed a motion criticising the practice of euthanasia in the Netherlands.

Yet anyone who saw the programme must have been convinced that death can sometimes be a friend. Death destroys a man, as E. M. Forster said, but the thought of death preserves him. That is what the saintly Dutch doctor has found too – that patients who know they are free to choose to die often find the strength to live longer, or to wait for a natural death. The thought that one can sometimes choose death is a very great freedom from humiliation and fear. I shall never understand the passionate opposition to euthanasia; it is not as though anyone wants to make it compulsory, or even, strictly speaking, legal. This is a case where, as so often, double standards are called for. Killing people must be illegal, but under certain carefully controlled circumstances doctors should not be prosecuted for it – this is what used to happen in the Netherlands before it was formally legalised, and it happens here too, actually. It seems to me the obvious way round the obvious objections.

In any case we shall soon all be driven to mass euthanasia. Now that we all live so long, once we have squandered our meagre savings, we shall have to choose between the overnight train to oblivion and what is known as 'care in the community'; when even a few social workers are too expensive, this presumably will be provided free by convicted thugs, who have, according to the quaint current fashion, been sentenced to community service. I read that a weird man who pretended to be a doctor at an accident and started sticking needles into someone was sentenced to a period of community service. I would rather take my chances of hell in the hereafter.

Reprinted from the Sunday Telegraph 19 March 1995

A right to autonomy

Gillian Tindall,
writer

Here are some words from an eminent Professor of Education, decorated for his courage and resourcefulness in war. Speaking about death, with which he had a close acquaintance, he pointed out that:

'Already many doctors admit to withholding treatment to a patient whom they are convinced is dying... Some of us would go further and would have positive action by doctors to end a dying and suffering life made legal. This too we know already sometimes happens and no court action follows... But now I should like to put forward a third [suggestion] ... This would make a reality of the right of individuals to decide when and how they die. Personally, I would like to see accepted by a large section of society, and established by law, the right of the individual at his own request to be helped out of life in such a way that this last act could be performed in the most humane, civilised and considerate way possible.'

So is this from a submission made to the All Party Parliamentary Group on Choice at the End of Life, which deliberated long and hard to produce the draft Bill which Lord Falconer finally took to the Lords in 2014? Or perhaps it comes from a recent debate in the newsletter of Dignity in Dying, or maybe from their more cutting-edge sister-organisation Healthcare Professionals for Assisted Dying? Or maybe it is from the Society for Old Age Rational Suicide, which aims with low-profile discretion to carry the debate further?

Actually, no. It is from an AGM address to the Voluntary Euthanasia Society in 1973 by Professor Harry Rée OBE, DSO, and no one then present regarded these views as particularly advanced, let alone unacceptable. VES was founded in 1935, before the decent old word 'euthanasia' ('good death') had become tainted with Nazi irrelevancies, and emphasis was firmly on the voluntary – on the choice of the individual to dispose of his own life as he saw fit. Essentially, human rights lay at the heart of the movement, though these were a much less fashionable topic then than they are today.

I knew Harry, and in the 1980s he induced me to join the VES committee for a few years, on the typically pragmatic grounds that if sane people like him and me did not take a responsible interest in it 'it will get into the hands of nuts and wets.' (Since the small but vociferous colony of nuts who regularly turned up at the AGM included one man who insisted that the Government should provide the entire population with cyanide pills, because a nuclear catastrophe was unavoidable, I could see Harry's point.) As I then did a good deal of journalism, sometimes I would be allowed or asked by this or that national paper to write on the subject, typically when some high-profile person such as Arthur Koestler had decided to take his dying into his own hands, or when a Court case about the act of a kindly doctor or a devoted spouse was making news. We have, you may say, moved on from there: the DPP made the decision in 2010, now endorsed by Parliament, that it is not in the public interest to prosecute someone who assists in a suicide for compassionate reasons. This has brought some common sense and honesty into a legal trap that should never have been set in the first place.

Where we have not moved, however, is toward the fundamental concept of its being a human right to determine your own end – rather, we have retreated on the matter. Today, Dignity in Dying is a far larger and more main-stream organisation than it was in its VES days. The 'nuts', at least, seem to have taken their obsessions elsewhere. But in its understandable desire to be extremely respectable and not to frighten anyone, those steering Dignity in Dying tended, for a number of years in the mid-2000s, to favour an anodyne and intellectually down-market approach. Several years ago a couple of long-term members, feeling that the newsletters contained little but Tales to Touch your Heart, suggested that perhaps it might be a good idea to inject rather more principle back into the campaign? No one, after all, has ever managed to formulate a philosophical argument as to why an individual should not be able to renounce his *own* right to life. Could this essential point perhaps be mentioned in a newsletter, not of course to advocate suicide among the physically healthy, against which there are all sorts of cogent arguments, but at least to provoke a focussed discussion on a fundamental level?

But the idea was at once vetoed, on the grounds that it would shock and alarm the Opposition. What is meant by this term is a small but highly visible body of self-styled 'Pro-Lifers' who seem constantly on the look-out for grounds, however far-fetched, for declaring 'We are on the slippery slope to the gas-ovens.' Since their dedicated aim is to express shock and alarm, one might feel that the attempt to pacify could serve only to drive them into ever more tenuous pretexts for prophecies of doom. But those at that point employed to do PR for Dignity in Dying did not appear to have thought this matter through, or to be aware of past debates. When told that almost forty years earlier Harry Rée had raised the point about a basic human right to self-determination, in a meeting open to the public, they were not keen to know this. They had never heard of 'Mr Ree' they said. They revealed the disconcerting fact that the office staff no longer have access to archives dating from before 2000.

Such a failing in institutional memory is hardly helpful in formulating on-going policy. It also naturally tends to alienate long-term members, and it did. There were well-informed fears at this point that DinD, however useful and well-respected, was so committed to re-branding itself as cosy and non-threatening that it was alienating many of its most potentially useful and dynamic supporters. The anxiety was that DinD, having become somewhat wet in Harry Rée's terms, would only have itself to blame if it were overtaken and sidelined by a cruder mass movement for change, not necessarily of a well-informed kind.

Happily, this has not taken place. More recent AGMs have shown far more focus, with really well-informed speakers. DinD has played a key role in the wide-ranging consultation and heart-felt discussion that has attended the drawing up of Lord Falconer's Bill. Evidence has been gathered from countries and states that have already taken some steps in the same direction, enormous thought has gone into proper safeguards against abuse (which aren't actually as difficult to erect as the Opposition like to maintain). There have been a number of previous, equally well-intentioned Bills that have failed. With over 80 percent of the population in favour of a revision in the law, it is clearly more than time that one should succeed. At the AGM of DinD in May 2013 both Lord Falconer and the distinguished medical Professor Ray Tallis made it clear, in speaking, that while each of them realised that the current Bill had its limitations and was not radical enough to satisfy every supporter of DinD, 'this is the Bill we have got' and that common sense suggested all should unite behind it.

This is true. One therefore feels somewhat hesitant, however intellectually justified, in quietly pointing out that both in the current Bill and in DinD circles, the original values of the voluntary euthanasia movement have been considerably modified. The present exclusive emphasis on allowing assisted suicide only for those already terminally ill does not address the more fundamental moral issue of individual rights. And whatever one feels about the desirability of allowing a terminally sick person to die quickly rather than lingering for weeks or months in pain, nausea, indignity or attendant distress, the word 'allow' pulls me up short. We don't attempt to make restrictive rules today about other major areas of life. We don't tell people whom they may or may not marry, or that they must marry; we don't force them to have children or forbid them from doing so. We urge them to be responsible for their own decisions but we also let them, in the decent name of free will, lead unhealthy or dangerous lives if that is that they want.

Long term, should the discourse around dying really be about 'allowing' an individual to decide that enough is enough? Should we really have stringent tests for 'eligibility', which risk creating a restrictively narrow window between 'not ill enough yet' and 'too ill to take a competent decision'? Doesn't the focus on the terminally ill side-step the central issue about personal autonomy? It certainly excludes all those who, for sane and well-considered reasons, do not wish to go on living in a dilapidated state deprived of most of what, for them, has made life worth while. And, more fundamentally, should we really adopt such a negative, defensive approach to the Great Imponderable we are all – yes, all – eventually going to meet?

These considerations arise before one even starts to comment on the morally indefensible situation arising from Britain's current equivocal attitude to what has been called 'suicide tourism' – dying patients transporting themselves expensively to Zurich to take advantage of something permitted there which is against the law in the UK. As a relative of someone who took the Swiss route to death has said: 'We actually tolerate assisted suicide now. We just do it off-shore, for those who can afford it.' It is also common knowledge that the rich and powerful, the kind of people who have homes around the world, do not have much difficulty in securing the services of some private medical advisor to give them appropriate help when they feel the time has come.

Looking back through a file of yellowed cuttings from my past life, I see that in the *Times* in 1983 I wrote, concluding an article 'A generation is a long time in the field of what is considered right. I am willing to bet that, within my own lifetime, ordinary people will look back with as much disapproval on the days when there were no proper arrangements for a timely death as we now look back on the dark ages before contraception.'

I was in my forties when I wrote that, already ten years after Harry's measured address along the same lines. A generation has passed, and 'within my life time' has a very different dimension. My contemporaries confide their fears about old age – which are *never*, contrary to 'Pro-life' myth, about being bumped off too soon but about being forced by well-intentioned but ill-advised doctors to go on too long. A fault line runs here through our social structure. Both medical research and hospital culture are dedicated to what is called 'saving lives' but which often might be more accurately described as merely prolonging lives, with results that may be far from beneficial or welcome. Meanwhile the still-active elderly murmur to one another about stocking up on sleeping pills – and whether hypothermia might be worth bearing in mind?

Anyone who has seen Michael Haneke's darkly brilliant film *Amour*, about an old couple imprisoned in a life worse than death, will understand the desperation engendered.

And it is worth making the point that the wife in the film does not, contrary to the misperception of some reviewers, have Alzheimer's: she is fully aware but is trapped, by a bad stroke, in speechless, incontinent immobility. Inside herself she knows what she wants, and she has communicated this to her husband while she was still capable of doing so.

It is true that Alzheimer patients and grossly incapacitated stroke patients do present a formidable moral and practical challenge. We all of us, almost without exception, hope that our lives will end before we reach such a pass. But the whole issue of people who cannot any longer help themselves or express themselves gets hastily shoved into the tray marked 'Too Difficult', and any Advance Directives about refusing treatment that have been signed when the person was still *compos mentis* are, once again, only likely to be of help if he or she is actually dying. The unwillingness even to look straight at such problems, let alone to discuss them, is understandable, but does suggest a lack of moral fibre in those who are eager to claim they have right on their side. The beloved Mary Stocks, economist, social campaigner and Member of the House of Lords some forty years ago, was told when going round a home full of demented old people that most of them were 'quite happy in their way.' 'Maybe they are,' she said, 'But I do not want to be happy in that way, and nor do I wish my family to see me being happy like that.' She had understood that it is the overall integrity of a person's life that should be preserved and respected, along with their expressed wishes, not that life's last degraded remnants.

The moral challenge posed by an otherwise healthy person who suffers from intractable clinical depression is even more complex, and would require a chapter to itself.

Given that such a person is not actually prevented from killing him or her-self, the topic hardly seems to come under the heading of assisted suicide. However, I do recognise that, if we are eventually to have an honest debate about people's fundamental right to decide about their own death, as Harry Rée believed in the 1970s and an increasing number of people believe today, we are going to have to take on the ramifications of this problem as well.

All social adjustments change the mental landscape. Some results we can usually predict, others may take us by surprise, other confident or dire predictions may turn out to have been quite wrong. But while we are so afraid of allowing people to decide about their own death that we do not even want to examine the idea, the debate about assisted dying will not go away. Far from it.

Easeful death for the very elderly

Mary Warnock,
baroness, former mistress of Girton College, Cambridge.
Educationalist, Chair of the Commission of Enquiry into
Human Fertilisation and Embryology

The older we get, the more realistic we usually become about approaching death, and the more we hope for a good death. Euthanasia in the strict sense is what we all want, whether we will need medical intervention to achieve it or not. I prefer the terms 'euthanasia' and 'assisted suicide' – not sanitising these words with euphemisms like 'assisted dying.'

Like many people of my age, I have witnessed the death of a close relative – my eldest sister who died in 2010 at the age of 101. She did not have a good death, and though its badness lasted only two months, it was avoidable badness, and too long-drawn out. She got pneumonia and was taken to hospital where she was given masses of different antibiotics. It was plain that she was dying, but no one admitted this; they spoke as though their one aim was to help her recover, and get her back to where she had been before. She became unable to swallow and was doubly incontinent, and increasingly distressed and agitated. Her last few days were spent, mercifully, in unconsciousness.

This sad story makes me even more convinced than I was before that everyone must make an Advance Decision, and, if possible, appoint someone to make decisions on their behalf. Universal understanding of Advance Decisions, and access to proper forms on which they can be made are essential now that we are all living much longer, and it is the responsibility of GPs to bring it about. There should be explanatory notices and copies of these forms in every surgery, and, at least in the case of everyone over eighty, or with particular health problems, doctors should steel themselves to talk about how their patients would like to die, and what would constitute a good death. And especially they should talk about how to avoid a bad death, and how the doctor is committed to helping in this avoidance.

Doctors appear to be hard-wired not to mention death, even though they know quite well, as we all do, that all are mortal. And it is to be hoped that they know that their duty is as much to make death bearable as it is to fend it off, for this is what we all trustingly believe that they will do, until we witness the contrary. The fact is that most doctors are not much interested in death. A dying patient is not their concern, but the concern of nurses and relatives. Once most doctors believe that they have done all that can be done to cure a patient, that is to prolong life, and have failed, then their interest wanes. If doctors seem incapable of mentioning death to their patients, how much more incapable are they of bringing it about? Instead they should try to embrace the idea that to bring about a good death for a patient is simply to continue the duty of caring for that patient, of acting in the best interests of that patient.

Dying in hospital, though it may be long postponed by advances in treatment and in technology, may also be lonely and horrible, because there are not enough nurses to care for the old in the most basic ways, by spending time with them, by helping them to eat or drink, and talking with them. All such neglect contributes to a bad death, even, or perhaps especially, for those who remain mentally competent, and able to recognise with horror what is happening to them.

Nothing that I have written so far bears on what is the most intractable problem of all those that we must face when considering the death of the old, and that is, of course, the problem of dementia. We all know the increasing numbers of those old people suffering from some form of dementia, and we all know that the annual rate of increase is rising fast. There is certainly a strong argument for enabling patients with dementia to have an Advance Decision that would be fully and properly respected. This, once again, points to the absolute need for the public to be educated about Advance Decisions. Specifically, it shows the need for early diagnosis of dementia. For, in its early stages, dementia does not render its victims mentally incompetent; they are well able to make decisions with regard to their future (witness the admirable pronouncements of Terry Pratchett), and they are still able to retain the sense of who they are and who they have been, which is lost in the final, most bewildering and frightening stages.

I simply do not want to be remembered as someone wholly dependent on others, especially for the most personally private aspects of my life, nor can I tolerate the thought of outstaying my welcome, an increasing burden on my family, so that no one can be truly sorry when I die and they are free. Our life, for us, is a narrative, with a beginning, a middle, and an end. We want it to have an end that is fitting, not an end that trails pitifully on into chaos and darkness. Euthanasia ought to mean death that is good, in the sense that it is timely.

We must hope that Society can get used to the idea of a good death being in the interest of the very old, when they have, one way or another, ceased to enjoy their life. I believe that this change is perhaps not so far off, if only we can persuade the priests and the doctors to listen.

This is an edited version of a talk that Baroness Warnock gave to a SOARS audience, in London, on September 17, 2010.

POSTSCRIPT FROM 'EASEFUL DEATH: IS THERE A CASE FOR ASSISTED DYING?' BY MARY WARNOCK AND ELISABETH MACDONALD, OXFORD. OUP. 2008.

One of the fears most commonly expressed is that, if assisted death were an option, patients in the last stages of their illness might have pressure put on them to ask for it, when it was not what they really wanted. It is not difficult to imagine feeling that one's children were getting impatient, either for their inheritance or simply for relief from the burden of care, and that one had not so much a right to ask for death, as a duty to do so, now that it was lawful to provide it. There undoubtedly exist predatory or simply exhausted relatives. But it is insulting to those who ask to be allowed to die to assume that they are incapable of making a genuinely independent choice, free from influence. (Indeed, there are people so determined to confound their children, if they see them as vultures hovering over a hoped-for corpse, that their will to spite them by staying alive may outweigh their wish to escape their own pain.)

6

Religion and Philosophy

The Christian case

The Rev. Dr. Paul Badham
*Emeritus Professor of Theology at Trinity Saint David
University (Lampeter Campus). He is author of
Is there a Christian Case for Assisted Dying?*

The last two attempts to change the law on assisted dying were blocked by well-organized lobbying from Christian organizations and by the unanimous opposition of the Bench of Bishops in the House of Lords. This is sad because this opposition does not represent what most Christians want. The latest opinion polls show that 78% of occasional worshippers support a change in the law. The figure is lower for more regular Church goers, but even so, 61% of weekly Churchgoing Anglicans and 57% of weekly Churchgoing Catholics would like the law changed.

The most important reason for this is that the religious arguments against assisted dying don't stand up. To claim that only God should determine the hour of our death is something that no one today can consistently believe. If they did they would be just as opposed to human interventions to prolong life as they are to assisted dying. If it were seriously thought that only God should chose the moment of our death, we would not resuscitate people whose hearts had stopped but would simply accept that God had chosen that moment to end that human life. Thankfully no one takes that line. Similarly Pope John Paul II's claim that 'suffering in the final stages of life has a special place in God's plan of salvation' would in practice run counter to all attempts to palliate human suffering and hence would be equally unacceptable on both sides of the debate.

For some the commandment 'Thou shalt not kill' is decisive. But that command is better understood as forbidding murder, rather than making an absolutist stand against all killing. This is shown by the fact that the Old Testament law code endorses killing in warfare as well as authorizing capital punishment for a wide range of offences. Historically, the commandment was never invoked against heroes who committed suicide to avoid a humiliating death.

Some Christians say that they oppose assisted dying because they want to uphold the sanctity of life and that they see life as a gift of God to be treasured and valued. But this argument is irrelevant to the debate because supporters of a change in the law believe equally strongly in the sanctity of life. They see themselves upholding the sanctity of life when they allow people to die when their lives become a travesty of what a human life should be. Moreover from a New Testament perspective 'The gift of God is eternal life' and on that understanding the gift of life is in no way diminished by death.

However, these religious arguments rarely surface in public debate. Instead Church leaders switch to assertions about what they think would be the consequences of allowing assisted dying for the well-being of the old and ill and for the development of palliative care. In the latest declaration from the Church of England, Lord Falconer's bill is opposed on the supposed ground that 'Any change in the law would negatively redefine health care … and would have far-reaching and damaging effects on the nature of our society.'

There is no evidence to support this claim. These predicted consequences have not happened in any of the European countries or states of the USA which have authorized assisting dying or voluntary euthanasia. On the contrary what their evidence shows is that countries where people are willing to give assistance to those who want to die are more, not less, likely to show comparable compassionate help to those who want assistance to live on for as long as they can.

To claim that 'a right to die would become a duty to die', because the old and ill would feel under pressure to ask for an assisted death, is falsified most clearly by the Swiss experience. The Swiss have permitted assisted dying for over seventy years but the fact that on average the Swiss live two and a half years longer than we do, and that they live longer with terminal illness, shows that this argument is nonsense. It is worth googling the OECD or the WHO websites on comparative health care. It becomes apparent that the Swiss have four and half times as many hospital beds as we do and far more doctors and nurses. The hundred or so foreigners who travel to Switzerland each year to end their lives in the Dignitas clinic in Zurich must be set against the

30,000 foreigners who annually travel to Swiss hospitals and sanatoria for the latest and best medical treatments.

Similarly, it is false to claim that palliative care could be put at risk. The Oregon Hospice Association fought bitterly against the passage of the Dignity in Dying Act in their state. Moreover, when the Act was passed they appealed all the way to the U.S. Supreme Court to have the Act declared unconstitutional. However American appeals are very slow and it was eight years before the Supreme Court finally ruled that States could make their own laws in this area. At this point the Oregon Hospice Association issued a new position statement acknowledging that after eight years of seeing how the Act worked, 'Absolutely none of our dire predictions has been realised.' Instead, the numbers dying in hospice care had risen from 22% to 51% during the first eight years of the working of the Act and numbers have continued to rise ever since.

Similarly, the European Association on Palliative Care found that in the Netherlands and Belgium, palliative care has improved since assisted dying or voluntary euthanasia has been legalized. Indeed Luxembourg introduced a universal right to palliative care at the same time as it introduced its euthanasia law. Why should the same not happen here? I conclude that the religious arguments against assisted dying do not stand up and that the practical objections based on fear of what might happen are equally groundless.

On the more positive side, I believe that there are good religious grounds for supporting assisted dying. Jesus taught that the whole of religious law and prophetic teaching could be summed up by saying that you should love God and love your neighbour as yourself. His 'golden rule' for interpreting this command was the axiom that you should 'always treat others as you would like to be treated yourself.' I suggest that there are no moral issues where the teaching of Jesus is more directly relevant than in relation to assisted dying. Opinion polls repeatedly show that what most of us want for ourselves is the option of an assisted death if we should ever find ourselves suffering unbearably in the final stages of a terminal illness. If this is what we want for ourselves, then this is what we should want for others.

According to St. Paul, the great new insight of Christianity was its emphasis on 'compassionate love' (in Greek *agape* and in Latin *caritas*). It was far more important than faith or hope or willingness to be martyred. This again is highly relevant to the current debate. When someone's sufferings are so great that they make repeated requests to die, it seems a denial of that loving compassion which is supposed to be the hallmark of Christianity to refuse to allow their requests to be granted. If we truly love our neighbour as ourselves, how can we deny them the death we would wish for ourselves in such a condition?

Cancelling our captivity

John Harris,
Professor of Bioethics, University of Manchester

Cassius.

…Cassius from bondage will deliver Cassius:
Therein, ye gods, you make the weak most strong;
Therein ye gods, you tyrants do defeat:
Nor stony tower, nor walls of beaten brass,

Nor airless dungeon, nor strong links of iron,
Can be retentive to the strength of spirit;
But life, being weary of those worldly bars,
Never lacks power to dismiss itself.
If I know this, know all the world besides,
That part of tyranny that I do bear
I can shake off at pleasure.
Casca.   So can I:
So every bondman in his own hand bears
The power to cancel his captivity.

(Julius Caesar Act I. Sc. III.)

The problem of assisted dying is primarily one for those people who tragically do not have in their own hands the power to cancel, in Casca's words, their captivity. Those who, in short, need assistance with dying. Two important ideas bear crucially on the ethics of assisted dying and something useful can be said about both. One concerns autonomy and the other involves a response to vulnerability.

I suggest that there is only one thing wrong with dying and that is doing it when you do not want to. (Doing it painfully is a problem about pain not about dying). It follows that there is nothing wrong with doing it when you do want to. I do not believe there is any rational person who would not take the bargain that they would only die when they wanted to, and never when they did not want to.

This in essence is the argument from autonomy, bearing in mind that choosing the place, time and manner of my own death is no more in principle damaging to others than is anything else I or you do that others do not like or would prefer we had not done.

Respect for persons requires us to acknowledge the dignity and value of other persons and to treat these as ends in themselves and not merely instrumentally as means to ends or objectives chosen by others. This means respecting others' autonomy. Autonomy is the ability to choose and the freedom to choose between competing conceptions of how to live. It is only by the exercise of autonomy that our lives become in any real sense our own. We are shaped by the decisions we make, and, without the freedom to choose what we do and how we live, we cannot have any personal identity at all. If we cannot choose our path through life, including its destination and as far as it is within our control the nature and manner of our life's end, we are nothing!

The ending of our lives often determines life's final shape and meaning, both for ourselves and in the eyes of others. When we are denied control of the end of our lives, we are denied the capacity to give our lives their ultimate meaning. As Ronald Dworkin memorably put it: '*Making someone die in a way that others approve, but he believes a horrifying contradiction of his life, is a devastating, odious form of tyranny.*'

Autonomy is the underlying rationale of laws allowing patients to refuse life- sustaining medication, which our law does allow. To permit this and to deny medically-assisted death is inconsistent.

Many objectors to medically-assisted death emphasise their concern to protect the vulnerable. I yield to none in my concern for the vulnerable. But there are two groups of vulnerable people to whom we owe concern, respect and protection. One consists of those who might be pressured into requesting death. The others are those, like Tony Nicklinson, who are cruelly denied the death they seek. We are surely not entitled to abandon one group of vulnerable people in favour of another. We have somehow to protect both.

Those who might be encouraged to die are and remain free to refuse. They are not victims unless they make themselves victims. Those seeking assisted death are the more vulnerable because they are truly coerced, absolutely prevented from obtaining the remedy they seek. They seek death and are denied it: these are genuinely coerced and are certainly the victims of tyranny.

Thus, concern for the vulnerable does not, as so many falsely believe, tell us we should forbid assisted dying. On the contrary, it tells us we should permit it, with safeguards, as Joel Joffe's Bill (in 2006) and other current proposals, also do, thereby protecting both groups of vulnerable people to whom we have responsibilities.

Some invoke the spectre of the 'slippery slope' The only response, when threatened with a slippery slope, is a choice: 'skis or crampons.' We can always decide further up or further down; the direction of travel is assisted by appropriate footwear. Competent human agents always have the appropriate equipment to make choices – it is called a brain.

Consider this situation, widely known as 'the policeman's dilemma': A lorry driver is trapped in the blazing cab of his vehicle following an accident. An armed policeman is on the scene and sees that the driver cannot be extracted before the flames get to him and he is burned alive. The policeman can let him be burned alive or can give him a quick and relatively painless end by shooting him in the head. The driver says; 'please shoot me, don't let me be burned alive!' All decent people will know the policeman to have been justified in such a case.

Those opposed to euthanasia must give one answer to the policeman's dilemma, and condemn the driver to an horrific death. Decent people will want to act compassionately in circumstances like this and are entitled to the protection of the law when they so act. They should not be condemned or even criticised for doing what is right. A person is a creature capable of valuing its own existence. Self-consciousness, coupled with fairly rudimentary intelligence, are the most important features of personhood because they permit the individual to value her own existence.

The harm of ending a life is principally a harm to the individual whose life it is, and must be understood principally as the harm of depriving that individual of something that they value and want. Persons who do not want to live are not harmed by having their wish to die granted, thus voluntary euthanasia will not be wrong on this account. The principle of respect for persons is a cornerstone of medical ethics and is endorsed by the law in most jurisdictions. This principle is always engaged in end-of-life decision making because such decisions will be ethical only in so far as they plausibly demonstrate such respect for the individual whose death is hastened by them.

It is because we accept that the meaning, purpose and indeed the distinctive uniqueness of an individual's life is governed largely by acts of self-definition and self-creation that we are concerned to protect those attempts at self-creation even where we are convinced that they are misguided or even self-harming.

We need welfare, broadly conceived in terms of health, freedom from pain, mobility, shelter, nourishment and so on because these things create the conditions in which autonomy can flourish and our lives be given their own unique meaning. However, concern for welfare ceases to be legitimate at the point at which, so far from being productive of autonomy, so far from enabling the individual to create her own life, it operates to frustrate the individual's own attempts to create her own life for herself.

If we respect the life plans and choices of others, it will matter to us that those plans and choices are not frustrated. It should make no difference to us (and certainly does not to them) that the frustration results from omissions rather than actions. Respect must apply both to acts and omissions, to doing and refraining. I agree with Lord Mustill in the Bland Case (in 1993) when he says of the difference between so called active and passive courses of action – *'However much the terminology may differ, the ethical status of the two courses of action is, for all relevant purposes, indistinguishable.'*

The ethics of assisted dying

Antony Lempert,
GP and Chairman of the Secular Medical Forum

The role of the healthcare professions has never been to prolong life at all costs. The heart of medicine is to work with patients to improve the quality of their lives. Although they often go together, quality and quantity sometimes have to go their separate ways.

The UK doctors' regulatory body, the General Medical Council (GMC), reminds doctors that: 'there is no absolute requirement to prolong life irrespective of the consequences for the patient and irrespective of the patient's views.'

Whilst this cannot be seen as an endorsement of assisted dying (AD), the sentiment is clear that patients should be allowed to decide when enough is enough.

A request for an assisted death should always be treated as a cry for help. Sometimes help to carry on living is available; at other times a death-wish may be a reasonable request in the face of intolerable, unrelievable suffering. This is why AD is supported by the majority of the general public and by many doctors and nurses.

There are four widely-agreed fundamental principles of medical ethics;

- Autonomy: The right to decide for oneself what happens to one's own body;

- Beneficence: Doing what is best for the patient;

- Non-maleficence: Not causing unnecessary harm; and

- Justice: Individual and societal.

Until relatively recently, autonomy played second fiddle to the concept of beneficence as determined by the doctor. Even into the 1970s for example, it was not uncommon for doctors to collude with relatives anxious that patients didn't suffer by being made aware of their terminal illness. This approach frequently backfired as the anxiety of ignorance and the barrier of deception increased suffering. In turn, how could relatives trust that they were being given the full picture when they became ill?

Such medical paternalism is no longer acceptable. Personal autonomy is now embedded as a core principle of good medical practice. Doctors must make every effort to involve patients in decision-making. The NHS motto for autonomy is: 'No decision about me, without me.' Autonomy, guided by informed patient choices should not be overruled even when a choice is considered unwise, such as the potentially life-threatening refusal of an emergency blood transfusion by an adult Jehovah's Witness patient.

Dying patients in particular often have strong views about the treatment options or indignities they are, or are not, willing to suffer. In practice, though, people's views are being disregarded. Patients, suffering unbearably, with no realistic prospect of improvement, who have made their own reasonable assessment, and have decided that they would prefer to die sooner rather than later, are denied help. Even with consensus between patient, relatives and the attending medical team, anguished relatives and sympathetic doctors are legally restricted from taking active steps to help people to die with dignity. Faced with the cruelty of this paternalistic disempowerment, some feel truly abandoned in the last days of their life.

The final experience for many people is the increased suffering from illness progression, a botched suicide attempt or the desperate slow starvation and dehydration employed as a last resort by those without the physical ability to take more active measures.

In 2010 Debbie Purdy's successful legal challenge to the Director of Public Prosecutions (DPP) clarified who is most likely to be prosecuted for assisting suicide. Doctors with the necessary expertise to assess patients properly and to offer a swift, painless death should expect to be prosecuted if they assist. Even providing advice and information about the available options could lead to a doctor's prosecution. Instead, doctors must somehow support patients through the agony of a protracted death.

Some doctors employ the doctrine of double effect; a specious, religiously-inspired solution to the apparent problem of distinguishing between alleviating symptoms and actively shortening life, both of which may result from the same treatment option. By stating that their sole intention when using such a treatment was to ease suffering, the doctor jumps through the necessary hoops because any stated deliberate intent to shorten life would lead to prosecution. Paradoxically the doctrine may increase suffering; instead of ending a person's life intentionally, using the most appropriate method, other treatments with additional side effects may be employed. This can result in a more prolonged death with additional unpleasant symptoms.

Reasonable concerns have been expressed that AD might hinder good palliative care or place vulnerable patients at risk. Evidence from Oregon, where AD was legalised in 1997, shows that about 90% of AD patients were enrolled in hospice care – a higher percentage than similar patients not seeking an assisted death. The European Association of Palliative Care reported in 2011 that AD neither obstructs nor halts palliative care development. On the contrary, it is possible that there will be a missed opportunity when patients avoid approaching doctors who they know won't help. A thorough re-assessment of the available treatment options might afford some patients sufficient quality of life to continue living. The evidence shows that the people who have accessed the Oregon law, in the main, have been the most articulate and empowered rather than the most vulnerable.

In the absence of coherent UK legislation it is worth
scrutinising the existing situation with regard to vulnerable
patients. The 2010 DPP guidance explains that relatives
who assist a loved one to die may limit their risk of later
prosecution if they act 'out of love and compassion and
in accordance with the dying person's wishes.' But it may
well be impossible for prosecutors to make a post-mortem
determination of relatives' intent, or to know for sure what
the patient's actual wishes might have been. People are being
helped to die 'under the radar' by distressed relatives without
medical expertise and with no safeguards. Robust regulation
would protect patients from non-voluntary euthanasia, would
allow for further assessment, a more humane death than a
pillow or plastic bag over the head, and would serve to protect
relatives from later prosecution.

Fifteen years of assisted dying in the Netherlands have
shown a significant reduction in the number of people killed
without their explicit consent, i.e. non-voluntary euthanasia.
A 2009 study showed that roughly three thousand deaths
annually in the UK are already via euthanasia. Without AD
legislation these patients have no automatic assessment for
treatable symptoms, no safety-net, and often no medical input.
The current situation is an unsafe, unregulated, unmonitored,
muddled mess. The 2012 Falconer commission on Assisted
Dying described the current legal status of assisted dying in
the UK to be 'inadequate and incoherent'.

For most dying patients, the greatest fear is not death but
dying badly. Those of us who regularly care for dying patients
know that suffering often extends beyond pain and may be
compounded by loss of dignity, loss of sense of self, and the
agony of watching a treasured life disappear. Each person

will experience different emotions or responses to the same situation and will have different values; this is precisely why autonomy is so important.

In Oregon, many more lethal prescriptions are approved than are eventually used. The comfort that this option gives some people cannot be underestimated. It is often sufficient just to know that if life becomes intolerable then at least there's a Plan B, as Tony Nicklinson called it. Tony had locked-in syndrome, communicating through an eye-blink recognition computer. When the High Court refused Tony's request for an assisted death in August 2012 he starved himself and died six days later.

With such compelling arguments, why is AD not already legal? By far the most powerful and persistent obstruction remains the pervasive and privileged influence of religion. Arguments against AD often rest on groundless fears and religious concepts of sanctity of life and community autonomy. In 2006, Lord Joffe's Assisted Dying bill was itself suffocated by organised obstruction from the Anglican bishops who stifled the debate. Twenty six bishops remain privileged with automatic seats in our second parliamentary chamber, accorded moral authority because of, or in spite of, their chosen beliefs which include resurrection and virgin birth.

The personal choices of autonomous patients, religious or otherwise, should be respected. Equally, society must not be held hostage to a narrow religious morality, premised on incredible hypotheses, which is increasingly impoverished by developing international ethical and human rights norms.

All patients deserve patient-centred medical care with compassion, dignity and personal autonomy at its heart.

Assisted Dying legislation would represent just that. It is a personal tragedy for many people and their loved-ones that they have to suffer unnecessarily because their reasonable autonomy is frustrated by unsubstantiated fears wedded with ancient religious privilege. Whether or not they need to use it, robust assisted dying legislation would afford huge comfort to many people, and would protect patients and their relatives.

A Basic Human Right ...

Professor Julian Savulescu,
Editor, Journal of Medical Ethics

Imagine that you find yourself in a room. You are not sure how you came there. It is dark, pitch black in fact, and cold. You are frightened and you want to get out. You try to turn the knob but the door is locked. You don't have the key. Who should keep you in this room, if they have the key? Imagine it is your house but someone else has the key. They should give it to you. You should be allowed to leave that dark, cold room.

Of course, if the room is a prison, in which you are confined because of some crime, you must remain. You must serve out your punishment. Or perhaps if the house and key belong to someone else, you have no claim to be let out of the room. But your body does not belong to God or the King, as many people once thought. It belongs to you. And so you should be able to leave this body when and how you choose. To keep a person trapped in this life is a grave affront to the liberty of the person and human dignity.

There are two ethical grounds for voluntary euthanasia and assisted suicide which are usually given: respect for autonomy and beneficence. I will consider these in turn. In Western liberal society, the foundation stone of ethics and law is liberty and individual autonomy. Autonomy comes from the Greek, *autos nomos,* which means 'self rule' or self-determination. It was first used in relation to Greek city states that were given the power to determine their own affairs and fate. In the last couple of hundred years, it has been extended to individual people – that each person is free and should be the servant or slave of no one. Each human being should be allowed, or even helped, to form and act on his or her own conception of how their life should go, what kind of person to be and the meaning for their own life.

It is a consequence of freedom and diversity that people will choose to live in different ways. Some will choose jobs in banking, others in plumbing, others in law, some will want to have a family, others won't. Some will choose to remain married and faithful, others will never marry and others will choose partners of the same sex or both sexes.

What view should the State take of these different 'ways of living' as John Stuart Mill put it? The State is the only body that legitimately possesses the power to exercise authority over individual liberty. Mill, the 19th century British utilitarian, famously argued that the sole ground for the State to restrict the liberty of its citizens was when those citizens threatened to harm others. Harming themselves was never sufficient warrant.

We frequently harm ourselves. When we engage in any risky activity, we raise the chances of self-harm. Examples include driving, action sports, smoking, unhealthy eating and lifestyle, unsafe sex, smoking, drinking and taking other drugs. The state bans some of these, such as taking certain recreational drugs and driving very unsafely, but these prohibitions are at least partly grounded in protecting others.

Minimal levels of incursion on liberty may be justifiable when the social benefits are great. For example, seat belts are required by law because they have such overall beneficial effects, reduce health care costs and represent an almost zero infringement in important freedoms. However, large infringements of individual liberty are only justifiable in states of extreme emergency, such as epidemic or war.

Paternalism is the practice of deciding what is good for another person and restricting that person's liberty to promote that person's good. Mill thought that this was only justified when the person was incompetent in some way, such as suffering from some relative cognitive deficiency (for example, children or those with dementia) or lack of relevant information. But where the incompetence could be corrected, that should be done and then the person allowed to decide for himself what was best.

How does medically-assisted rational suicide (MARS) fit into this framework of respecting personal autonomy and liberty? The default position should be not to interfere in a person's choice unless that is directly going to harm others. So allowing assisted dying should be the rule, not the exception.

It might be objected that MARS harms family members who do not agree with it. This may be the case. But it is in the end the individual's own life. We can try to persuade the person to change his or her mind, provide information and even ethical arguments but if people are of sound mind and in possession of the relevant facts, their own decisions relating to their own lives must be respected.

Consider a parallel case. Jehovah's Witnesses believe that if they forgo blood transfusions and other blood products they will have a better chance of enjoying eternal paradise. This interpretation is not shared by any other denomination. It is likely that this particular interpretation of the Bible is irrational. Nonetheless, their decisions to refuse blood are respected, provided the person is competent and informed and acting of their own volition.

Jehovah's Witnesses may even refuse blood when it costs them their lives. It is illegal to transfuse them in the face of a valid refusal (albeit one based on an irrational belief) even if their families request treatment. In the case of children, though, courts will intervene to save the child's life when parents refuse transfusion because that child is not yet deemed competent.

The lesson to draw from the respect society accords Jehovah's Witnesses is that respect for autonomy is fundamental, even when it results in the foreseeable and avoidable death of a person and even when the desires that motivate a lethal course of action are based on beliefs not shared by most people.

One might object that Jehovah's Witnesses do not intend to die. They merely want to refuse a blood transfusion and they foresee that it will probably cause their death. The distinction between the moral evaluation of intention and foresight, which underlies the Doctrine of Double Effect, is a specious one. We are responsible for the effects of not only what we intend to do, but also for the foreseeable effects of our actions.

The Doctrine of Double Effect states roughly that it can be permissible to cause harm provided one is intending to achieve some worthwhile end and one merely foresees but does not intend the bad consequence. This doctrine is used to justify bombing in war that foreseeably kills innocent civilians – so called collateral damage. The death of innocent civilians is a side-effect of the strategic aim of destroying, say, a munitions factory or a terrorist training camp. The doctrine is staunchly defended by the Roman Catholic church and it is deployed to justify giving morphine and sedatives to relieve pain in terminal cancer, with the side-effect of shortening life. I believe this doctrine to be specious but even if it were valid, it would not preclude MARS.

It is my belief that very few people who request MARS really want to die. They do not intend their death in the sense appealed to by the doctrine. What they want is to escape the dark room of their confinement, their suffering, decrepitude or other unpleasant aspects of living. If miraculously there were an escape that did not involve death, if there were cures for the ills of age and the diseases that grind them down, I suggest there would be little appetite for MARS.

While marvellous, modern medicine is not miraculous. Despite its enormous achievements, the human condition is still to suffer and to undergo the vicissitudes of disease and aging. So, if we allow Jehovah's Witnesses to refuse blood resulting in their death (hoping to go to heaven), we should allow people to access voluntary euthanasia. Another objection – or disanalogy – is that while Jehovah's Witnesses merely refuse blood transfusion, voluntary euthanasia and assisted suicide both involve a deliberate action on the part of others to effect death. The difference is between negative freedom (freedom from interference) and positive freedom (the freedom to request assistance by others).

It is true that voluntary euthanasia and assisted suicide require that others do something to help the person to die. Should the state prevent this exchange or interaction? The only role of the state in regulating human interaction is to prevent harm to others, or unfair exploitation of one of the parties in the exchange. If I want to die and you want to help, and we both understand the facts and are competent, what business is it of anyone else to prevent us going about our business?

I have so far largely ignored the reasons why people request euthanasia, for the rationality or justification of their reasons is not the central issue in respecting autonomy. If there is any important liberty, it is the liberty to decide how and when we exit this world. There can be good reasons to die, which brings us to the second usual justification for assisted dying: beneficence, or the moral obligation to provide benefits or good to others.

The idea that one person could benefit another by assisting his suicide might be initially puzzling. Surely the worst thing you can do a person is helping to take away all that he has, his life. However, when life becomes dominated by pain and suffering, hopelessness, fear, anxiety and other negative states, it might be said to be no longer worth living.

Theoretically, this justification seems sound. But drawing the line is the problem. When precisely does life cross from being worth living to not worth living? A logical way of deciding this is to appeal to the person's own values. Quality of life is subjective and only the person who lives the life can judge how good or bad it is.

It is certainly true that there is context relativity in all value judgements. What may be a burden for one person may be a benefit for another. One person is terrified by heights; the rock climber craves them. For one person, something is a pain worth enduring; for another it is unbearable. Some adapt to great disabilities; others don't. There are, however, problems with a purely subjective view of worth of life. Surely we can autonomously desire things which may not be the best for us? Surely, sometimes we can be mistaken about our own good?

This is the basis for the common objection that despite profound disability, life remains worth living. Daniel James is the youngest Briton so far to access assisted suicide. He was 23 when he died. His spine was dislocated when a rugby scrum collapsed, severing his spinal cord. His parents faced prosecution for assisting suicide by taking him to Dignitas in Switzerland.

'The couple, who run a stud farm, were interviewed by detectives. They said that their son had tried several times to kill himself before he 'gained his wish' and added that he was 'not prepared to live what he felt was a second-class existence.'

'His death was an extremely sad loss for his family, friends and all those that care for him but no doubt a welcome relief from the 'prison' he felt his body had become and the day-to-day fear and loathing of his living existence, as a result of which he took his own life,' they said.

Mrs James had defended her son's decision previously, saying: 'He couldn't walk, had no hand function, but he had constant pain in all of his fingers. He was incontinent, suffered uncontrollable spasms in his legs and upper body and needed 24-hour care."[1]

His parents and others in his family did not want his suicide, but supported his decision. The public prosecutor rightly decided not to prosecute the parents. At the time, there was significant public criticism of his actions, with commentators maintaining that he would adapt to his disability. This might have been true. But the first justification of assisted dying is individual liberty, not objective assessment.

Objective evaluations of the worth of life seem necessary, though, when it comes to making decisions about incompetent patients with severe disabilities. One way round this is for individuals to express their own wishes in advance of mental deterioration. They could say; 'if I am never able to speak, or recognise my close family, and am incontinent, then I do not wish to live.' Advance decisions which refuse life prolonging medical treatment, even simple treatment like antibiotics, have the force of law if they have clearly been made with adequate information about the relevant circumstances, are applicable to those circumstances and there is no evidence that the person has competently changed his or her mind. Such an approach could be extended to voluntary euthanasia decisions.

Take the example of Lisette Nigot. The *Sydney Morning Herald*[2] reported in 2002 that: 'Lisette Nigot was not ill. She was not in pain. But she was 79 and, quite simply, did not want to live to 80. So last week the retired academic took a fatal overdose in her Perth home, leaving a suicide note describing the euthanasia campaigner Philip Nitschke as her inspiration. Later, Dr. Nitschke [the leading Australian pro-euthanasia advocate] released that note, which Ms Nigot had pinned behind her bed.

'After 80 years of a good life, I have [had] enough of it,' she wrote. 'I want to stop it before it gets bad.' The French-born Ms Nigot, who is believed to have appeared in one of Dr. Nitschke's how-to-commit-suicide videos, would have turned 80 on December 15. Her final words were, 'The life of an individual, voluntarily terminated, is of small importance compared with the death statistics relative to crime, accident, war and other similar causes of human demise which are viewed by society as a whole with regret, but accepted with relative equanimity. Why is there pressure against helping or allowing people who have had enough of living ... to fulfil the longing for final peace?' The story of her life and death became the subject of a documentary *Mademoiselle and the Doctor* by Janine Hosking.

Another example of autonomous suicide is the suicide of the philosopher, Michael Bayles, who committed suicide on August 6, 1990. He was born in Charleston, Illinois, January 21, 1941, and so died in his fiftieth year. His suicide was carefully planned and is as much an expression of Mike as his varied writings in ethical theory and applied ethics, philosophy of law, and political theory. Mike's argument for the moral acceptability of suicide is that, as he put it, 'only humans can choose when they will die' and that 'to fail to exercise that choice is to deprive oneself of a distinctive freedom.' A person's life is a story, he suggests, and a person ought to consider how the story ought to end, with suicide an option under appropriate circumstances. 'If', he says, 'what makes life a good story is happiness or the pursuit of projects, then a long, drawn out ending without either is a bad end of what may have been a good story.'

Bayles had been very productive in the years leading up

to his death though he took on fewer and fewer projects. He wanted to die without unmet obligations. 'He had, in the three years before his death, seen to publication his *Principles of Law* and what Joel Feinberg has called 'a groundbreaking theory of procedural justice with applications not only to legal practices but to social institutions generally.' And the day he committed suicide he received word that his book on H. L. A. Hart had been accepted for publication. Bayles died by his own hand. But had he requested assistance, should others have been prevented from helping? Bayles ended his life the way he chose.

Some wrote that Bayles was depressed, and others have said that Nigot undervalued life after 80 and all she could have done. Both of these statements may have been correct. But what matters for voluntary euthanasia to be justified is not that a person makes the right decision, but that they make his or her own decision. The suicides of both Bayles and Nigot appear to have been the expression of an autonomous desire to determine when and how they die. As Nigot acknowledged, the hand of death is never far from our shoulders. Decisions about death are an inescapable part of the human condition.

We do have some power to affect our time and circumstances of dying now by suicide. And this right to suicide may give us more options than we realise, in the following way. Courts have acknowledged that artificial feeding and hydration are forms of medical treatment that can be withheld or withdrawn. But what of feeding and drinking by mouth? What goes into our bodies, and how, and in which circumstances is an ethical issue; even food by mouth. Political dissidents have the right to starve themselves to death. Individuals have a basic human right to refuse to eat and drink which must be respected.

Because of this right, I have argued that we may not need new laws regarding assisted suicide. If people can end their lives by refusing to eat and drink, they can do this now, or in advance through a living will. No one has the right to force-feed a person who has competently refused food and water. And such a passage to death could be eased with effective palliative care, just as the deaths of people who refuse medical treatment can be eased with palliative care.

I have called this idea Voluntary Palliated Starvation. It is one way in which perhaps even now we have the ability to control when and how we die. It will not deal with cases of human beings who have never competently expressed the desire to die (non-voluntary euthanasia) but it may ease the passage to accepting voluntary euthanasia. I believe it is only a matter of time before every civilised society legalises assisted suicide and voluntary euthanasia. We don't have choice about whether, when and how we enter the world but we can and should have a choice about when and how we leave it.

References:

1. http://www.telegraph.co.uk/news/majornews/3689907/Parents-of-rugby-player-in-Dignitas-assisted-suicide-will-not-face-charges.html

2. http://www.smh.com.au/articles/2002/11/25/1038173695743.html

Dementia, MARS and voluntary euthanasia

Colin Brewer

This section will focus particularly on what we may call 'preventive' or 'anticipatory' deliverance. With most other conditions where the patient may consider MARS, he or she is likely to remain in control of the final decision (including the decision not to invoke it) at all times unless or until death occurs naturally. In most cases, mental capacity will not be in question unless a delirious state develops due, for example, to a high fever or serious metabolic disturbance. Even then, unless it is truly terminal, delirium of this type often responds to treatment, thus preserving or restoring mental capacity. With dementia, the patient does not remain in control, because once dementia reaches a certain stage, mental capacity will be lost and therefore MARS, as we have defined it, may not be a legal or practical possibility. Although Dutch law and practice permit voluntary euthanasia for dementia in the absence of mental capacity if a mentally competent patient has clearly asked well in advance to have euthanasia once that capacity has been lost, such requests are rarely acted on. Here are two stories that illustrate both how British citizens typically view late stage dementia and some of the practical problems it throws up for health professionals. For as Baroness Warnock noted in Section 5, 'The most intractable problem of all those that we must face when considering the death of the old ... is, of course, the problem of dementia.'

In the early 1980s, I worked for two half-days a week as the psychiatric advisor to an NHS clinic for sexually-transmitted diseases. It soon became clear that there was very little need for my psychiatric expertise and so once I had taught the staff some basic psychiatry and interview skills, I started doing my share of ordinary venereology, having had experience of the specialty as a junior ship's surgeon on large cruise liners.

Because I often saw half a dozen patients every hour (some just needed follow-up laboratory tests after successful treatment) it occurred to me that I could easily carry out simple and informal patient surveys just to satisfy my curiosity. In those days, it was not thought necessary to submit such proposals to ethical committees or NHS bureaucrats and for one of the surveys, I decided to ask about the sort of care my patients would want if they ever became severely demented. Nobody ever asked: 'What is dementia?' The qualifier 'Alzheimer's' was not so widely used then but everybody knew that dementia meant the progressive and permanent loss of memory and the gradual destruction of the personality – 'identity annihilation', as some commentators have called it. In those days, there were fewer old people's homes but the large mental hospitals still existed and most of them had dementia wards where people with advanced dementia were nursed until they died. Several of my patients had personal experience of dementia in their family.

'If you were ever admitted to such a ward', I asked my initially surprised but always cooperative interviewees, 'I am interested to know how you would want to be treated. Please choose from one of three options.' The first was: 'I would like Matron to put something into my tea to end my life as soon as possible.' The second was: 'The Matron option is a bit too radical but at the first sign of pneumonia or other life-threatening illness, I very definitely don't want to be treated and hope I will be heavily sedated to help me to die.' Option three was: 'I would like to be treated just like any other patient and be resuscitated if I have a serious illness.' None of them chose option three. They were about equally divided between options one and two.

The other story involves a visit to a private psychiatric hospital in rural Kent, whose owners were trying to persuade me to admit my patients there. I never did, because it was geographically very inconvenient but I wanted to see its interesting architecture, which included a neo-Gothic folly and an *art nouveau* villa that housed the alcoholism unit. The villa had originally been built for a mad Egyptian royal and his servants, since he was too grand to mix with ordinary bourgeois schizophrenics. On one of the general wards, an elderly man in a neat suit and tie was energetically pacing the corridors and muttering to himself. My surmise that he had Alzheimer's disease was quickly confirmed, with the additional information that he had been a well-known academic psychiatrist and the co-author of a respected textbook. I remember thinking what a sad and ironic end for a psychiatrist and how he would probably – like my venereal patients – have hated his life to be prolonged. However, I also reflected that even if he had specifically asked in advance for something to be put into his tea, it might in practice be difficult to do so, even if it were legal. It could be terrifying for a confused old man to be reminded of his previous request and told that the time had now come. That may partly explain its rarity in the Netherlands.

'Elderly care physicians and relatives were found to be reluctant to adhere to advance directives for euthanasia. Not being able to engage in meaningful communication played a crucial role in this reluctance.'[1] The kindest way to honour such a request would probably be to slip something into a routine cup of tea without any announcement but bureaucrats are not the only people who don't like that sort of thing. Nevertheless, despite the major ethical and practical considerations, there seems to be a growing feeling in the Netherlands – and doubtless elsewhere – that dementia should be added to the list of conditions for which MARS (and in this particular situation, VE) is a rational and medically acceptable option for those who want it. Significantly, the title of a recent Dutch paper about this debate is: 'Would we rather lose our life than our self?'[2]

Alzheimer's is bad enough but it is not the worst of the dementias. That distinction probably belongs to Huntington's Disease (HD – sometimes called Huntington's Chorea). HD is a hereditary dementia with 50% of offspring being at risk. It doesn't usually appear until after the sufferer has produced children but there are now diagnostic and predictive tests for people and embryos at risk. Many potential sufferers prefer not to know their diagnosis but of those who do want to know the genetic status of their potential offspring – normally-conceived foetuses or embryos created *in vitro* so that the affected ones can be identified before implantation – nearly all want those that carry the disease to be aborted or not to be implanted.

That is not because – as with abortion for Down's syndrome – prospective parents fear that the offspring would prove to be difficult or challenging children with limited intellectual ability. HD can occasionally start causing problems during adolescence but most sufferers show no signs of disease until well after they have flown the nest.

Indeed, during their adolescence, it is their affected father or mother who is likely to start causing problems or become overtly demented. What makes HD even nastier than Alzheimer's disease (apart from the strong hereditary element) is its very slow onset and prolonged course, death typically occurring in the 50s or 60s some 20 years after the first signs. Furthermore, it is accompanied by progressively more severe twitching and writhing ('chorea' shares the same Greek root as 'choreography') so that patients are not just demented but distressing to look at, especially for their offspring who know or fear that the same terrifying fate may befall them. In the circumstances, it is not surprising that there is a significantly increased incidence of unassisted suicide in identified HD patients, usually when the disease is at a relatively early stage.[3] The reasons for suicide presumably vary but a desire to avoid reaching the advanced stage of HD must surely be prominent.

Without being dishonest or dismissive about the realities of the condition, it is not obvious to me how a therapist or counsellor might effectively dissuade someone carrying the Huntington gene who, having seen the future, wants very much to avoid being there when it happens. Yet the end-stage of HD is not very different from end-stage Alzheimer's and some cases of Alzheimer's progress almost as slowly as HD usually does. Some dementia sufferers may hope for a breakthrough in treatment but one can hardly criticise those who don't want to take the risk that any breakthrough may not come in time to save them. In any case, a very recent review does not give many grounds for optimism. 'Relatively few clinical trials are undertaken for [Alzheimer] therapeutics, considering the magnitude of the problem.

The success rate for advancing from one phase [of development] to another is low, and the number of compounds progressing to regulatory review [i.e. near to being licensed] is among the lowest found in any therapeutic area'.[4] Dr Rodney Syme's description in Section 5 holds for dementia of all kinds. '[It] is characterized by what I have described as the 'infantile triad' – incontinence of bowel and bladder, inability to communicate and being spoon fed – to which I now realize I should add immobility and total dependence. Shakespeare described this as the seventh age of man – 'a second childishness and mere oblivion, sans teeth, sans eyes, sans taste, sans everything.' This is not how I want to end my life. I am sure I am not alone.' It is not surprising that older people fear developing dementia 'more than diabetes, cancer heart disease or stroke'.[5]

I sometimes think that Ibsen's most-censored play 'Ghosts' needs to be re-written with HD replacing syphilis of the brain – GPI or General Paresis of the Insane – as the disease that is central to the plot. Thanks to penicillin (to which syphilis still unfailingly responds) GPI has lost its former terrors, though it was almost as common in its day as Alzheimer's is in ours. Like congenital syphilis, HD is passed on from an affected parent, though the mechanism is genetic rather than bacterial; and like syphilis, HD is sometimes the result of irregular or unsuspected sexual liaisons, as with the dissolute but outwardly respectable Capt. Alving in 'Ghosts.' However, the main reason for dragging a long-dead Norwegian playwright into this discussion is that one of the most electrifying parts of the play comes near the end, where Capt. Alving's artist son, young Osvald, realises that he is losing his mind from GPI. (Ibsen's description of the affected brain as looking 'like cherry-red velvet' is medically inaccurate but memorably vivid.) Osvald makes it clear to his horrified mother that he plans to commit suicide with morphine, precisely because he thinks he cannot trust her to do the job for him when he can no longer do it for himself, though the play ends without that particular question being resolved. 'But this is so horribly revolting', says Osvald. 'To be turned into a helpless child again. To have to be fed, to have to be … Oh! It doesn't bear talking about.' Those are essentially the reasons given by people with early Alzheimer's who want to go to Dignitas. I am pretty sure they were an important consideration for the people who took part in my impromptu survey and for those in the larger and even more persuasive surveys to be discussed shortly.

Many contributors to this book emphasise that what concerns them most about the way they may die is not the prospect of unrelievable pain but of unrelievable and progressive loss of dignity. Most pain can indeed be adequately controlled and even the failures and indignities of terminal care described in Section 10 have rarely to be endured by patient or family for more than a few weeks. In contrast, the indignities of dementia – as feared by the patient in the early stages even if largely experienced by the family towards the end – often start well before the terminal stages and commonly persist for many months or even years.

For many people, an additional consideration is that they do not want their families to have to watch them living and dying in this sorry state. This may be a minor and secondary motivation for MARS for some patients but a primary and important one for others. As Baroness Warnock puts it: 'I simply do not want to be remembered as someone wholly dependent on others, especially for the most personally private aspects of my life, nor can I tolerate the thought of outstaying my welcome, an increasing burden on my family, so that no one can be truly sorry when I die and they are free.' To our opponents, such sentiments are held to reflect dangerous pressures in society. To most people, I think they will be viewed as altruism. Furthermore, what we spend here on a week's residential or, *a fortiori,* hospital care for one person with advanced dementia would fund quite a lot of rather useful treatments in countries where in addition to high infant mortality, many adults die of easily treatable or preventable diseases long before they get anywhere near our normal retiring age. Among other organisations, *Médecins Sans Frontières* will benefit in my will from the money that I hope will not be spent on caring for my own body when my brain has gone. I find that thought quite comforting.

The usual progress of Alzheimer's dementia – and of other varieties – is a slow and steady decline into fatuity and incontinence, though as with all illnesses, some patients have a more (or less) rapid course than the average. In a recent British post-mortem study, the mean duration of the disease was 7.1 years. 25% of cases died within four years, 50% within seven years, and 75% within ten.[6] Current drugs for Alzheimer's can make that decline even slower and few patients would not want to give them a trial. However, they can only delay the inevitable. They cannot prevent it. Developments in genetic testing may make it easier to predict both the likelihood of developing Alzheimer's and the speed of decline, though if HD is any guide, many actual or potential sufferers will not wish to know either of those predictions.

It therefore follows that sufferers who prefer MARS (or

self-deliverance) to living with steadily diminishing awareness and dignity until they die need to make the necessary arrangements well before they lose mental capacity; and therefore while they may still have at least a few months of life that might bring them and their social and family circle some pleasure to set against their declining abilities. This is not very different in principle from patients with a progressive neurological disorder – e.g. motor neurone disease – deciding to go to Switzerland before their loss of mobility or the need for assisted breathing makes travel too difficult. If MARS becomes legal in Britain, such neurological patients will be able to delay their planned deaths by weeks or months because travelling to Switzerland will be unnecessary. However, for Alzheimer patients planning MARS, it is not loss of mobility that may determine the timing but loss of mental capacity and that is not negotiable.

Several recent publications show that the results of my informal survey in the 1980s were very similar to those of larger and more sophisticated studies today. A British survey published in 2007 questioned 725 members of the general public in London and the South East. 'In the face of severe dementia, less than 40% of respondents would wish to be resuscitated after a heart attack, nearly three-quarters wanted to be allowed to die passively and almost 60% agreed with physician assisted suicide. ... Our survey suggests that a large proportion of the UK general public do not wish for life-sustaining treatments if they were to become demented and the majority agreed with various forms of euthanasia.'[7] That as many as 40% *would* want to be resuscitated may reflect the intriguing additional finding that: 'White respondents were significantly more likely to refuse life-sustaining treatment and to agree to euthanasia compared with black and Asian respondents.'

I don't want to digress too much about this last point but I would guess that religiosity was an important factor in the significantly different levels of treatment refusal, since the black and Asian respondents were almost certainly more religious, as a group, than their white counterparts. A very recent report from the Netherlands[8] describes the responses of three groups to two hypothetical 'end-of-life' scenarios. One involved cancer, the other dementia but in both cases, the patients have reached the stage where rational communication is no longer possible. In the dementia scenario, 'you … no longer recognise your family or friends. You refuse to eat and drink and you retreat more and more into yourself. To communicate with you about medical treatments is not possible any more.' Respondents were asked to state their preferences in this situation about artificial feeding and hydration, antibiotics in the event of pneumonia, resuscitation in the event of cardiac arrest and artificial respiration.

The preferences of 5661 respondents who were members of the Dutch equivalent of Dignity in Dying and had completed Advance Decisions were very similar to those of a representative sample of 1402 Dutch citizens who were not members and had not completed an Advance Decision. In both groups, a large majority 'want to forgo all four presented treatments' for both cancer and dementia. The remaining group consisted of 1059 members of a 'Christian-oriented' patient organisation which, in contrast to conventional Advance Decisions, encourages its members to complete a 'wish-to-live statement.' This predictably rejects 'actions with the purpose of actively terminating life' but also, in theory, rejects 'excessive, medically futile' treatments at the end of life' as well. In practice however, of this largely Protestant group, 71% definitely or probably wanted artificial feeding and hydration, 67% wanted antibiotics for pneumonia, 59% wanted breathing assistance and 47% wanted resuscitation after cardiac arrest, even when 'personality annihilation' had occurred and meaningful communication was impossible; and almost certainly never would be possible again.

Unsurprisingly, especially given the progressive bureaucratisation of British medicine and the pervasive post-Shipman paranoia, what most of the public apparently wants is not what it is likely to get, at least if a survey from Finland is any guide. Over 500 Finnish doctors were asked how they would deal with two clinical scenarios, one involving a terminal cancer patient, the other a patient with advanced dementia. Only 17% said that they would give active [i.e. resuscitative] treatment to the cancer patient but 43% of them would give it in the case of dementia.[9] Another factor – not much discussed – is that private nursing homes naturally like to keep their beds filled and dead patients pay no fees.

Ironically, the situation would be very different for a patient in a persistent vegetative state. In such a case, a judge would probably let the doctors stop tube feeding so that death from dehydration would occur in a few days, as happened in the case of Tony Bland, described in Section 1. This is not normally considered a nice way to go but of course, as a vegetable, the patient won't feel any discomfort. Only his or her family will. However, if he is only half-vegetative (which is a reasonable description of advanced dementia) he will often be fed and watered until he rots, which is literally what will happen if he gets severe bedsores.

It is sometimes said – or hoped – that people with severe dementia are not suffering as much as observers fear they are, because progressive brain failure makes them unaware of most aspects of their existence. Loss of short-term memory may well protect them from recollections of unpleasant things that they experienced in previous days or weeks. After all, during a general anaesthetic that is just a little bit too light, patients may move or cry out in response to painful stimuli but they usually have no recollections or complaints after they wake up. However, we cannot be sure that similar mechanisms or similar consequences are involved in patients with dementia. In any case, the failing brain quite often conjures up disturbing phantoms and fears that are not less disturbing for having no basis in reality. Nobody who has seen frightened and confused dementia patients, sometimes fighting off their blameless carers and screaming in terror or anger, can confidently deny that such routine scenes in the nation's nursing homes and hospitals involve both severe distress and great indignity.

References:

1. de Boer ME, Dröes RM, Jonker C, Eefsting JA, Hertogh CM. Advance directives for euthanasia in dementia: how do they affect resident care in Dutch nursing homes? Experiences of physicians and relatives. J Am Geriatr Soc 2011 Jun; 59(6):989-96.

2. Hertogh CM, de Boer ME, Dröes RM, Eefsting JA. 2007. Would we rather lose our life than our self? Lessons from the Dutch debate on euthanasia for patients with dementia. Am J Bioeth 7(4): 48–56.

3. Di Maio L, Squitieri F, Napolitano G, Campanella G, Trofatter J, Conneally M. Suicide risk in Huntington's disease. J Med Genet 1993, 30; 293-5.

4. Cummings JL, Morstorf T, Zhong K.. Alzheimer's disease drug-development pipeline: few candidates, frequent failures. 2014 Jul 3;6(4):37.

5. Batsch NL, Mittelman MS. 2012. World Alzheimer's Report 2012: Overcoming the stigma of dementia. Alzheimer's disease International: London, England. Available at: http://www.alz.co.uk/research/WorldAlzheimerReport2012.pdf; (Accessed 11th Aug 2012.)

6. Armstrong RA. Factors determining disease duration in Alzheimer's disease: a postmortem study of 103 cases using the Kaplan-Meier estimator and Cox regression. 2014;2014:623487.

7. Williams N, Dunford C, Knowles A, Warner J. Public attitudes to life-sustaining treatments and euthanasia in dementia. 2007 Dec;22(12):1229-34.

8. Van Wijmen M, Pasman H, Widdershoven G, Onwuteaka-Philipsen B. Continuing or forgoing treatment at the end of life? Preferences of the general public and people with an advance directive. J. Med.Ethics. Published online September 2nd 2014. 10.1136/medethics-2013-101544

9. Hinkka H, Kosunen E, Lammi EK, Metsänoja R, Puustelli A, Kellokumpu-Lehtinen P. Decision making in terminal care: a survey of Finnish doctors' treatment decisions in end-of-life scenarios involving a terminal cancer and a terminal dementia patient. 2002 May;16(3):195-204.

The 2014 House of Lords debate

Michael Irwin

On June 5, 2014, Lord Falconer, a former Lord Chancellor (2003 to 2007), formally presented his Assisted Dying Bill to the House of Lords. (Although this was called the 'First Reading', no debate on a draft Bill ever takes place on this occasion.)

Essentially modelled on what has been possible in the U.S. State of Oregon since 1997, this Assisted Dying Bill would enable mentally competent, terminally-ill adults (that is, individuals who are expected to die within six months) to end their lives by taking a lethal substance after they have been assessed by two independent doctors.

The last time that a Bill of this kind was debated in the House of Lords was in 2006, when Lord Joffe's Bill fell at the Second Reading due to a 'wrecking' amendment which was tabled by peers opposed to a change in the law. This time, opponents did not feel confident in trying to repeat this negative action because of a recent Supreme Court judgment that Parliament should debate the issue.

Following the usual procedure, Lord Falconer's Bill was given its Second Reading, in the House of Lords, on July 18, 2014. At the end of this long debate (nearly ten hours), no objections were raised to the draft Bill going to the 'Committee' stage (when members of the House of Lords examine, in very considerable detail, all aspects of the draft).

Following this 'Committee' examination of the Bill, it will return to the House of Lords for still further debate; this is now called the 'Third Reading.' If a majority of Peers vote in favour of Lord Falconer's Bill on this occasion, it has to be sent to the House of Commons for further detailed consideration. Only if a majority of MPs support the Bill will it finally become law in England and Wales.

At the Second Reading in the House of Lords, on July 18, 2014, sixty-four peers were in favour of the draft Bill and sixty were opposed (and two took a neutral position).

Opponents of the Bill were obviously influenced by the recent Supreme Court decision, and so decided not to oppose this Second Reading – unlike what happened in 2006, when the Joffe Bill was defeated, 148 to 100 votes, at its Second Reading. In this debate, a new record was established for the number of speakers in one day in the House of Lords – 126 Peers – mainly because there was a limit of four minutes for each speaker. Some of the important remarks made by these peers, on July 18th, are listed below. In reading them, please remember that most come from speakers in support of the Bill, and that this Bill is only focused on the 'terminally ill.'

LORD FALCONER OF THOROTON – 'The current situation leaves the rich able to go to Switzerland, the majority reliant on amateur assistance, the compassionate treated like criminals, and no safeguards in respect of undue pressure. … Critics of my Bill cite the voluntary euthanasia laws of Belgium and the Netherlands as an example of a slippery slope. In fact, it is not a slippery slope but a deliberate path chosen by legislators in those countries.'

LORD DUBS – 'I support the Bill, because I do not wish to deny other people something that I might want myself some day in future.'

LORD LESTER OF HERNE HILL – 'Patients have the right to life. They also have the right to personal autonomy and dignity.'

LORD WIGLEY – 'Those lucky enough to have the material resources and family support can go to Switzerland to end their lives, whereas those without the resources or family support have to struggle on from day to day, suffering pain and anguish with no means of relief in their reach.'

LORD JOFFE – 'In Switzerland, arguably the most conservative country in Europe, lawful assisted dying has existed for 60 years.'

LORD AVEBURY – 'Palliative care is effective in the large majority of cases of terminally ill patients, but it is not effective in all.'

EARL OF GLASGOW – The Bill is about personal choice and the alleviation of unnecessary suffering.'

LORD BLAIR OF BOUGHTON – 'In Oregon ... evidence neither of a slippery slope, nor of the elderly being pressured.'

BARONESS WARWICK OF UNDERCLIFFE – 'I strongly believe in personal autonomy, and there is no more crucial point in life where that seems relevant than when one is close to death. ... [The Bill] will give the individual the control that they want over the last days of their lives.'

LORD BIRT – 'I can see no reason at all for denying individuals the right to manage their own imminent, irreversible and prospectively painful, wretched or deeply distressing death – in their own interest, and in the interest of the loved ones that they will shortly leave behind.'

BARONESS BLACKSTONE – 'The same freedom of choice that applies to how we live should also apply to how we die. ... Those who argue that palliative care can always ensure a peaceful and painless death are flying in the face of evidence ... it would be more compassionate to accept this and to reflect on a system that combines palliative care with legally assisted dying for those whose suffering has become unbearable.'

LORD HARRIES OF PENTREGARTH – 'If we are moved by compassion for people who have only six months to live, how much more do we feel compassion for someone who may have a totally incapacitated life ahead of them for years … it is totally inconsistent to argue for autonomy in the case of those who are dying and not others who may be in even greater distress.'

LORD BAKER OF DORKING – 'I believe that God is a loving, compassionate and caring God, and that he would not wish to subject any of the creatures which he has created to long periods of suffering, which can in fact be mitigated or eliminated.'

BARONESS MEACHER – 'The guiding principles for every doctor in all their work are, of course, to follow the best interests of the patient and to respect a competent patient's autonomy, wherever that takes them.'

LORD BROOKE OF ALVERTHORPE – 'I am frightened of dying too, as I get older; it is an issue that comes into my head virtually every day, in a way that it did not when I was younger. … It leads me to think about whether I can continue to control everything in my life – and I have controlled a great deal of it, for much of my life.'

VISCOUNT CRAIGAVON – 'I wholeheartedly support palliative care and its extension, but we have had numerous descriptions and reports of conditions where in 10% or 15% of cases such care is not successful or not wanted. Individual choice should be respected.'

LORD STONE OF BLACKHEATH – 'The word 'choice' is key here. If people with religious conviction or medical professionals opposed to assisted dying do not want this option, they could simply choose not to partake ... a law which enables assisted dying would stop people living the end of their life in fear of a terrible death.'

THE EARL OF SANDWICH – 'What right has the palliative care community to provide the ultimate comfort if it allows suffering and falls short of providing the ultimate relief? I agree that doctors are in a separate category and I admire those who already take the law into their own hands.'

BARONESS TONGE – 'I sometimes feel that the people in this category, who may have locked-in syndrome or a long-term neurological condition are, in the words of Article 3 of the European Convention on Human Rights, being subjected to torture or to inhuman or degrading treatment.'

BARONESS WHEATCROFT – 'Compassion has always been the route of the best doctors – and this Bill is all about compassion.'

BARONESS WARNOCK – 'If one sacrifices oneself in a modest way for one's family, that is also thought virtuous. I do not understand why one should not be allowed to exercise that virtue at the end of one's life, and not have it assumed that this is an idea that has been put into one's head by somebody else. It is not, it is there already.'

BARONESS ROYALL OF BLAISDON – 'The goal must be to allow people who are suffering at the end of their life to choose to die. This, I believe, is a matter of compassion and human dignity.'

LORD ABERDARE – 'I believe that I am responsible for my own life and how I live it, including the right to end it if I find it no longer bearable.'

BARONESS RICHARDSON OF CALOW – 'Why should it be

considered shameful for me to wish to protect my family
and friends from the burden of watching me slowly die?... I
would wish to protect my family from having to watch me,
from putting their lives on hold and making a rota to make
sure that somebody is with me at all times. I would want to
protect them from having to bear my anger, frustration and
sheer peevishness, which often accompanies pain. ... For the
elderly, death often comes as a friend, and for the religious
it comes with hope and promise.'

LORD SHERBOURNE OF DIDSBURY – 'There are many
distinguished people with deep religious convictions, and
many in this House, who support this Bill.'

LORD DAVIES OF STAMFORD – 'Terminal sedation is a
euphemism for giving the patient a dose of an opiate –
usually diamorphine – or perhaps a barbiturate. It would
not be sufficient to kill the patient, because that would be
illegal in this country, but sufficient to send the patient into
a permanent coma. Then, no further means of life support
are supplied.'

LORD CAREY OF CLIFTON – 'I have the greatest admiration
for the work of our hospices, but even the best palliative care
does not meet all needs. Dr. Rajesh Munglani, the well-
known expert in pain management, writes that he frequently
sees cases of excruciating pain that are unresponsive to
powerful analgesics and can be alleviated only by very
heavy sedation, to the point of unconsciousness. ... Being a
Christian is quite compatible with supporting the Bill. ... If
we truly love our neighbours as ourselves, how can we deny
them the death that we would wish for ourselves in such a
condition? That is what I would want.'

LORD BROWN OF EATON-UNDER-HEYWOOD – 'It is clear that

many people are deeply unhappy with the law as it stands. We defy their views at our peril. The peril is that we lose respect for the law. That is indeed a slippery slope ... The noble and learned Lord, Lord Neuberger (President of the Supreme Court), said, 'there seems to me to be significantly more justification in assisting people to die if they have the prospect of living for many years a life that they regarded as valueless, miserable and often painful, than if they have only a few months left to live.'

Lord Crisp – 'I am sure that there will be others whose conditions are not covered by the Bill but who will be comforted by the thought that this is a step towards a wider right to assisted dying.'

Lord Elder – 'The House is about to rise for two and a half months and there will be few sitting Fridays between then and the House rising for the General Election. The chances of this Bill going through Committee, Report and Third Reading, even before it gets to the Commons and assuming that it is passed here, means that in reality any Bill passed on this draft is a very long time away.'

Baroness Neuberger – 'Six months seems arbitrary and ... possibly unkind because suffering that is longer than six months is suffering that we should take even more seriously.'

Lord Shipley – 'In principle, I believe individuals have a human right to exercise their own choice to end their own suffering. It is a right that I would like for myself, to be taken with my family.'

Baroness Murphy – 'There has been talk about the risk or fear about the doctor-patient relationship, but the country in the world that has the best trust in its doctors is the Netherlands – that is research evidence.'

LORD HARRISON – 'If this Bill fails, the law will still lack clarity in regard to medical staff who administer 'easeful death.' Giving a double helping of morphine to the dying is compassionate but it is a sleight of hand in which we all collude.'

LORD BERKELEY OF KNIGHTON – 'The days are gone when a country GP visiting a patient he or she had known for decades could quietly and gently ease them on their way. Perhaps some still do – I know many doctors who have done it. However, in curtailing the ability to carry out this compassionate care, through the forensic analysis of deaths, I believe we have created the need for the Bill.'

LORD FINKELSTEIN – 'Failing to legislate for assisted dying is substituting our reason – Parliament's reason and the state's reason – for that of the dying person on the grounds that we are of sound mind and strong, and the dying person is not. ... We live as free people and now we want the right to die as we have lived'.

LORD HOLLICK – 'We live in a democracy where citizens have the right in personal matters to make up their own minds and to act accordingly. Society should respect and protect the right to choose how you wish to die in the same manner we respect other important personal freedoms.'

LORD LOW OF DALSTON – 'I am disabled. ... It is curious that the leaders of disabled people campaign for choice and control in every other aspect of life but balk at it in this one. I wish to speak for the overwhelming majority of disabled people who do not welcome the tendentious advocacy of their self-appointed spokespersons but, rather, wish to see this Bill progress.'

LORD HASKEL – 'We also have to move with the times.

As a society, we are becoming a lot more aware of choice. Personal choice has become one of our freedoms. As a result, our society is moving away from moral certainties towards personal choice.'

LORD LAYARD – 'We have 17 years of evidence from Oregon, where no single instance of undue pressure from family and friends has been discovered.'

LORD PEARSON OF RANNOCK – 'I fear that those noble and Christian Lords who oppose the Bill because it breaches the sanctity of human life may not have got that quite right. I am no theologian, but it seems to me that Jesus Christ was somewhat careless with his own earthly life. After all, he did not need to go to Gethsemane and the cross.'

BARONESS MALLALIEU – 'There is a strong probability that on the very next appeal on this issue, the relevant provisions of the Suicide Act will be found inconsistent with the European Convention on Human Rights, which provides the right to private and family life. ... It may be a strong word but I believe that the law at present is cruel. ... I also respect those who have spoken from strong religious belief of the sanctity of life, but they should not try to impose their certainties on others who do not share them.'

THE EARL OF ARRAN – 'None of us here today asked to come into this world. Should we therefore not have the choice as to how we might wish to depart from it?'

LORD BEECHAM – 'The Liverpool (Care) pathway has its supporters, but it also has its critics. Its use without the consent of the patient is surely a denial of individual choice. Even with the consent of the patient, it is difficult to argue that it is fundamentally different in substance and effect from what the Bill proposes.'

The quality of death

Peter Tatchell,
Human Rights activist

> *'To live badly is not to live, but to spend a long time dying.'*
>
> **Democritus of Abdera, circa 420 BC**

We live in a strongly materialist, consumerist society, where wealth and possessions are too often one-sidedly deemed indices of success and happiness. In truth, while a certain quantity of income is necessary for comfort and fulfilment, what's really important to most people are quality of life factors, such as a loving partner, family and friends; a safe, crime-free neighbourhood; affordable, warm housing; friendly supportive neighbours; good education and healthcare; and a clean, pollution-free environment.

These are the true measure of a fulfilled, contented life – and cannot be easily monetarised or commodified. Just as important as quality of life is quality of death: the opportunity to die with dignity and without prolonged painful, debilitating incapacity. Where is our consistency and compassion if we care that a person lives a good quality life but not that they suffer an undignified, degrading death? Quality of life and quality of death are two equal humanitarian entitlements. The former without the latter is incomplete.

To suffer prolonged physical pain and emotional distress, with no hope of respite, is a terrible fate – not just for the dying person but also for their loved ones too. I know. In 2005, I was witness to my cousin, Priscilla, being dragged down to an agonising death from lung cancer and secondary tumours, including malignancies in the brain. To see her relentless degeneration, knowing the doctors gave her no chance of survival, was bad enough. More heart-breaking still was to see her daily convulsing, choking and gasping for breath. It was akin to prolonged torture.

Once all hope was lost – when no medical intervention could save her life or stop her intense suffering – it was cruel and inhuman to let her suffer more. I wanted her to live but also, at that end stage, I wanted her to be allowed to die peacefully and gracefully. Bearing witness to Priscilla's demeaning, agonising death convinced me that dying with dignity is a human rights issue – equally as much as the human right to live with dignity. The right to live humanely and to die humanely are merely two different aspects of human rights and human dignity.

At the onset of her decline, while still of sound mind, my cousin should have been allowed to designate that beyond a certain point of no return she would be allowed to die a calm, dignified, gentle death. That, to me, would have been the kinder, more humane option. It is what I want for myself: to die with dignity, without long drawn out suffering or humiliation. In the same way that I have sought to take personal command and responsibility for my life, so I would like to be able to do likewise in death. It is my body and my right.

Christian attitudes to suicide

Colin Brewer

The Rev. Paul Badham argues persuasively that Medically Assisted Rational Suicide (MARS) is not incompatible with Christian faith and principles. In this section, I want to review briefly the historical development of Christian attitudes to suicide because I believe that 1500 years after they were codified, they still have a significant influence on legislation and debate.

Although most of the opposition to MARS in Britain (and the USA) comes from Christian organisations and individuals, early Christianity, arising as it did in a Graeco-Roman world in which suicide was widely regarded as an honourable choice in certain situations, had no strong views about suicide. Early commentators noted that the several suicides mentioned in the Bible were discussed in fairly neutral or even positive terms and some of the early fathers of the church even regarded the death of Jesus as containing elements of suicide.

During the debate in the House of Lords on the Suicide Act of 1961, which decriminalised suicide but made assisting it a new offence, Baroness Wootton reminded her fellow-peers that: 'Early Christians were very much disposed to suicide ... They assumed that by an early departure from this life they could escape not only its miseries, but also its temptations, and ... would thus [obtain] a clean passport to the blessed state of the next world.'

This attitude – or at least, the attitude of the Christian authorities – changed when Christianity ceased to be a persecuted cult, or just one cult among many others and

became Rome's state religion. In that same debate, Lord
Justice Denning (later a famous Master of the Rolls) said that
'for nearly a thousand years suicide has been regarded as the
most heinous of felonies ... [because our religion] decreed
that ... to commit suicide was invading the prerogative of
the Almighty, by rushing into His presence uncalled for...'

Until 1824, he added, 'suicides were buried at a crossroads
with a stake through their body and until 1882, a suicide had
to be buried by night; and ever since 1882 up to this day,
according to the law of the Church of England, a suicide is
not entitled to Christian burial.' It is Catholic law too. Both
churches get round it now by pretending that all suicides
are mentally ill. (As the philosopher C.E.M. Joad put it, do
not attempt suicide in England 'for fear of being regarded
as a lunatic if you succeed and a criminal if you fail.') Even
in 1893, a *Lancet* editorial protested: 'For a jury to return
a verdict imparting insanity to a man without any evidence
beyond the bare fact of suicide is an unworthy evasion.'[1]

The poet A. Alvarez also emphasises, in his classic personal
and historical study *The Savage God*, that early Christianity
did not condemn suicide. It was only after two or three
centuries, with the rise of the Donatist sect (who, as Baroness
Wootton indicated, actively embraced martyrdom and suicide
on the principle that if heaven's our destination, let's travel
express) that the Church started to worry about empty pews.
One historian described how some Donatists 'announced the
day on which, in the presence of their friends and brethren,
they should cast themselves headlong from some lofty rock.'

St. Augustine was the most prominent of the church
leaders who decided that suicide was a worse sin than murder
because a suicide was not only leaving life before God allowed

him to do so but was, in effect, criticising God too. A suicide would also be guilty of the sin of despair. In 562 AD, The Council of Braga denied funeral rites to all suicides. In 620, The Council of Toledo ordained that even attempted suicides would be automatically excommunicated.[2] The Catechism of the Roman Catholic church states: 'Everyone is responsible for his life before God who has given it to him. It is God who remains the sovereign Master of life. We are obliged to accept life gratefully and preserve it for his honour and the salvation of our souls. We are stewards, not owners, of the life God has entrusted to us. It is not ours to dispose of.'[3]

This, I believe, was very much the view of the late Dame Cicely Saunders, rightly praised and honoured for her promotion of hospices and palliative care. Nobody who met her, as I did (we got on surprisingly well) can doubt her compassion but she held the fundamentalist – or at any rate, post-Augustinian – Christian view that even though suicide is not now a crime, it is still a sin. I heard her say this at a conference in the late 1980s. She wasn't very keen on Advance Decisions either at that time.

When Islam swept over the Christian world, it seems to have absorbed these attitudes, along with several others. 'The Prophet said, 'He who commits suicide by throttling shall keep on throttling himself in the Hell Fire (forever) and he who commits suicide by stabbing himself shall keep on stabbing himself in the Hell-Fire.'[4] In contrast, other world religions – Buddhism, Confucianism, Hinduism – while certainly not encouraging suicide at least do not vilify the deceased, refuse conventional funeral rites or ritually desecrate the corpse. Interestingly, Byzantine Christianity's position was very different from Rome's. The 6th century Code of Justinian took a sympathetic view of suicides, provided that they were not trying to escape punishment for a crime.[5]

Christianity has often worked very closely with the rulers of the day. After the 7th century anathema on suicide, those rulers soon adapted Rome's view that people were the property of God and could not remove themselves from life without God's permission. Kings decided that people were their property as well as God's and treated suicides, unless suffering from obvious insanity, as enemies of the state. Non-insane suicides generally had their property confiscated by the state, the church, or both and many suicides were therefore ruled insane by sympathetic juries to protect them and their families from legalised pauperisation.

Despite Christianity's historical distaste for suicide, until relatively recently it seems to have had much less of a problem with homicide. Just over 300 years ago, a young Edinburgh student, Thomas Aikenhead, was hanged for expressing disbelief in God and he was hanged with the full approval and encouragement of the religious leaders of the time. That was the last such execution in Britain but similar manifestations of religious intolerance continued in France until the 1770s and in Spain until 1826 – the Inquisition's last victim being a mere post-Enlightenment deist. They still happen under Islam.

Care Not Killing is a Christian-oriented organisation, particularly concerned with protecting disabled people from what it fears will be increased pressure to end their lives, especially at a time when the rising costs of health services are rarely out of the news. One of its patrons, Nola Leach, is also active in another Christian organisation called, simply, CARE, whose website has a Prayer Diary. The prayer for

Nov 27th 2013 was this. 'Lord, thank You for the centuries-old Christian heritage on which England, Northern Ireland, Scotland and Wales have been built.' As well as vicious and vengeful attitudes to suicide, that 'heritage' includes hanging sceptical students, supporting slavery and devaluing women. Its Catholic and Islamic equivalents include all of those but the Catholic heritage also includes endorsing, until barely a century ago, the castration of pre-pubertal boys, the better to sing God's praises in the Vatican choir.

Our religious opponents often claim or imply moral superiority to those of us without religious beliefs but some of them seem to have no sense of shame. Why should we automatically respect sermons on human rights and the sanctity of life from the spiritual descendants of Torquemada and John Calvin? How can these people argue that their religion confers on them some kind of intrinsic moral wisdom when those same religions have a history of being viciously cruel and intolerant for so many centuries and of being so reluctant to admit their mistakes? The encyclical *Humane Vitae,* issued by Pope Paul VI in 1968 is perhaps best known for its reassertion of Catholic opposition to artificial contraception but it also contains assertions of Papal wisdom and authority that could just as easily have been uttered by political leaders who were as totalitarian in their day as popes used to be. Indeed, the tedious and routine claim of religious apologists that Stalin and Hitler show what happens when atheists take control ignores the fact that Communists and Nazis were as much in thrall to their own quasi-theological ideologies (complete with sacred texts) as any religious leader.

Humane Vitae asserts: 'It is in fact indisputable, as Our Predecessors have many times declared, that Jesus Christ, when he communicated his divine powers to Peter and the other Apostles ... constituted them as the authentic guardians and interpreters of the whole moral law.' Yet this apostolic 'authenticity' and the implication of a hot-line to heaven evidently did not prevent popes (and their equivalents in other religions) from endorsing some extremely ungodly activities, many of which would have been deemed unacceptable by free citizens of the ancient Roman and Greek empires. Of course, not all Christians supported these horrors and few would try to justify them now. Surveys indicate that even practising (as distinct from nominal) Christians are almost as supportive of MARS as the four-fifths of the general public in Britain who consistently favour legalisation. However, in Europe and America, it was the non-conformists, the deists and the atheists who did much more to end the horrors than the established religions and their leaders.

The CARE prayer for Jan 5th 2014 urged us to praise God 'for the beauty and fruitfulness of all You have made.' That 'all' presumably includes the bacteria and viruses that used to kill half of our children before they reached puberty, not to mention cancer, motor-neurone disease and Alzheimer's. We doctors spend our entire professional lives trying to defeat some of God's creations and it is probably no coincidence that the first person to publish an atheist tract in England and live to tell the tale was a doctor – Matthew Turner of Liverpool. It was 1781 before he felt that it was reasonably safe to do so. If we accept the notion that only God should decide when we die, then surely all life-saving medication and surgery are in some sense interfering with God's plans. (Plans, incidentally, which apparently include the absence of effective interventions for most illnesses until about the last hundred years of the many millennia of human existence).

The well-documented over-representation of Christian doctors in British palliative care[6] means that many of them must find it very difficult or even impossible to accept patient autonomy in this most crucial and fundamental area. Is it unreasonable to suggest that such doctrinaire views make them, in some very important respects, unfit – or at any rate, much less than ideal – for a medical specialty that deals every day with human beings holding diverse views on one of the most important stages of our life?[7]

Based on a speech to the Cambridge Union,
January 16th, 2014

References:

1. Editorial, The legal fiction of the insanity of suicides. *Lancet* 1893. 972.

2. Alvarez A. *The savage god: a study of suicide.* London. Weidenfeld and Nicholson. 1973. *Passim*

3. Catechism. Part three. Article 5, item 2280

4. Hadiths. Sahih al-Bukhari, 2:23:446

5. Code of Justinian Title 50. Concerning the property of those who commit suicide.

6. Seale C. The role of doctors' religious faith and ethnicity in taking ethically controversial decisions during end-of-life care. J Med Ethics 2010 Nov;36(11):677-82

7. The motion was that 'This House Would Legalise Assisted Dying'. The opposers included a speaker from the organisation 'Care Not Killing.' The motion was carried by 207 to 67 votes with 54 abstentions.

Acts of suicide

Professor Anthony Grayling,
philosopher and first Master of New College of the
Humanities, London

I am going to talk about compassion and about autonomy. Both of these points are of very great importance. The kindness that we feel towards our fellows in society makes a claim on us to consider the circumstances in which they find themselves in difficult times of their lives. Remember that we are talking here about assisted dying, not actually talking about death – that is something that happens when the dying process has come to an end. We are talking about an experience which is a living experience – something experienced by the person undergoing it, and we are talking about the degree of compassion, the degree of kindness in our preparedness to help somebody going through that experience.

The autonomy point speaks to this because if you think about what we have in mind when we talk about the right that an individual has to make decisions about important things in their lives – for example, how and when they die and whether they find life still worth living or not, and whether they are in a position to help themselves to die – they can legitimately claim the help of their fellows in society to be released from their suffering. When we think about that, we think about something fundamental which is a 'right.' Those of you who have been studying what has happened, in the last decade in this country, in the number of cases which have come up before the Courts – the Diane Pretty case, for example; the Tony Nicklinson case more recently – you would have noticed that the legal representatives of those that are seeking the license from society to end their lives or to be helped to end their lives, to be assisted in the process of dying, appeal to the human rights that are now embodied in our English law. This is the European Convention of Human Rights, which by means of the Human Rights Act, came into effect in the year 2000.

There are three Articles of that Act that are relevant. The second Article is the right to life, the third is the right to be protected from inhumane and cruel treatment, and the eighth which accords privacy to individuals. The concept of privacy there is a broad one which entails that individuals have the scope, the margin, to make these important decisions for themselves – decisions, for example, about whether they marry, have a family, and in the arguments put before the Courts, the right to make decisions about how long they live.

In 1961, the Suicide Act of that year decriminalized suicide. It may be surprising to know that prior to that time, if you attempted suicide and failed, you could be prosecuted for doing so. There are still plenty of jurisdictions, where if you do not succeed in killing yourself, you can get into trouble for it. The 1961 Act decriminalized suicide, but it left a provision saying that anybody who helps someone, who aids or abets or encourages someone to commit suicide, is liable for criminal prosecution. So, this means that somebody who is incapable of committing suicide who wants to and now has a right implied in decriminalization is in a Catch-22 situation: they cannot end their lives if they need to, because, if they can get anyone to help them, that person might be prosecuted.

Now, I would like you to reflect a little on these rights. Think about the right to life. Suppose I imprison you in a very small cage and I give you some bread and water occasionally to keep you alive. Am I respecting your right to life? Surely not. Surely a right to life is a right to a certain minimum quality of life. And, given the complexity of human nature and the human mind, the quality of life which is implied is something of quite a high degree of complexity, A right to life is a right to a life worth living, and, when in the judgement of the person living it, that life has ceased to be worth living, it behoves us to respect the judgement that person has made – and, as an act of kindness and compassion, to help them if they are not able to help themselves to be released from a life that they find no longer worth living. So it seems to me that it is implicit, in the second Article of our Human Rights Act, an acknowledgement of the fact that life should be of a certain minimum quality and the only person who can make a judgement about that is the person living it – the person experiencing the process of dying.

Article 3 says that we must not subject people to inhumane treatment. Surely it is the case that, if someone wishes to be released from life cannot take an action that would bring about that desired result for herself or himself and they ask us, they plead with us, to help them to be released, surely it is inhumane and cruel to deny them that? I think that those two expressions – inhumanity and cruelty – actually apply to those people who deny to people who have a settled and clear-minded intention to leave life, if, they deny them that, then they are being inhumane and cruel to them.

And, lastly, Article 8 – the right to privacy or your right to self-determination. Surely that should be the final word in this matter because it implies that, in the end, and ultimately it is only the actor himself or herself who can make those judgements and those choices, which affect the entire quality and aim of the direction of life's purpose that can infuse into life its meaning and which, when life has become intolerable, can choose to end it and to ask, if necessary, to be helped to be released from it.

These are tremendously important ideas because they are ideas that come out of the very concept of a life worth living, of a full rich human life, the end of which and the manner of the end of which is an important part of the story of that life, and to think that by legal means, that by opposition, particularly when the opposition is based on very tendentious principles (most of the opposition comes from the idea that life is not for an individual to make choices about ultimately) because life is given by some other agency, a transcendent agency, a deity or deities, who, having been the givers of life, are the only ones entitled to take it away. This is a view which has its roots in the metaphysics and the morality of people who lived several thousand years ago. We, now, that we have much more respect for individuals and also the means to provide individuals with genuine help when they need it, should be thinking differently, more sympathetically, and with much greater kindness.

So, for these reasons, I ask you to support the motion that we should legalize Assisted Dying.

*Text of address to the Oxford Union debate on
'Assisted Dying' on October 18, 2012.
Union voted 167 to 139 in favour of the motion)*

7

A death in the family

Up the slippery slope

Virginia Ironside,
journalist and author

M y mother had always made me promise that I would make sure that if she was terminally ill she would be snuffed out 'like a candle.' She didn't want to remain guttering till the end. But even in the good old days when doctors were far more free with the morphine jabs, it was still difficult to get her wishes fulfilled.

After another setback in her treatment – my mother had cancer and was talking gibberish most of the time except when she had a blood transfusion when she'd beg me to get the doctors to end it all – the doctor in charge called me into his consulting room. 'Nothing to worry about!' he said breezily. 'We'll have her up and going to the opera and playing tennis in no time at all!' As any idea of exercise was anathema to my mother who had twice tried to commit suicide, and since going to the opera was her idea of hell, I broke down.

'She doesn't want to live!' I said. It was to no avail. It was only when, an agonising week later, that a nurse took me aside. 'Your mother has no hope,' she said bluntly. 'I'm a Roman Catholic, but I beg you to ask the doctors to do something. She is terrific pain, physical and mental.'

So at that point I went in and begged with a vengeance, and soon a morphine shot was administered and she died that night. 'Thank you, darling,' she said, when I told her what I'd arranged. Shortly afterwards, an elderly friend of mine who'd been in pain for a couple of years, asked if I could buy her a coffee grinder to grind up her pills, and some coloured felt pens so she could write a visible note on her door, warning people to call the police before entering. But because of the law I was obliged to tell her that I couldn't fulfil her requests. She should try asking someone else but not to tell them what she wanted the purchases for.

Recently, another elderly friend of mine, who longed to die and refused food, was woken every two hours during her final weeks by a nurse practically force-feeding her and trying to pour soup down her throat, despite the pleadings of her daughters.

There is an extraordinarily skewed view that life is worth living at all costs. The truth is that life is only worth living if it's worth living. We are compassionate enough to our animals, putting them out of their misery if they're suffering – indeed it's approved of, although sometimes to put an animal down causes more pain to the owner than the pet – but when it comes to humans, who actually have minds of their own and can often tell us what they want, our hands are tied.

Recently I was talking of my endorsement of euthanasia at a forum about old people. The rest of the panel (though privately I knew some agreed with me) seemed nervous about coming to support the idea fully in public. And members of the audience were outraged. 'I know a ninety-five year-old who even though bedridden, a widower and unable to see is living a full life!' said one, imagining that I would like to see the happy old gent bumped off, the last thing on my mind. I felt completely isolated. But afterwards two young people came up to me. 'We agree with you,' they said. 'Our mother is a slave to our grandfather who lives with us. He used to be a lovely person, kind and fun, but now he's incontinent, subject to rages, deeply unhappy, doesn't know who any of us are, but when he had pneumonia instead of letting him go they filled him with antibiotics to face another year of hell.'

I want to be able to decide my own death because I want to have control of my life. My poor son has been given so many living wills by me I'm surprised he doesn't pop over and bump me off straight away. The last thing I want is for my hard-earned money to be squandered on nursing a distorted and unhappy version of myself for years when it could help my grandchildren. There is a lot of talk of giving dying people 'dignity,' but frankly where's the dignity in having your bottom wiped by a stranger, even a kindly one? Or, come to that, even your best beloved?

One problem is that laws on the Right to Die are made by people who haven't reached old age. They don't know, yet, that as we get older, many of us find that not only do we fear death less than when we were younger, but that we might even welcome it. Two people recently have gone to Dignitas not because they have a terminal painful illness but simply because they don't find life today worth living any more. They have, quite simply, come to the end of the line. For some it can be an awful struggle trying to continue being a Game Old Girl or Perky Pensioner when you're over eighty. Suddenly death starts to look less like an enemy and more of a friend.

There's a lot of talk about slippery slopes. But why are slopes always slippery? A slope, yes, but 'slippery' implies something out of control, a fear that if we allow, under strict regulations with the endorsement of two doctors, the possibility that we might be able to have our lives ended in a compassionate manner by a professional, that soon everyone over sixty will be rounded up in a van and bunged into gas chambers. Nonsense.

The other argument against self-deliverance is that old or sick people will be pressured by their loved ones to agree to be got rid of by their families. Not only is this view extremely insulting to most old people who can easily withstand family pressure – on the whole we're a curmudgeonly bunch, not people who give in easily – but it's also insulting to the doctors who would have to check that the people who wanted to die were totally convinced of their views and weren't being coerced.

There is another problem less spoken of. Unless loved ones can really detach themselves from their own feelings and allow the person who wants to die to do exactly what they want, they find it very difficult to go along with the idea of endorsing a loved one's right to die. It feels unloving and certainly bad-mannered to say: 'Okay, if you really want to die, fine.' Whatever they may feel privately, they may feel compelled to resist the views of a parent or sibling or friend. Similarly, saying you want to die is tricky. The sub-text always appears to be 'However much I love you and you love me, however good and kind you are to me, you can't give me enough to overcome my desire not to exist.' And that belief, if it's articulated, can seem terribly unkind to loved ones.

Some people say 'But if you want to die, why not do it yourself? Why involve anyone else?' The reason is that when it comes to my wanting to die I may not be capable, physically or mentally, of doing it myself. But even if I were, I'd hate to get the dose wrong or botch up the attempt, resulting in my living a life perhaps even worse than the one I had originally, and becoming more rather than less of a burden. I want someone to tell me what is the right dose, what's a completely fool-proof method. Not being a doctor I simply don't know this myself.

Often when I've explained my views to friends, they say: 'Ah, but when it comes to it, you might change your mind! What would you do then?' Of course I might. And if I do I will say so. But I hope I don't change my mind. The survival instinct is, after all, only another instinct. It has no reason to it. It doesn't have always to be listened to. As we suppress our murderous instincts and our greedy instincts and our sexual instincts when they're inappropriate so, I think, I hope I would be willing to suppress my survival instinct if it kicked in at the wrong time – at the end of my life when, having made an Advance Decision while I was normal and rational, I'm sick, unhappy, in pain, confused, a burden and unable to cope for myself.

Laura and me

Angela Neustatter,
journalist and writer

A few months before she died, my dear friend Laura, 60, accepted that her fast-moving cancer could no longer be treated and she would almost certainly be gone by the end of the year. She and her beloved husband were wrapped in grief, and Laura talked of how almost unbearable it was to know she would not see her children, both in their twenties, mature and have families of their own. Yet alongside this railing against the dying of the light was anguish at knowing she would almost certainly disintegrate, becoming ever less of the fiercely independent, hugely loving person she was. The Laura so admired as the dynamic, efficient heart of the family, a fine counterpart to her husband's artistic, intensely sweet but often other-worldly role in the family.

In this near future of diminishing returns, she visualised how it would be to become physically and maybe mentally incompetent, possibly incontinent, graceless, and a relentless drain on her family's physical and emotional resources. She suffered greatly knowing she would have no control over all this if it came to pass. And least of all if, as she rightly predicted, the pain would become increasingly worse and the pain medicine less and less able to deal with it.

Laura lived in the Netherlands and so, rather than accept this destiny because there was no alternative, she chose the option offered. In that enlightened country, she could go to see her doctor at the time she was still fit enough and *compos mentis* enough to go through the rigorous consultation required as she made the decision to opt for assisted suicide should she want it. To be sure her family could be there with her when she went.

It was heart-warming to see the sense of release and relief that having this in place brought Laura. When I visited soon after, she looked better than for some time: her bobbed hair was buoyant because she had washed and brushed it to the familiar wild curly bob. She had put a spot of make-up on to the once rosy but now pale and thinned cheeks; her lips gleamed with crimson gloss.

She pointed to the drawer of her writing desk and where the document for her right to euthanasia was kept, along with a file with all the preparations made for her funeral. She always had been dazzlingly efficient and practical and so it was at this time. She had sat with her family and planned the final ceremony, going with them to choose the grave where she now resides.

In the end Laura did not call on the doctor for her end. She deteriorated suddenly, very fast. Her husband and children, realising what was happening, stayed with her round the clock. The end, her husband tells, was mercifully brief because Laura, her body brittle and fleshless as a bird's skeleton, was wracked with an appalling pain that had her howling and writhing. She could not sustain life and so, held by everyone, she quietened and was dead. The sadness was immense, but also the relief that Laura did not have to suffer any longer. In fact she had set in motion the plan for chosen death, telling her husband just the day before that she now wanted to die and for him to make the appointment with the doctor.

Her husband is a Scotsman who grew up in a fiercely religious family where God's will was the thing and there could be no recourse to a medically orchestrated death, no matter what. He was relating this to me, his blue eyes fiery even as tears coursed down his face, and saying how fortunate it was to live in a country where you have the right to choose death before a total melt-down of dignity. How much that had meant to Laura.

Yet if I, living in the UK, find myself facing the same prognosis and future as Laura, there will be no such relief and release in knowing I have some say over my death. And how terribly wrong, so lacking in decency and humanity our society is, forcing courageous, desperate people who are physically unable even to take their own lives, to suffer the ordeal of going to court, begging for their loved ones to be allowed to assist them in passing. And how does this denial of what seems a most fundamental human right play in a society which seems remarkably unworried by the proliferation of cars, arms, poisons in our air, in cigarettes, alcohol in our guts, among a great many other stoppable things that end the life of people who would like to stay around, thank you very much?

I see the same grim paradox here as in the pro-life line with its sentimental adherence to the idea that all life is sacred and yet a marked unwillingness to pay more in taxes to care for the unwanted children born, or to take them on themselves. With older people and sick people there is much righteous ranting and raving about how badly our elderly are treated, how someone who is never going to get better, or enjoy life fully again, must be kept alive at any price.

I know the arguments about the dangers of evil families talking their elders into a precipitate end, of doctors abandoning the Hippocratic pledge to get a few elderly ailing patients off their books, the fear that a young person facing a seemingly relentless future of harsh treatment for a terminal illness might actually prefer a peaceful way out. And each one poses a moral dilemma that needs addressing. But not the door slamming definitively on the very idea.

Perhaps a good beginning is to face our own fear of death, and if we have no faith which promises afterlife, then we must come to terms with the notion of absolute finality. We live in a society where the idea that we can and should go on and on is a triumph: where the egomaniac rich invest millions in trying to find a way to become immortal. I don't want to die but that is because, approaching 70, I still feel fit, I am able to use my brain, to work, to care for my granddaughter, and I do not need caring for myself

Should that change and I foresee a future in which all these things are gone and in their place I become a failing, flailing, dependent, demanding person who will be a burden to those caring for me, it seems to me only right that a society that bangs on about the individual's freedom should allow me to take that freedom in getting help to end it all. We live in an age where, with few qualms, we use technology to create killing machines of a grand order, yet giving a known doctor who has no vested interest, other than common decency, the right to administer a gentle technological end is apparently a step towards the horrors of mass slaughter, with Harold Shipman clones running amok.

If it were you in crucifying pain, knowing death will certainly come, paralysed so that you can do nothing for yourself except think, or some such thing, wouldn't you want the right to choose whether to put an end to your suffering? I suspect many of us would opt for the quiet dignity, the relief which came to Laura, knowing she had the means to end her life and her family's suffering with a visit from the family doctor administering the drug that would end it all, helping her husband and children through the process.

My mother the murderess.

Deborah Moggach,
author

In 1985 an elderly acquaintance of my mother, Annette Harding, decided to end her life. She was nearly blind, friendless (she had never married and had no family) and suffering from cancer. She lived in sheltered housing in Primrose Hill and my mother, who was training to be a Samaritan, visited her from time to time, but didn't know her well. One day Annette spoke of her decision and asked my mother if she would sit with her while she took an overdose of pills. She was a member of EXIT and had all the procedures in place – the right dosage, a 'Do not Resuscitate' sign to hang round her neck and a plastic bag in case the pills didn't do the trick. She was absolutely determined to end her life but didn't want to be alone. She made my mother promise that if the pills didn't work she would put the bag over her head until she stopped breathing.

Needless to say, this was a huge thing to ask another human being to do. My mother, Charlotte Hough, was a strong-minded, unconventional woman – she wrote and illustrated childrens' books and had just published a thriller – but even she was somewhat daunted. She agreed to do it, however, and went round on the evening in question to hold the old woman's hand. The trouble was, the pills didn't work. Four hours later Annette was unconscious but still breathing, and as dawn broke my mother knew that the warden of the sheltered housing would soon be visiting for his morning check-up. So she put the plastic bag over Annette's head, tied it with ribbon and held it there until the breathing stopped. Then she took it off, put it into her handbag and quietly left.

She was deeply shaken and told me what she had done. I was alarmed for her, and also pretty angry that Annette had asked her to do such a thing and put herself at risk. But basically I was filled with admiration, that my mother had been so courageous – indeed, loving. I knew I would never have dared do it myself. The trouble was, my mother was a rather indiscreet woman and told a couple of other people too. One of them must have betrayed her, because the next day I was cycling past an *Evening Standard* placard and it said THRILLER WRITER ARRESTED FOR MURDER. 'That's neat,' I thought, and then slewed to a halt. Christ, it was *my mother*.

The case caused a furore. It opened up the debate about the right to die, about a wholly altruistic act of mercy, about how we choose to end our lives. The Old Bailey was packed with supporters as my mother was charged with murder and pleaded not guilty. The case hinged on whether the pill dosage was in fact strong enough to have killed Annette, without the help of the plastic bag. If it was proven that the plastic bag did it, my mother would get a mandatory life sentence. So halfway through the trial her counsel persuaded her to change her plea – to guilty of attempted murder. My mother was unhappy about this – she didn't feel that was the case – but had no alternative.

She was sentenced to nine months' imprisonment. I'll always remember the moment she was led downstairs from the courtroom, disappearing into the underworld like Orpheus. Just the clanking of a key, the slamming of a door, and then silence.

Her prison experience was deeply traumatic. Though she had many letters of support from people all over Britain she was desperately lonely. Being older and more middle-class than the other inmates, she was mercilessly bullied. She only survived by counting the days to her release. I remember the letter she wrote during her last week: 'Nerves at breaking point ... I'm unfit for human consumption. And I thought one danced out, all wreathed in smiles, and took on the world! Nobody knows the first thing about prison life. You're literally PUT AWAY. And that's it.'

For months afterwards she was in a fragile state – alarmed at traffic, shaky, unable to carry on her career as a writer. Prison undid her, and seemed a horrifically harsh punishment for what was a true act of mercy. I wonder if she would have been treated differently today. I do believe that people's attitudes towards assisted suicide have moved on, but this has not been reflected in the law, which seems to remain in the Dark Ages. When many years later my mother suffered from dementia, and longed to die, I wished there had been someone around with her courage who might have helped her on her way. I was too much of a coward. And besides, I had seen what the result could be.

8

The activist's tale

My Journey

Jean Davies.
Former committee member of the Voluntary Euthanasia Society (Chairperson 1985-1990) and president of the World Federation of Right-to-Die Societies from 1990 to 1992.

In 1972 – or thereabouts – a friend, arriving first of a small group of friends coming for dinner, gave me a pamphlet and said 'You might be interested in this.' It was a single modest sheet produced by the Voluntary Euthanasia Society and I never asked her why she thought *I* should be interested. The other guests arrived and it was the following day that I read about changing the law so that anyone could choose medical help to a merciful death rather than just going on, and on, and on, with no remaining quality of life. It seemed to me one of the most sensible ideas I'd ever come across (and still does) so I filled in the form and sent off my £10 life membership. Despite its change of campaigning name to Dignity in Dying, the VES flourishes and with it my life membership.

A year or two later I was startled to be called to the staff room phone in the school where I was teaching by BBC Wales. 'We believe you are the VES representative in Wales. Can you come to the studio to do an interview?' Well, of course I could, outside school hours. And by 1980 I must have organised a Welsh Branch of VES because two of us went from Cardiff to a week-end Conference in Oxford. It was there that the World Federation of Right to Die Societies (WFRTDS) was set up and the speech I remember most vividly was by Ludovic Kennedy. He talked about the end of his mother's life and how, five months before she died, she said 'I've had a wonderful life but it's over now and I long to be gathered,' i.e. to die. Ludo himself thought she should have had that choice. He became president of VES and one of our most distinguished supporters.

The first biennial WFRTDS Conference was held in Melbourne in 1982 and I intended to go despite breast cancer treatment early in the year. But my husband's sudden death in June scuppered me so that Nice, 1984, was the first such Conference I attended. That was where Dr. Christiaan Barnard, the South African who was the first to do a heart transplant operation, was the keynote speaker. During this meeting I took Derek Humphry's advice to concentrate on VES in my post-early-retirement efforts to improve the world. So there followed 20 years of campaigning all over Britain and a large part of the rest of the world.

The 1986 WFRTDS Conference was in Mumbai. Speaking from the floor at that conference I said that relieving the health care services of expenses would play a part in my own decision to shorten my life. This was not well received. Today most people still avoid facing the fact that ageing societies pour away huge resources prolonging lives unwanted by their owners.

After 4 years as WFRTDS Newsletter Editor, I spent two years as President Elect then reached the dizzy height of being President at the Maastricht Conference in 1990. Dr. Tenrei Ota was the man who had first put forward the idea of having a World Federation and during the early years, the Japanese Society was far and away the biggest member society and the most generous financial contributor. Their aim was the refusal of treatment by the patient, usually known as *passive euthanasia*. Most of the rest of us were hoping to get *active help to die well*.

During these years I was deeply involved with the setting up of the European Division of WFRTDS. All communication seemed to take a very long time and the fact that I was the only one working in my native language didn't help. The Dutch Society, NVVE, was our tower of strength, being the pioneers in the whole field of voluntary euthanasia as far as gaining its legalisation goes.

The first Voluntary Euthanasia Society was, however, set up in Britain in 1935, its founders including H.G. Wells and Julian Huxley. By 1981 it was in deep trouble, partly because it was publishing a 'Guide to Self-Deliverance' but mainly because its secretary was being prosecuted and eventually given two years in prison for 'aiding, abetting, counselling or procuring a suicide.' It was hard running the Society with an unpaid volunteer as Secretary. Although the police did eventually return our office papers, they returned them in sacks and I don't think we ever did find the time to re-file them properly.

We survived, and in 1996 our (minimally) paid secretary rang me to say a publisher wanted a book for the general

reader to be called 'The Facts about Voluntary Euthanasia.'
and would I write it? Called 'Choice in Dying' with the rest
as a sub-title, it came out in April, 1997. Dirk Bogarde, a
strong supporter of VES wrote the foreword. This all sounds
like a lot of time and hard work on my part, and indeed it was.
The travelling was done by train or in economy class seats in
planes. Lectures and debates were often ill-attended, radio
and television appearances too few. Letters did appear in
the press however and some articles in academic journals.

The benefits, though, more than repaid all that effort.
In New Zealand and Australia, I had in-laws who happily
provided hospitality. Often I was invited by a local VES or
Humanist group and one of their members would welcome
me as a guest. There were many colleagues attending the
World and European FRTDS meetings who also became life-
long friends. Since I had retired from paid work in 1984, my
time was my own, so staying on after a Conference to visit art
galleries or concerts, or even go on tours were all perfectly
possible. 'Palace on Wheels.' a train-based tour of Northern
India and a coach-based tour of Kakadu Park in Northern
Australia were the most memorable of these.

Now I am 85, still living in the centre of Oxford but in a
retirement development. There are 91 flats and I've lived here
for more than 10 years. During that time we have all aged.
Many have died. It is safe to say that in aging, it is losing our
minds that we dread most and those few residents who have
failed to wake up one morning have been the most envied.

For myself, provided I am not totally incapacitated by a
stroke, I intend to bring my life to an end at a time of my
own choosing. The book 'A hastened death by self-denial
of food and drink' by Dr. Boudewijn Chabot, outlines what I

propose to do. It is worth noting that when Tony Nicklinson was recently denied a merciful death by our judicial system, he achieved it for himself, by that method, four days later.

When the time comes, I shall simply stay in bed and refuse food and drink, having made arrangements beforehand with my adult children and my GP. The advantages of doing this rather than 'letting nature take its course' include the fact that my children can be there when I die. That will happen within a fortnight at most so they will have a chance to get here, even from the other side of the world. It will spare them the long drawn out misery of possibly years witnessing my slow deterioration. It will satisfy my wish for personal autonomy. It will release medical resources to the benefit of those who want to go on living.

Granted this is not voluntary euthanasia as practised so long and carefully in the Netherlands, nor is it the self-administered drug legally provided to the terminally ill by Dignitas in Zurich, Switzerland. But it is kinder to my GP whose role will be to prescribe the necessary drugs to keep me comfortable. It seems to me that to linger on for a few days is a small price for me to pay. And in any case, one's own bed seems to me the most desirable place to die.

In this country, the law on assisting people to die may not have changed but its practice has and the same goes for medicine. We know that we shall not be prosecuted for assisting a suicide provided we can demonstrate that it was the dying person's decision and that our motive was not in order to benefit by the death. Our doctors are encouraged to inform patients and discuss all treatment options with them – including non-treatment options. We no longer speak of 'doctor's orders.' Eventually the law will change and just as medical help is available to achieve a good birth, it will also be there to achieve a good death.

EDITORS' NOTE.

In September 2014 in her 87th year, Jean decided to activate her planned starvation because several medical conditions were making her quality of life increasingly intolerable. She died peacefully, without direct medical assistance but under medical supervision and with appropriate palliation, after being able to say farewell in person or by telephone to her many friends and admirers.

'I'll see myself out, thank you'

Dr. Libby Wilson,
retired GP, founder of Friends At The End in 2000 and its convener until 2013.

I have never been one who plans far ahead. The only real ambition I ever had was to become a doctor, in which I succeeded more than 60 years ago. Since then I have had to make decisions at various turning points in my life but the paths I chose were decided on practical grounds, not by long term goals. I did not intend to have a large family but after six children in quick succession I opted for sterilisation in a distant city where the gynaecologists I knew at home would not be embarrassed by having to refuse my request. In those days this operation for both men and women was regarded as 'mutilation.' I worked as a part-time assistant in general practice for 18 years, until my husband was invited to the chair of medicine in Glasgow. I did not want to go, I had several satisfactory projects going in Sheffield but I really had no choice. I had to decide whether to continue in general practice or concentrate on sexual health and family planning. At a later date I was offered a consultancy in sexually transmitted diseases (known as venereology in those days) but turned it down in favour of full time family planning and sexual health – anything below the belt in fact. A year before I was due to retire I was asked to go to Sierra Leone to work for Marie-Stopes International, a contraceptive charity. It took me all of two minutes to decide to accept.

I recount these milestones in my life to illustrate my attitude to planning my death. I have always been pragmatic. I am good at making practical arrangements for planned future events with foreseeable consequences. I have, for example, travelled to Australia eleven times, always stopping at the major cities to visit relatives and friends. The problem with my own death is that I have no knowledge of the form it will take. My decisions in the past have been practical reactions to situations which have arisen but dying can take so many different forms and prediction is futile. One hopes that one might die unexpectedly in one's sleep – go to bed relatively healthy and never wake up – but this is extremely unlikely. If I develop cancer I would refuse all adjuvant therapy and hope to be able to take a lethal dose when what remained of life became burdensome.

More probable, but less acceptable, is having a stroke. Here an Advance Directive is essential but will not necessarily accelerate my death. My family would undoubtedly try to carry out my wishes if I was no longer able to take the necessary steps (literally and figuratively) to reach one of the helpful organisations in Switzerland to which I already belong. The most difficult situation is that of developing dementia and not recognising one's mental incompetence in time to make the required arrangements.

In reality I expect I will end up in terminal care in some NHS facility, feeling too ill and remote from reality to be concerned. As long as it is not in some Catholic hospice with pink sheets and an elderly priest trotting round saying 'Bless you my child' indiscriminately to all the dying inmates. I do have plans about the disposal of my body and my funeral. I would have liked a burial at our West Highland holiday home on the shores of Loch Sunart but the ground is so stony that it would require a digger, hired from over 30 miles away, to excavate the grave. This would be a great waste of money better bestowed on my needy grandchildren. I like cremation but it is relatively polluting, so a green burial is my choice, in a wicker or cardboard coffin, (I'm too heavy for a shroud!)

I have still to decide on the music but it must include 'Ilkley Moor Baht'at,' partly because of my and my family's long connection with Yorkshire but also because it should be the recycler's anthem. 'Tha' catches a deadly cold, is buried and eaten by worms who, in turn, are gobbled up by ducks. The ducks are consumed by 'us' -'then we shall all have eaten thee.' And everyone knows the tune. 'Celebrations of the life' are a wonderful modern interpretation of what used to be solemn participation in consumption of funeral baked meats. I hope all my large extended family and my friends far and near will enjoy a terrific party to remember me by.

9

No laughing matter?

Mortality as fact

Steve Jones,
Professor of Genetics at University College, London

Every French schoolchild who takes the 'Bac'
(the secondary school graduation test that has
been there since Napoleon) must sit a compulsory
paper on philosophy, and write an essay on 'Is it possible
to think about death?' The recommended reading includes
works by St Augustine, Heidegger, Kant and Voltaire and
everyone – from intending electrician to professor – must
attempt it. The curriculum advises that they separate the
physical, moral, psycho-physical and metaphysical aspects
of the subject. (Parmenides: 'Can one say anything about
nothingness?' – discuss).

Faced with such questions at the age of eighteen I would,
I imagine, have given it all up and become a bus driver and
it's hard to imagine that the Gradgrind School of Education
that now reigns in our native land would countenance such an

economically irrelevant topic. Even so, like it or not, mortality is a Fact as undeniable as is that of the Graminivorous Quadruped with Hard Hooves that must be Shod with Iron and is one that occupies the attention of seventy-year-olds perhaps rather more than that of the average British teenager.

That attention, of course, is new. I start my first year lectures in genetics by asking the students to look at the person to their left, and to their right; and I tell them – with a modicum of accuracy – that two out of three of them will die for reasons connected with the genes they carry, for cancer, heart disease, diabetes and the rest of today's killers all have an inherited component (which is not to deny the importance of the environment). I then cheer them up by reminding them that had I been lecturing in Shakespeare's time, two out of every three would be dead already. Even in Charles Darwin's day, around half of them would already have departed.

And that has led to the biggest shift in attitudes to mortality in human history. Until not long ago, the Grim Reaper was a familiar and unwelcome visitor to every household, whatever the age of the person who opened the door. In the modern world in contrast, most people can be confident about when they will breathe their last, not because – as in the days of the Patriarchs – the old die older but because the young die old.

We live in an era of death postponed. The average life expectancy for British men in 2011 was 77.9 years and for women 82.3. Each figure was up by almost three months compared to the previous year. Since the end of the War the average age at which a citizen can expect to survive for another ten years has risen by a decade. In 1945 it was seventy, but is now close to eighty. The debility of old age has also been pushed back. Today's octogenarians have the health of people ten years younger during the sixties. Things continue to get better. Since the middle of the nineteenth century, longevity has increased by six hours a day, with no signs of slowing down. At that rate, most British children born since the beginning of this century will see in the next.

Most of this improvement has come from sewage engineering rather than from high-tech medicine, but whatever lies behind it, the fact remains that we live in a far more predictable world than ever before. Part of that includes a more certain insight into our own mortality. No longer do we dice with death, with the odds stacked against us, every day of our lives; instead we gamble more and more in a game that in the end we are bound to lose. As we know, more or less, when that will be, surely it cannot be too difficult to accept the fact and plan for the inevitable exit in a way that would have made little sense until not much more than a century ago. Human ingenuity has brought us (almost) eternal life on this Earth and a decent dose of the same thing should be allowed to propel us into the next world (if there is one – discuss).

As the sound of the Hooves Shod with Iron draws ever closer, one must contemplate whether philosophy or science should reconcile us to our fate. For me, I go with science, in the form of some yet to be invented narcotic that brings joy to life while bringing it to an end. On the other hand, the French are the most pessimistic nation in the world (more so than even the Afghans and the Iraqis) so that perhaps it is not a good idea to remind the rising generation of such uncomfortable facts quite so early.

Ready for a good death

Will Self,
author

I'm looking forward to committing suicide – really, I am, and I hope to nudge you in the direction of considering it, when – and this is the important point – the right time comes. Why? Well, the facts are pretty persuasive when it comes to the business of British dying: we're living longer and longer, while our deaths are becoming commensurately more protracted. Such is the brilliance of contemporary medical science – at least in our privileged realm – that we can be kept breathing long past the point where our existence is anything save miserable: miserable for us, miserable for our loved ones, and miserable for those who have been appointed by either the state or a private health plan to minister unto us.

There was a time, in the not so distant past, when either sepsis or infectious disease, or the very act of parturition itself did for most of us considerably in advance of the Biblically-mandated three-score and ten. But nowadays the majority can reasonably expect to live long enough for senility to set in, and sclerosis or sarcoma to finish us off. It's often said that there's an epidemic of cancer, or heart disease, or Alzheimer's in our society – but what there really is an epidemic of old age itself, all these pathologies being merely its inevitable sequels. What I am emphatically not proposing is that anyone, of whatever age, or in any particular physical or psychic state, should necessarily kill themselves – I have friends in their nineties, who may be debilitated and depressed at times, but who nonetheless enjoy life intensely. Often it seems to me that these aged ones have endured long enough that they are not so much hanging on to life as caressing it gently, in the awareness that this – like all bodily experiences – is of necessity transitory. But what I do emphatically believe is that those who feel decrepitude to be insufferable should have the stoicism and the self-love needed to let go of their lives.

Of course, for people of some religious persuasions the notion that self-love entails suicide is anathema; for them all human life is inherently sacred, no matter that the body which lives this life is effectively mindless, or wracked by pains still transmitted by stubbornly vigorous nerves. It's for this reason that in our society – one governed by Judaeo-Christian moral precepts – the suicidal individual was traditionally deemed *felo de se* literally: 'a felon of himself.' Nowadays, while we may take a rather more secular view of these matters – neither prosecuting those who, as it were, botch the job, nor quarantining for eternity the cadavers of ones who got away – nonetheless the taboo against killing yourself remains so strong that few can dare to contemplate it, even in extremis.

And there are so many of us in extremis: as our population ages our hospitals, care homes and hospices are full of people for whom the expression 'quality of life' has purely an ironic application. There is one thing and one thing alone, that gives the lives of many of the terminally ill what little quality they do, and that's diacetylmorphine. At least, that's what the medical profession term the drug – to the general population it is better known as heroin, and it was called this because in trials conducted by the pharmaceutical company Bayer, those who took it said they felt 'heroic.' That was almost a century ago, but the ascription remains apt, for now so many of us play out the final tragic act of our lives in this narcotised state.

Doctors and nurses will tell us that they can calibrate the dosage effectively enough for the moribund to experience no pain and yet remain lucid, but from what I've seen palliative care at this late stage largely consists in rendering us oblivious of everything – and in particular our own imminent demise.

Both my mother and my father died of cancer while heavily sedated. In my mother's case the nursing staff made no secret of the fact that they were upping her medication, while withdrawing nutrition, with a view to hastening her end. My father died at his home, but was visited four or five times a day by medics bearing barbed gifts. On the morning after he died the first task I had was to gather up all the pain-killing medication in the house – morphine in oral solution and pill form – and return it to the hospital. I don't judge those who find themselves passive participants in this awful situation – and I absolutely understand why it happens: for those without any belief in transcendence there is nothing beyond this life, and so we cleave to it for all we're worth. We may tell ourselves that when things get bad enough we'll make a dignified exit, but somehow things don't ever get quite bad enough until they're excruciating and we're incapable of acting. I've observed what might be termed a 'creeping normalcy' in the existence of the terminally ill: with each successive stage of greater incapacity, indignity and discomfort, somehow managing to be incorporated into the daily go-round. Besides, few of us really understand how to end our lives painlessly and effectively – this is just another crucial bodily matter that we have left, along with all the rest, to the professionals.

And this is why the whole debate about assisted dying is really a shadow play, behind which lurks a still darker and more discomfiting dilemma. Of course there are those with terrible conditions – locked-in syndrome, various forms of paralysis – who may wish to die, but be quite unable to do so without help, but for the vast majority of us suicide will be achievable for some time after we know that we are incontrovertibly dying, if, that is, the right means are readily to hand. But instead of stating this boldly and clearly, we collude with the medical profession – who, at an unconscious level, are always only too pleased to increase the ambit of their own expertise – and ask of our legislators that suicide be rendered simply another medical procedure.

It's not, though. Rather the decision to take one's own life is, I would argue, part of affirming personal dignity, and also expressing love for those who love us. To kill yourself may well be, somewhat paradoxically, a life-affirming thing to do: surely, in the great gyre of our experience, its giddy highs and equally dizzying lows, the cultivation of the resolve needed to end it all, if required, can be part of a wider sense of acceptance, and so lead to serenity. Yet as things stand, our impotence in the face of our extinction means that a vast amount of medical resources are expended in the last few weeks of people's lives purely in order to render our deaths insensible and insensate – when I see politicians campaigning relentlessly on their defence of the National Health Service, I often think that this is the unacknowledged subtext: Vote for me, and I'll make sure you cease upon the midnight with no pain.

I don't say any of these things idly – like many of us in middle age, my last few years have been heavily marked by an increasing awareness of both my own mortality and that of those who I love. Nor do I wish to offend religious sensibilities, or upset anyone who is either terminally ill themselves, or caring for someone who is. While not a

Christian myself, I still concur absolutely with the sonorous words of the committal service for the dead: 'In the midst of life we are in death'; and it's because of this that we should all keep constantly in mind that we cannot hope to understand how to have a good life, unless we also ready ourselves for a good death.

Vacation Parc

Stewart Lee,
stand-up comic.

The brown ducks are dabbling, and the willow branches hang down to drink the grey lake. Above the reflective steel roofs of the leisure complex and the dining department, cumulus clouds billow over the bare treetops. Through the glass sliding doors of the cabin the cold winter sun whitens the whole world and I wonder about breakfast. Once I would ride to the dining room bolt upright on my bicycle, wending between the woodland walkways and the wooden homesteads, the wind blowing my long hair, waving at my neighbours. My mouth would grow wet at the thought of boiled puffin eggs, slippery strips of fish, crisp fresh bread, and all the sliced meats. Now I wait for the boy to bundle me into the trailer and tow me to the table, and bring a selection from the smorgasbord to the table by the window where I sit always alone. Nowadays, the menu, somehow, never quite matches the meal. The tastes are too familiar, and the churning of my jaws and the subsequent opening of my oesophagus are painfully predictable. On the way back through the wood we will stop to stroke the lambs in the petting farm, and watch through the windows as the children whoop in the waterslides, where I once slid myself, but slide no longer. Yes indeed, I have had a wonderful time at Vacation Parc, but now, if you don't mind, I would like to leave. And I have asked the camp administrator to process my request.

As the bicycle pulls up outside the cabin the boy helps me to my feet, and I see her waiting under the awning. I gesture for The Administrator to enter – the doors are never locked here – and she begins to boil a little pan of water for tea. I have not, it is explained, fulfilled the duration of my allotted stay though, she concedes, it has been a long stay, and she appreciates that many, but by no means all, of the amenities that make Vacation Parc so popular may not overlap entirely with the Venn diagram of my own current interests, preferences, needs, as they now stand, as opposed to what they may have been at other points during the sum total period to date of my time in the Parc. The Administration as a whole, it is explained, are looking into ways of expanding the range of services available but, as she is sure I understand, financial considerations mean the fiscal initiative for these improvements, well let's not call them improvements, let's just call them calculated switches of activity focus, may have to be initiated by client-customers within the complex themselves, perhaps by forward planning through some kind of lifetime subscription scheme, rather than expecting the Parc itself, and its other client-customers, to bear the full brunt of increased expenditure brought on by the expectations of those fortunate enough to enjoy stays in the Parc significantly longer than initially projected. And yet, at the same time, she concedes, even though it may not be possible at this stage for the Parc to commit to underwriting life-quality-alteration schemes of this nature, it would also be in neglect of its duty of care were it to allow client-customers to terminate their own stays significantly ahead of the provisionally agreed departure date. I agree. And then I ask her what would happen if I just walked out of the gate.

The next day it is raining, and the red squirrels run around the shore of the lake agitatedly, burying acorns for future feasts, planning ahead. When the boy bicycles me back from breakfast in the protective plastic sheeted trailer, the cabin door is already flapping ajar. Through the half open blinds, I see a black shadow sat on the sofa, drinking furtively from a small silver flask, and reading a magazine. As I hobble into the hut, hanging on to the handles screwed into the wall for support, the priest pockets his hooch, rolls up the magazine and slides it into his velvet cassock, smoothes his silver hair, and looks for a place to stub out his cigarette. 'Now, now, what's all this nonsense?' he asks, and invites me to sit down next to him. Don't I find the puffin eggs delicious at the moment? And doesn't the lake look beautiful in the low sun? The winter months, he feels, are especially beautiful, apparently, and that, he explains, is because they contain within them the promise of life to come, but that life to come will not come unless we first endure the winter months themselves. Life at Vacation Parc is a precious gift, and it is not polite to refuse a precious gift. Life beyond Vacation Parc might be beautiful too, but we can only attain the promise of that beautiful afterlife if we accept the gift of our stay in Vacation Parc with good grace. I hear the boy outside the window, rolling up the protective plastic sheeting and stowing it in a compartment under the trailer now the rain has stopped. I wonder if he has been listening. I am not unhappy, I explain to the priest. I have enjoyed my time at

Vacation Parc. I do not need the promise of another life. I have been satisfied with this one. And then I ask him what would happen if I just walked out of the gate.

The next morning, snow has fallen. Out through the window, the red squirrels are nowhere to be seen and only a few ducks have made tentative excursions on to the frozen surface of the pond. The boy is waiting for me when I awake. He lays a blanket over me in the bicycle trailer. 'If you're warm enough,' he says, 'I thought we might take a slightly longer route to the breakfast building this morning.' We head west, towards the skyline where the sun sets, out through the fringes of the lodges and into darker deeper woodlands, along a wide path slashed intermittently by smaller routes. At the crest of a hill a vast wooden cross, made from two tree trunks, bisects the horizon. And beyond it, the track slopes down towards what I assume is the gate.

The boy brings the bicycle to a halt a few hundred yards from it. To my surprise the gate is entirely unmanned, standing in splendid isolation at an apparently random point in the trees, without a fence or a wall attached to either side of it, just a wooden pole about nine feet long lying horizontally across two supporting struts, positioned a little above waist height. Beyond it the track stretches off through the forest to where the light fades, into an unknowable darkness. But I am not afraid of it. 'You asked the priest what would happen if you just walked out of the gate,' said the boy, 'but you can't. You're not steady on your feet. You'd fall.' I don't understand the point he is trying to make. He says he expects that I am hungry and slides back up onto the saddle.

After breakfast, the doctor is waiting on my doorstep. The boy helps me out of the trailer and, unusually, escorts me into the cabin. The doctor follows. While the boy lowers me into an armchair, the doctor walks towards the sliding glass door that looks out onto the frozen lake. He stands with his back to me and stares out at the snow. 'I appreciate your concerns of course,' he says, 'but you must understand that as regards this matter, I am afraid my hands are tied.' I ask him what would happen if I just walked out of the gate. He shrugs his shoulders, turns, smiles at both of us, and leaves.

The next morning the snow has frozen into a slippery sheeting that coats the hard earth. Nevertheless, the boy has struggled on the bicycle, towing me in the trailer behind him, out west through the woods once more, past the hilltop cross, and down the hill towards the gate. We stop a few hundred yards from it, and he asks me to stand, while he turns the trailer over on its back and unscrews the wheels and the axle, leaving only the smooth underbelly of the structure exposed. Then he turns it back over and invites me to sit in it. 'Like I say, you'd never be able to walk out through that gate alone, but the ground is icy and slippery, you're facing downhill, and momentum alone ought to carry you under the barrier, if you keep your head down, and then you just slide on out into the… well… whatever.' And he gives me a soldierly salute, and cycles away without a backward glance.

I was surprised at myself. I sat in the trailer for a few hours, warm enough wrapped in the woollen blanket, and watched the red squirrels bouncing around the boughs and the thrushes pecking at the unrelenting ground. In its own way, it had all been quite wonderful. But now, as I looked ahead of me, into the west, the sun was setting, and slowly, calmly, and at the moment of my own choosing, I finally and faithfully allowed my full weight to fall forwards.

Glenn's last tape

Karl Sabbagh,
writer, documentary maker and publisher

The videotape shows a man sitting at a table, slightly slumped, in a room. He is wearing a grey T-shirt. The walls of the room are a neutral colour, and hanging behind the man is a reproduction of an Italian renaissance painting, a Madonna and child. On the table in front of him is a collection of objects – a lit candle in a candlestick; a pottery bowl; a glass, half-full of some liquid with two plastic straws in it; a bottle of wine; a box of tissues. There are more bottles – of wine and spirits, and blackcurrant juice – on a table behind him. In the background a radio is playing pop music. The man leans forward. He has a cigarette in a holder in his hand and he lights it shakily from the candle. As he puts the cigarette in his mouth, a fast-speaking DJ announces the next record in Italian and the music changes. By a macabre twist, the next song is Elvis Presley singing 'Are You Lonesome Tonight?' Macabre, because this man is at the loneliest point in his life. He has sent his friends away and is about to die.

When the actress Miriam Margolyes telephoned me in April 1998, I thought it would be one of her usual chats, enlivened by a mixture of hilarity and scatology, discussing the latest house she had bought or sold, telling me about her filming plans or discussing the lives of mutual friends. But this call was different. She wanted to tell me about the death of a friend, or at least, the planned death, of a man called Glenn Scott, a Canadian teacher of fine arts who lived in Hamilton, Ontario, and was moving to Rome.

Miriam had first 'met' Glenn on the internet, through the Compuserve Italian Forum, where people with a love of Italy exchanged tips about restaurants, tourism, accommodation, and Italian culture. Glenn was a frequent contributor, amusing, urbane and observant, and he gathered a large number of friends on the internet, most of whom never met him in person.

Glenn, Miriam told me, was an expert on the Italian Renaissance and had spent many years teaching students in Canada, using videotapes that he filmed himself in Italy every summer. A few months beforehand, Glenn had been diagnosed with motor neurone disease, known in North America as ALS, amyotrophic lateral sclerosis, the illness that has kept Stephen Hawking immobile but alive. In Glenn's case the doctors had no doubt that his disease would lead to progressive loss of muscular power, with a slow, agonising, and inevitable decline towards death. But Glenn wasn't having it. He loved life too much. It was not his style to decline slowly in his house in Canada, bedridden and increasingly incontinent until he lost the ability to breathe and suffocated to death. He wanted to find another way to die, one that allowed him a better quality of life in his closing months, weeks and days.

The reason Miriam called me, a writer and documentary maker, was that Glenn had expressed the wish, born partly of anger at his plight, to publicise his condition. In particular he wanted to draw attention to the injustice of a situation in which it was not legal for a doctor to give him a lethal injection at the moment when he wanted to die – before extreme discomfort set in. He felt that the law condemned him to live longer and die more appallingly, and he wanted to change that law or at least thwart it in his own case. So, as he announced to his friends, he was going to sell his house, cash in his life insurance, and use the proceeds to fund a final sybaritic trip across Europe, eating, drinking and being as merry as his deteriorating condition would allow. His final destination – on earth – would be Rome, a city he had filmed, lectured about, explored and come to love, and where he wanted to die – at his own hand.

This was the crux of the story he wanted to tell, that he had to end his own life earlier than he would like, at a stage when he still had the use of the hands he needed to achieve the deed. It wasn't ideal, since he knew he could probably have weeks more of enjoyment – of a sort – if someone else could administer the drugs that would kill him. But, as he put it baldly to me when we first met: 'I intend to take my life, but I must be able to do it myself, and I must do it without implicating anyone else. The laws simply do not allow for disabled people to kill themselves.'

When I first heard about Glenn, while I could see that he might have an interesting story to tell, I was a little apprehensive about following up Miriam's suggestion. I wasn't sure that I had the necessary social skills to discuss someone's suicide plans with him in a matter-of-fact way. But from the moment Glenn picked up the phone in Rome, where he had recently arrived at the end of his long and hectic trip across Europe, all apprehension vanished as I discovered someone who was very quickly to become a friend, and almost as quickly to die.

It was clear from that first telephone conversation that Glenn had already spent many months preparing himself for the end of his life, and the decisive date might not be far away, so I found a cheap air ticket, and on a sunny May day I flew to Rome, to the leafy street where Glenn had rented an apartment. His illness was now at a stage where he needed 24-hour assistance, and a young man called Jim, a male nurse and carer, had come to provide that. Jim answered the door and showed me into the dining room, where Glenn was sitting in his wheelchair, having lunch with several friends, including a Canadian woman, Mary Forsyte, who had known Glenn for many years. Over chewy salami and good Italian wine we talked desultorily about the weather, the food and the internet until Glenn finished lunch.

After lunch, Glenn wheeled himself into the next room and we sat and talked for an hour or so. Glenn's voice was losing its strength, occasionally breaking into falsetto, and his conversation was punctuated by bursts of coughing, triggered sometimes by bouts of laughter. The laughter was one of the first things I noticed about Glenn. He was never morbid or self-pitying about his condition.

'This disease has some advantages,' he said. 'Given a menu of fatal diseases – God, that's a restaurant to avoid! – given a menu of fatal diseases, I find it rather nice that there's nothing the doctors can do, because there are a whole lot of diseases where doctors can do all kinds of things that are excruciatingly uncomfortable and painful, and they lose their patients in the end anyway.'

It was clear that the experience he was going through provided fuel for insights, anger and jokes in equal measure. For example, having decided to have a good time across Europe on his way to Rome he realised that he would need some kind of incontinence device to help him urinate while in a wheelchair.

When he telephoned a young woman in a drug store in Canada she asked him what size he wanted for the end that fitted over the penis – Small, Medium or Large? Glenn said 'Large' but the young woman clearly thought he was just trying to impress.

'We sell a lot of these,' the young woman said, 'and most people buy a Medium and a Large and off they go. Then, nine times out of ten they come back and order the Medium.'

''I still think you should send me the Large,' Glenn had said to the young woman, and she said: 'Well, congratulations!'

Glenn told this story with glee, and relished what happened next, when he later found a message on his answerphone from the young woman saying 'In spite of our discussion, I have sent you Medium.'

'Off we went with Medium,' Glenn continued, 'and when I arrived in England, in Stoke on Trent, I tried it on. It was like the Boston Strangler had got a hold of me, so definitely Medium was not the answer. I started looking in the Yellow Pages, and after a few phone calls I found a shop called Wardles. We went there and I explained to the woman what I wanted and she said 'Well, we don't usually sell these things this way, but considering that you're visiting and so on, I'll open up that section.' Off she goes and she brings out a selection of these things, and a size chart. The size chart was a piece of plastic with holes of various sizes in it, the type of thing where if you're having people in and serving spaghetti, there are different-sized holes depending on how many people you have coming, dinner for two up to dinner for six, that kind of thing. And she handed me this thing, and I said, 'What do you want me to do with this?' and, well anyway I knew what size Medium was in millimetres, so we did a little conversion and came up with a larger size and off we went with those.'

The money from his life insurance and the sale of his house meant that he could stay in the best hotels, travel first class and pay for a companion, Tom, to accompany him. His regular e-mailed reports to the Italian Forum were written with gusto:

'The Manoir (des Quatre Saisons) has the feeling of a private club,' he wrote. 'The service is of course impeccable but the focus is on the food. It would take too long to describe all the various things that we had, but they included a starter of autumn vegetables with pheasant and truffles; a mousse of Jerusalem artichokes. Main courses of an extraordinary roasted plaice, turkey jus and Rosemary butter; and a saddle of hare wrapped in bacon and cooked in red wine with juniper berries. The garnish for this dish was fine leaves of cabbage that were transparent, apparently deep fried and very thin. I chose our wines: a Chablis Premier Cru and a couple of bottles of Aloxe Corton 1993. There was quite a wonderful selection of cheeses from the trolley and then came dessert. Here the choice was difficult so we chose two: an iced blackcurrant parfait terrine and a warm apple tart with cinnamon ice cream.'

But the video footage he and his companion shot of the journey showed a man whose good humour – and large appetite – occasionally evaporated in the face of a deteriorating physical condition. An undignified hoist up the steps of Winchester cathedral, a painful walk with a stick on the terrace of a French auberge; a messily-eaten gourmet meal in an Italian restaurant – they were pictures of a man trying to lead the good life with a frustratingly clumsy body. As someone who had had such a short time to come to terms with disability, he was often overcome by small gestures of kindness from others. He told me about a call to American Express he'd made, to tell them that his signature was deteriorating.

'Of course you never know where you're getting connected to – it could be anywhere in America. And I got a young woman on the other end and started explaining the problem to her, that I had this disease, and my signature was changing and so on, and she wrote this on my file on the computer so that it would come up if it was ever questioned. At the end of this she said, 'Well, you're all fixed up and you won't have any troubles with your signature', and then she said a prayer.'

Glenn couldn't speak for a moment, and then he said: 'I thought that was very moving, to find that corporate America and the people in the front line are just as human as anyone else.'

In one of his e-mails he described another incident that affected him, on his journey:

'After a not very graceful entrance to a small bistro in the Place des Vosges in Paris, Tom and I tucked into large bowls of *moules marinieres* for our late supper. With my clumsy hands I was generally making quite a mess of things but persevered. Across from us was a table of six people talking up a storm and enjoying their evening. They left before us and had to squeeze past our table (Paris has some of the smallest tables on earth.) The woman who had been facing in my direction patted my shoulder on her way past me. She didn't say anything; she just patted my shoulder in a simple gesture of encouragement. That can mean an awful lot. I will never forget her.'

And so Glenn arrived in Rome, in January, 1998, in the quarter of the city that he would inhabit for the remainder of his life. Choosing where he was to die had not been a difficult decision:

'I *had* to come back to Rome, it was very simple,' he told me. 'I told my friends that one of my greatest fears was never seeing Rome again...' He stopped, overcome with emotion. It was one of the few occasions on which I saw him break down, not out of self-pity or fear but because he was remembering how he felt in Canada when he contemplated the fact that he might never see Rome again.

'That probably sounds like an incredible statement,' Glenn said when he had recovered. 'How could anyone feel like that about a city? But Rome has so many connotations for me, not just intellectual ones. It's actually the city itself. Rome is a city I know and love – this is actually my thirtieth year of coming to Rome. In my younger, more foolish years I was known to kneel down and kiss the streets when I got into the city from the airport.'

But the city now was a very different place, seen from the groin-eye-view of a wheelchair occupant:

'Grocery shopping from a wheelchair was a new experience, particularly in the crowded aisles of an Italian supermarket close to Christmas. I am considering bringing out a cookbook called 'Cooking from the Bottom Shelf.' If there was anything important on those upper shelves and we weren't specifically looking for it, we don't have it. But I love shopping for food, particularly here in Italy, and it was a good outing for me.'

Over the last few weeks of his life Glenn became known and recognised around the area of his apartment.

He described in his e-mails a special relationship he developed with babies:

'First, the baby is simply curious as it is about the other babies being pushed around in great numbers around five in the afternoon. But then the eyes began to widen as the bulk and size of this incredibly large baby approaching begins to register. As we get closer the eyes get even larger as the bulk of my stroller and its rather large wheels becomes apparent. This may be the awakening of a basic instinct in Italian male babies and their intense interest in cars. The baby seems to be saying to itself, 'I wonder where he got that cool set of wheels?' Or, 'Holy Cow, just how long do I have to stay in this thing?' Or, 'These foreign babies are something else!' Or, 'I'm going to ask papa about this as soon as I learn how to talk!' Sometimes as I pass, the baby will twist in its seat looking backwards over its shoulder following my progress in rapt fascination.'

Nothing Glenn said or did seemed trivial. He was as passionate about a good glass of wine as he was angry about the fact that he was soon to die. He relished the small details of everyday life in Rome – a cup of espresso in a pavement café – as much as the view of St Peter's across the Tiber or the sculptures of Bernini. I found it difficult to believe that someone in his situation would not sometimes feel low, but he denied this:

'I can honestly say that I have not been depressed over any of the time since I found out. I've had great joys. I have pleasure every day. Rainy days are a little harder just because I can't get outside, but any day I can simply go out and do the shopping, sit at the cafe, have a coffee, do what many people in Rome do, for a few hours, then I've had a really good day.'

But then, early in January 1998, Glenn wrote on the Italian Forum:

'As joyous as Christmas was, New Year's Eve was as sad. The downside of the happiness of having friends visit is that they eventually have to leave. I had to say goodbye to five good and dear people, who had been so kind and caring, over only a few days and my equilibrium disappeared and the dam burst and for a few hours nothing would stop it. My attempts at meditation and thinking 'white' thoughts failed. From where I am sitting I can only liken the grief to having your friends die in ones and twos and leaving you behind. I know my friends are going through the same experience. Living and waiting with ALS is also having a lot of dispersed, very small but very sad funerals. My old friend Mary held me and sat with me and we weathered the storm.'

Nevertheless, in the next paragraph he bounced back, and, as usual, good food was at the centre of his happiness:

'Yesterday there was a splendid and festive party here at the apartment for 18 members and friends of the Italian forum featuring good conversation, food, wine, first meetings, old friends, food, conversation, computer toys, wine and food -- a proper pranzo lasting from 2:00 to 7:30 p.m. Several kinds of pasta (amatriciana and al grigio) prepared by the expert hands of Maureen Fant, lentils in tomato sauce with cotachino sausage (a traditional Italian New Year's dish guaranteeing good fiscal fortune) by Margaret Coffin, roast country lamb brought from Tuscany and prepared by Gary Topping, along with a jug of olive oil so fine money is not enough to buy it, antipasti, roast turkey, prosciutto, cheeses and so many things I have lost track of who brought what. Piero Amodeo also arrived ready to cook and serve. Wonderful bread and most special and delicious, 'neonati': newly born, very tiny fish mixed in yogurt and then formed into small cakes and rolled in a mixture of parmigiano, flour and parsley and quickly sautéed in fine oil to a crisp golden brown...

Many people have said to me and others that they hope they will die suddenly in their sleep. I can tell you that this way is much better. I would have missed some of the finest and most pleasurable and enriching hours of my life.'

Like everything else in his final months, he had been planning the details of his death for some time. And an important part of his death, as it had been of his life, was the internet, on which he became more and more dependent. Glenn found a recipe for the cocktail of drugs that he was to use to kill himself, and so he began to plan his death in meticulous detail. By the time I met him in May 1998, the plan was cut and dried. As he sat in his wheelchair describing the plan to me, he occasionally shifted in his seat from the discomfort of staying too long in the same position. His hands were clasped together, and one of them was much weaker than the other.

'The decisions have all been made,' he said, matter-of-factly. 'I'm the sort of person who has to have things planned out. It's when it gets implemented that's still undecided. That will be based simply on my capabilities, and this is why I'm so concerned about the loss of use of my hands. I intend to take my life, but I must be able to do it myself, and I must do it without implicating anyone else. There are some terrible stories about how far disabled people have had to go, such as burning the house down around themselves.'

Glenn knew that if anyone else helped him in any way, they could be liable under Italian law to a charge of murder.

Strangely, Glenn and his friend Mary Forsyte had talked about euthanasia many years before he had developed a terminal illness:

'Glenn and I have been in agreement about having a choice, long before he ever became ill, ' Mary told me, 'so I think it was very early on after his diagnosis that it just became a natural part of our conversation to include his plans. I am truly sorry that the situation is such that those of us who really care cannot be with him right at the end. It would be nice to have some Bach, a glass of Chivas and kind of celebrate but that's not possible.'

The method he chose involved several different drugs, and he had to work out how to administer them in a palatable and convenient way with his increasing loss of muscle power:

'If you have to take sixty or seventy pills it can be a tricky business,' he told me, 'and if you've got hands like mine, it's even more difficult, if not impossible. The other aspect of taking that many is that they're very bitter so you have to mix it with something else that conceals the taste. You also have to take another drug ahead of time to prevent you throwing the whole thing up. So there are all these kinds of details. I've been preparing for this as I see my abilities decline, and the first step was to remove the drug from the gelatine capsules. So that was done months ago, because it's much easier to mix without all those capsules on it. The mixing I can still do, but because I'm very clumsy with a spoon now, and my wrist will barely hold the weight of my hand, there's a risk of fumbling it. But I can still drink from a straw.'

So he decided to dissolve the various pills in a blackcurrant-flavoured drink.

'I tested one of the pills and the drink to see if it would

dissolve. It doesn't dissolve, it sinks to the bottom, so I have to make a mixture that has some substance to it, but not so much that it doesn't go through a straw. I bought some straws at the supermarket, but I found that they were too small, so I asked someone who was going out shopping if they wouldn't mind stopping at McDonald's and picking me up some straws, because McDonald's does serve horribly sweet thick things that you can drink out of a large straw. So I feel that as long as I can shake something, insert a straw and drink it, that I'm all right. But it makes me very angry that it is the law that is forcing me to do this, and probably doing it months before it's really necessary, even to my standards of quality of life. But there's no other way round it.'

There was another important part of the procedure that Glenn had also thought through months beforehand. 'I will have a video camera set up,' he said, 'with tape in it ready to go and a remote control, and a wide angle lens that will cover the room entirely.' When he felt the time had come Glenn planned to send his friends away, back to America or Canada. The videotape would then show that there was no one else around when he died.

'After a sufficient amount of time has passed, preferably enough time for my friends to arrive at their destination, then I'll simply film the whole thing so that there will be no doubt that I did it myself. I'm also leaving in front of me all the documentation – my doctor's diagnosis, prognosis, my will, my Italian will which deals with taking care of house-cleaning after the business. I've actually gone to visit the crematorium here to find out how much it costs. That was an interesting experience and I was a little naughty when I left and said to the dear woman who was quite kind,

"Alla prossima volta" ... "till next time."'

On June 5th, 1998, sensing that time was running out, Miriam Margolyes flew to Rome to see Glenn.

'When I saw him in his apartment,' she told me later, 'I had a feeling that this would be the last time that we met. Something had changed about him, he was physically very depleted and the spark, that special spark he had was gone. And he said "Miriam, I'm not enjoying life any more." I hugged him and I said "I don't know what to say, Glenn," and he said "there's nothing to say, it's all been said." And then he asked me to do something. He said "I want you to phone this apartment on Sunday and if there's no reply, will you please call the concierge?" So I did that, and there *was* no reply and then I phoned the concierge as he'd asked, and there was no reply there either so I tracked down his lawyer, Giuliano Lemme, and he got the landlord the next morning and they opened the door and they found Glenn, dead. He'd killed himself by sucking the contents of the sixty pills that he'd saved through a McDonald's milk shake straw.'

All Glenn's careful planning had succeeded.

After the death had been discovered, the Rome police were called and they confiscated the video equipment, along with the tape in the camera.

Ten days later a few of Glenn's friends, including Miriam and Giuliano, gathered in a bare anteroom in the basement of the hospital where his body had been taken. He had not wanted a religious funeral, but two or three friends read out extracts from letters they'd received, from other members of the Italian forum or from former students. In the background a persistent buzzing sound disrupted the peace and calm that

Glenn's friends had hoped for. It was the sound of an electric screwdriver being used to screw down the lids on other coffins in the basement. Glenn would have been amused.

After the funeral, the friends went for a meal in Glenn's favourite restaurant, and Miriam talked about her feelings:

'It's very strange not having him here and having left him in the coffin in that very curious waiting room where we were. But in another way, of course, he *is* here because we read bits of things that he'd written and his personality is extremely strong and it won't die and I don't feel solemn about his death, I feel great pride in his courage and focus. He was a cameraman and he had great focus, in life and death, and I feel great relief that he was able to die the way he wanted.'

But what of Glenn's last tape?

For months after Glenn's death, Giuliano Lemme tried his best to prise it out of the hands of the Italian police. But they were not to be moved. They said that they had their own inquiries to make and the tape was a key piece of evidence. As the weeks passed, Giuliano tried every legal trick he could think of. Eventually, the police agreed that a copy could be made, but on condition that a policeman attended the copying process. There was then a further delay because the tape was on the NTSC American standard, and most tape copying places in Rome were PAL or SECAM, the British and European standards. More weeks passed until a policeman could be spared for the three hours that the copying would take.

It was almost a year after Glenn died before I opened the package that arrived on my desk from Italy. Giuliano had managed to get the tape copied and, without looking at it, he sent it straight to me.

I closed my office door and put the cassette in the VCR.

I had often thought about the events of the previous May and June. I hadn't been a close friend of Glenn's; I had met him for professional reasons as much as personal ones; I saw it as a challenge to use my skills to help him tell the world, and in fact I had failed. At that point, partly because the tape had taken so long to retrieve, no one knew Glenn's story apart from the friends on the Italian Forum. Several broadcasters I approached to see if they would transmit Glenn's story, made excuses. One Channel 4 commissioning editor said 'no' because 'the BBC already showed a man dying in their *Human Body* series', and another turned it down because 'We're about to repeat a documentary about Dr. Kevorkian.' A BBC producer in charge of disability programmes said 'We don't believe in showing programmes in which disabled people kill themselves – it sets a bad example.'

But the events of Glenn's suicide had stayed with me. It is given to few of us to know when we are going to die, and even fewer to decide the time. And no one, you would think, particularly when killing himself, could be expected to die with equanimity, good humour and concern for his friends. So how had Glenn died?

I press the 'Play' button on the video.

After Elvis finishes singing 'Are You Lonesome Tonight?' the radio blares on with a rapid-fire Italian news bulletin. Slowly Glenn shifts round in his wheelchair to the table behind and picks up the bottle of blackcurrant juice. He turns back, and tries to pour it into the bowl. As the bottle rests on his crippled hands I have the momentary fear that it might fall on the floor. A paradoxical fear, since if it falls and spills Glenn will live; if he succeeds with the tricky operation he will die. Watching, I want him to succeed. Suddenly as he points the bottle towards the bowl it tips to one side, pouring juice on the table. Glenn tips it up again and pauses. What is he feeling? Has he left it too late, to a point where he cannot now do the deed? He tries again as the radio plays a soupy Italian song. This time the rest of the blackcurrant juice pours into the bowl. Carefully, painfully, he manoeuvres the bottle upright in his hands and slowly leans forward to put it on the table. You wonder why he bothers. Why couldn't he just let it drop from his hands? What does tidiness matter now? But Glenn has planned a dignified exit and untidiness is not part of the plan. Next, he rotates the bowl so that the side with the spilled blackcurrant juice on the rim is pointing away from him. He picks up a jar and shakes something from it into the bowl, probably the contents of the capsules. This time he lets the empty jar drop to the floor. He then picks up a spoon and tries to stir the mixture. He gets sticky blackcurrant juice on his hand and licks his fingers. Then, almost as if to throw a veil over the proceedings, the camera mysteriously goes out of focus. Behind the veil we can just see Glenn lean forward. He is probably taking a straw out of the tumbler it was in. Over the next few minutes he appears to lean forward, take a sip and lean back again, but it is difficult to be sure, the picture is so out of focus. As I watch this slow motion behaviour I realise that everything in this last film sequence directed by Glenn has a purpose. The banal Italian pop music on the radio is to provide the police with a timeline to show when the event actually occurred. The candle, slowly burning down, is to show that there has been no editing after the event, to remove evidence of an accomplice, for example.

The camera refocusses as mysteriously as it defocussed and we see Glenn pick up a glass of water with a straw and drink from it. Then he looks up for the first time, breathes heavily and shifts in his chair. He looks around the room. He seems to be thinking. The sobbing voice of the Italian singer rises in a crescendo. And then Glen speaks. 'I want to die...' he says, raising his voice above the music. 'I have done this myself. My greatest fear is that it doesn't work. No one else is involved in this so-called crime. I am killing myself.' He pauses, and as if on some weirdly intended cue, the music changes and the Procol Harum song 'A Whiter Shade of Pale' begins.

'I have prepared for this for months,' Glenn goes on. 'I have amyotrophic lateral sclerosis. There is no cure, there is no treatment. Death was inevitable. I could not dare to live life as a vegetable. I love Roma so much I had to come here. I apologise to the landlords for doing this on their property. All my dear friends, you have made up the meaning in my life. You are very special to me. I love you dearly.'

He then yawns, three times, and his head sinks on his chest. For the next hour or so, Glenn, apparently asleep, takes sporadic breaths. The radio music continues relentlessly, an anonymous, monotonous succession of pop songs. The Rolling Stones sing 'It's all over now' but it isn't quite, as a deeply unconscious Glenn takes his final three breaths. Shortly afterwards, the candle flame flickers and dies.

Glenn Scott died on June 6th, 1998. His friends told me that, after Miriam introduced me to him, he was buoyant at the possibility that the story of his death might now be told to a wider world. But there were already signs that public thinking was moving his way. Around the time of Glenn's illness, the state of Oregon brought in a law allowing physician-assisted suicide under stringent conditions. The person:

- must be terminally ill
- must have 6 months or less to live
- must make two oral requests for assistance in dying
- must make one written request for assistance
- must convince two physicians that she/he is sincere, is not acting on a whim, and that the decision is voluntary
- must not have been influenced by depression
- must be informed of 'the feasible alternatives, including, but not limited to, comfort care, hospice care and pain control.'
- must wait for 15 days

Glenn would have fulfilled every one of those conditions. In the year he died, fifteen Oregonians took advantage of the state law to die before experiencing the worst consequences of their terminal illnesses. Glenn, a Canadian, was not able to take advantage of that law.

The documentary described in this section can be viewed on YouTube at: http://youtu.be/9RXQLF9uTL0

10

Palliative care:
The promise and the reality

Let's all be Friends At The End.

Michael Irwin and Colin Brewer

Many of us, unless we are fortunate enough to die suddenly from something like a massive heart attack or stroke, can expect to receive some palliative care when we develop our final incurable illness. In the last few decades, palliative care has moved out of the shadows and is now a very important branch of medicine. In Britain, we have what seems to be internationally recognised as one of the best palliative care systems in the world and it has made a major contribution to the more humane treatment of the dying throughout the world. There is still a primary focus on patients suffering from cancer but the principles and practices of palliative care are increasingly being integrated into mainstream medical practice, both in and out of hospitals.

Opponents of medically-assisted rational suicide (MARS) often claim that one of the reasons that MARS and voluntary euthanasia have been so readily accepted in The Netherlands is that there are so few hospices in that country. There may have been some truth in that claim twenty or thirty years ago but if the Dutch at one time lagged behind Britain in this field, they now have good and well-integrated palliative care services. Indeed, investment in palliative care services tends to increase in countries where MARS is legal as in Belgium, the Netherlands and Oregon. In 2011, the European Association of Palliative Care stated: 'The idea that legalisation of euthanasia and/or assisted suicide might obstruct or halt palliative care development ... seems unwarranted and is only expressed in commentaries rather than demonstrated by empirical evidence ... There is scant evidence of the supposed underdevelopment of palliative care'.[1]

Unfortunately, some British palliative care clinicians – both doctors and nurses – seem to believe that if they try very hard, they can minimise or abolish the possibility that their patients will request MARS or even think of it. In their view, such requests can only mean that the patient is receiving inadequate palliative care and that with better treatment, the fears and concerns that led to a request for deliverance will not arise. They imply that they can adequately handle all problems likely to arise in the treatment of dying or progressively disabled patients. Many people now know – quite often from the experience of visiting family members in hospices – that this is not true.

Doctors are not always open about their end-of-life management practices but may be more revealing in anonymous surveys. In 2009, *Palliative Medicine* (the main British professional journal in this field) published the results of a survey[2] involving 2,869 British doctors in 2007-2008.

It found that one-sixth of all the deaths in this country were actually hastened by the deliberate, compassionate use of terminal sedation, invoking the 'double effect' doctrine. More surprisingly, perhaps, it also showed that about one thousand cases of illegal voluntary euthanasia and about two thousand cases of equally illegal non-voluntary (though doubtless compassionate) euthanasia, were occurring annually in Britain.

In her book *The Dying Process*, published in 2000, Julia Lawton described her study of the experiences of terminally ill palliative care patients.[3] It revealed with distressing clarity just how far some people can decline in hospices – physically and mentally – before they actually die. Lawton apparently began her study with no particularly strong views either way about palliative and hospice care (or deliverance) and simply encouraged patients, visiting family members and palliative care staff to talk openly about the everyday practices of the mid-1990s when British palliative care was already quite highly developed. Unlike most researchers in this area, she combined research with becoming a volunteer worker in a hospice and thus got to know the patients – and perhaps the staff as well – more intimately than most such studies permit. Some 200 patients died at the hospice during her time there.

Although she wondered whether published accounts of hospices by palliative care physicians might have been a little rose-tinted, she seems to have been rather surprised – even shocked – by what she found. It is a pity that Lawton's monograph is not better known than it seems to be among hospice staff, not to mention potential hospice patients – which is to say, nearly all of us. Apart from the unwelcome nature of its findings to many hospice workers, the reason may be that Lawton wrote as an anthropologist who used the methods of participant ethnographic study, first developed among exotic tribes by people like Margaret Mead. More to the point, she also writes – not surprisingly – in a classic ethnographic style. This is not really a criticism but phrases like 'the centrality of bodily unboundedness', 'rhetorics of individuality', 'contextual knowing' and 'self-identity is an existential cultural performance' are hard going for the uninitiated (which certainly includes us).

It is possible that what Lawton observed was not typical of terminal care at the best hospices in the country. Equally, it is unlikely that she just happened to choose one of the worst. It is also possible that there have been some technical advances since then, though faeces and vomit have not changed their smell or unwelcomeness. One of her main findings was the tendency of hospices to 'sequestrate the "dirty work."' While hospices like to present themselves as places where people can die in peace and dignity (and Lawton stresses that this was what many patients experienced) there were a significant minority of patients with intractable faecal incontinence who – to put it bluntly – stank the place out, despite the best efforts of the staff, and caused great distress to other patients and their visitors (and themselves). Hospices tried to keep such patients out of view (which meant that they often had little of the contact with other patients that some of them valued) but they could not so easily keep them out of smell, as it were. Sometimes, intestinal obstruction from tumours caused patients not merely to vomit repeatedly but to vomit their own faeces. Other examples of what staff called 'poor symptom control' included fungating tumours – i.e. in Lawton's words, 'the rotting away of a tumour site on the surface of the skin'.

One patient, Dolly, incontinent and with faecal vomiting,

regularly requested voluntary euthanasia for a week after her final admission. Eventually she stopped asking for it, because she stopped talking entirely. When staff attended her, she closed her eyes and 'totally ignored them.' Deborah stopped eating and drinking – and also speaking to the staff – for a week until death released her. Another patient, Kath, also asked to be put out of her distress after saying 'on repeated occasions' that 'you wouldn't put a dog through this.' The stench created by Annie – who lingered for six weeks – reached to the reception area and was so dreadful that badly-needed beds vacated by dead patients were not refilled. If staff could barely cope with this sort of thing, it is not surprising that family members often made their excuses and left. Hospice staff tended to define 'dying' as the point where a patient became comatose. Patients and concerned family members had a wider range of views. One ex-soldier said that he had seen many people die in his time but none of the deaths had been so 'cruel and disgusting' as his wife's.

Pain 'could not always be controlled.' In any case, effective pain relief often meant that patients simply became more aware of other – and more intractable – problems. Some patients died not in pain or incontinence but in terrifying states of delirium. Ironically, this sometimes included a belief that the staff were trying to kill them. Persistently and noisily distressed patients could naturally distress the staff as well, who admitted that they often administered heavy sedation in such cases because they disliked being confronted with such obvious and vocal failures of control. Heavy sedation may make patients quieter but can make confusion even worse.

Lawton's experiences led her to question the ideology, central to the hospice movement, of enabling patients to 'live until they die', because the quality of that last stage of 'living' was not just occasionally but quite often dreadfully poor. These failures were not, in general, due to lack of effort or compassion among palliative care teams. She gave many examples of the kindness of hospice staff, caring not only for their patients but also helping family members, often struggling to know how to behave in the presence of the dying. When most people died at home, the death-bed was not such unfamiliar territory, especially when premature death was not as unusual as it is today.

There should be a lot of common ground between palliative care professionals and right-to-die activists. Both groups use phrases like 'death with dignity' and 'a good death.' Both claim to value compassion and humane care but when it comes to patients' rights, palliative care clinicians generally have a rather one-sided view. Palliative care physicians often seem to value their own 'right' not to be distressed by requests for MARS (with its implication that palliative care has not delivered adequate relief) over the patient's 'right' – desired by the large majority of British citizens – to prefer and request a very different approach to dying.

Traditionally, palliative care has focused mainly on patients in the last few months or weeks of life. Increasingly, it is becoming involved both clinically and philosophically with a much larger and more varied constituency, ranging from mainly elderly people with dementia to generally younger people with progressive neurological disorders such as motor neurone disease or some forms of multiple sclerosis. There are also heart-rending and challenging cases like that of the late Tony Nicklinson with locked-in syndrome. Even if palliative care teams do not like dealing with such cases, they are the people who claim expertise in end-of-life management. They cannot easily avoid becoming involved in a debate in which the collective views of palliative care staff are increasingly at odds with the collective views of the people they have chosen to treat.

Some of them, however, try quite hard not merely to avoid debate but to prevent it. In March 2014, Dr. Philip Nitschke, a well-known Australian activist and founder of EXIT International was invited by doctors at Perth's prestigious Sir Charles Gairdner teaching hospital to give a presentation to a closed, doctors-only breakfast meeting. The invitation said that they had a 'poor understanding' of the issues involved and hoped to learn more. Dr. Nitschke assumed that 'Chatham House rules' (i.e. reportable but not attributable) applied to the meeting, as the convener later confirmed they should have been. It is difficult to imagine that Dr. Nitschke said anything that is not mentioned in this book (except perhaps for the pharmacological details of MARS and self-deliverance). Nevertheless, Dr. Mark Schutze, of the hospital's Department of Pain Management (and thus almost certainly much involved in palliative care) made a formal complaint to the medical registration authorities. Even though Dr. Nitschke is no longer in clinical practice, Dr. Schutze wanted him removed from the medical register.

Very recently, a few British palliative care specialists have broken ranks and started to speak, albeit rather cautiously, about the need to bring palliative care more in line with its patients. Professor Sam Ahmedzai, of Sheffield University, a hospice and palliative medicine consultant for 28 years, described in the British Medical Journal his 'journey from anti to pro assisted dying.'[4] Arguing that professional medical organizations should take neutral positions on MARS, he explained that his views changed following visits to Oregon and the Netherlands, where he saw good palliative care coexisting fairly amicably with MARS. 'It is patronising' he wrote 'to say that a few people should suffer unbearable distress and indignity because palliative care preaches that it values all lives – regardless of how meaningless they have become to their owners', adding: 'it is hypocritical to deny competent patients who are acknowledged to be dying the right to die in the manner of their choosing'.

At the AGM of Healthcare Professionals for Assisted Dying on November 6, 2013, Professor Ahmedzai repeated these views. He emphasised the need to continue clinical innovation but seemed to be advocating philosophical and ethical innovation as well, in order to provide a more patient-focused approach at the end-of-life, including the option of MARS.

In Flanders (the Dutch-speaking area of Belgium), and to a lesser extent in the rest of that country, voluntary euthanasia (as defined in the preface) has become an accepted part of its palliative care system over the last ten years. In the next section, we summarise a paper from a leading palliative care journal (printed in full as Appendix A on p 267) that describes in detail how this development came about. It demonstrates that if palliative care is truly patient-centred, there should be no problem about a dialogue between supporters of palliative care and supporters of active medical involvement in the timing of death. Belgium has had good palliative care services for a long time and the acceptance of MARS was not due to any lack of facilities. The Belgian paper specifically makes a point that bears repeating, if only because our opponents so often claim the contrary:

'After ten years of experience, an intermediate conclusion

is that some of the consequences of the introduction of euthanasia initially feared by its advocates or opponents did not materialise. ... Palliative care was not harmed by the introduction of euthanasia, but on the contrary was forced to develop further. The overall feeling is that end-of-life care in general has substantially improved.'

Good conventional palliative care will continue to be chosen by many patients and will enable many of them, in practice, to have a dignified death. Dignified, that is, both as they experience it and as their families will later recall it. Some of them will change their minds and ask for active deliverance if they find that palliative care does not provide the level of relief that they had expected. Others, expressing a clear preference for MARS, will decline palliative care from the start and for a variety of reasons though occasionally, they too may change their minds and opt later for palliative care. The Benelux countries and Oregon have shown very clearly that good palliative care systems can accommodate these diverse views and desires with remarkably little difficulty. One day, it will almost certainly happen here as well.

References:

1. www.commissiononassisteddying.co.uk/wp-content/uploads/2011/10/EAPC-Briefing-Paper-Palliative-Care-in-Countries-with-a-Euthanasia-Law.pdf

2. Seale C. End-of-life decisions in the UK involving medical practitioners. Palliative Medicine 2009 Apr;23(3):198-204.

3. Lawton J. The dying process. Patients' experiences of palliative care. Abingdon, Routledge. 2000. passim

4. Ahmedzai S. My journey from anti to pro assisted dying BMJ 2012; 9 July 2012 345:e4592

Assisted dying in Flanders: Summary of important paper

(Vanden Berghe P. et al. European Journal of Palliative Care. December 2013. 20(6) pp 266-272)

Colin Brewer

In an appendix [p 267], the editors have republished an important scientific paper, *Assisted dying – the current situation in Flanders*, on the gradual integration of assisted dying procedures with palliative care in Belgium since they were legalized in 2002. Here, we summarise its conclusions, which we think should be more widely known among both doctors and current or potential patients in the rest of the world.

Flanders is the northern, Flemish-speaking part of Belgium. It shares a border and a virtually identical language with the Netherlands. In both countries, voluntary euthanasia (VE) is legal, subject to clearly-stated statutory requirements but the history of VE in the two countries is different.

As mentioned earlier, Dutch palliative care was not very well developed in the 1980s when VE became professionally and legally acceptable, though not yet formally legalized. Although it has been well up to the best international standards for a decade or more, it was often claimed by critics that Dutch acceptance of VE in the 1980s reflected in part the underdevelopment of palliative care in the Netherlands at that time.

In Belgium, that criticism could not have been truthfully made. When VE was legalized in 2002, 'palliative care, initiated in the 1980s by volunteers, was already well developed' and in 2010, 'Belgium took joint 4th place worldwide on the quality of death index of the Economist Intelligence Unit.' Furthermore, as happened in Oregon after MARS was legalized, 'it can also be safely stated that palliative care was not harmed by the introduction of euthanasia, but on the contrary was forced to develop further'.

The co-existence of palliative care and VE did not happen overnight but it is significant that when VE and – in practice – MARS as well (see below) were legalized, two other related laws were simultaneously passed by the Belgian parliament. One affirmed the right of all patients to receive palliative care; the other concerned 'the rights of patients in general.' At first, a 'substantial' proportion of palliative care clinicians (and clinicians in general) were reluctant to become involved in the actual administration of VE/MARS. (I explain the double acronym later.) The authors suggest that there were two main reasons for this reluctance. Firstly – and very understandably – many palliative care clinicians felt that these procedures were both new and radical and that it was not something that doctors usually did. Secondly, there was a 'widespread opinion that optimal palliative care, starting with a thorough clarification of the patient's request for help to end their life, would eliminate the need for euthanasia.'

Yet after ten years of working in a context in which patients have a right to request VE/MARS, while all clinicians have the right to opt out of providing them on conscientious grounds, 'the caring practice of "euthanasia accompaniment" is part of the daily work of palliative care professionals, who support the treating doctor and team in all aspects of the patient's request, while only very occasionally carrying out euthanasia themselves.' This process means that the palliative care team continues to care for the patient, makes sure that no acceptable alternatives to VE/MARS have been ignored and provides support for team members.

This happened in some cases because palliative care clinicians recognized that patients were not actually getting adequate relief from palliative care interventions and that only VE/MARS provided a 'good death' as judged by the patient. In other cases, the patient simply rejected palliative care in order to seek and receive VE or MARS from another physician. Palliative care teams eventually realized that even when VE/MARS was carried out according to guidelines and 'good practice', the fact that it usually involved a last-minute transfer of care from the 'regular and familiar care team' (and sometimes also meant excluding dissenting family members) was not 'optimal care.' Gradually, palliative care teams became more positively engaged, 'at first only as witnesses', seeing this as a lesser evil.

This engagement inevitably exposed them to the benefits of VE/MARS. 'Whether or not all palliative possibilities had been exhausted, the patient was relieved and grateful that their final days did not have to last any longer.' This convinced most of them that VE could be part of genuinely good palliative care. Moreover, 'since the key reasons for euthanasia requests appeared to be a desire to be in control, fear of dependency and existential despair, euthanasia no longer seemed a failure of, or antagonistic to, palliative care, but something that could be served by it.' Gradually, palliative care teams became more involved with preparations for VE/MARS. Instead of abandoning their patients, they continued to care for them and provide the best possible symptom relief right up to the moment when patients chose to terminate their own suffering (and perhaps also the suffering of their carers and families). Indeed, it came to be regarded as bad practice for patients to be transferred from the palliative care team in their final few days or hours.

As early as 2003 – only a year after legalization of VE – the Flanders Federation of Palliative Care published its first guidelines on integrating VE and palliative care. A further 'framework document on treatment decisions in advanced disease' appeared in 2006 and further guidelines in 2011, which restated the value of specialist palliative care in 'difficult-to-treat symptoms and end-of-life issues' but added a very important rider. Multi-disciplinary palliative care clinicians, with their specialist clinical and communication skills, 'are well qualified to practice end-of-life care and also provide euthanasia accompaniment both in a [legally] careful … and caring way.' They should also support GPs in enabling patients to die at home, where possible, rather than in hospital. While the right of conscientious objection is clearly recognized, it is expected that clinicians who want to opt out do so 'clearly, forthrightly and, above all, in a timely manner', presumably so that patients do not have to make alternative arrangements in unseemly and distressing haste.

It is important to summarise some of the authors' reservations as well. The main ones are what they call 'proceduralism', 'legalism' and 'instrumentalism.' The first two mean that because VE/MARS is the only aspect of end-of-life (EOL) care that is legally defined, clinicians may think that 'meeting those legal conditions is in itself a sufficient condition for good care', though they note that the same problem may arise with guidelines and care pathways in other areas of medical practice. Because several EOL procedures involve difficult ethical and even legal decisions (e.g. terminal sedation, and withdrawing treatment or nutrition) there may be a temptation to by-pass them in favour of the one procedure that is clearly defined in law. Conversely, the lack of a clear legal framework for such procedures makes them attractive to some clinicians precisely because there is 'no obligation to declare them, and therefore no risk of questions being raised, or even prosecution being conducted'.

'Instrumentalism' means that EOL interventions such as VE/MARS 'are seen as an instrument to end a process of disease (or old age) that is demanding and difficult to bear, instead of letting it follow its course.' Increasingly, it seems, family members 'consider the dying process as undignified, useless and meaningless, even if it happens peacefully, comfortably and with professional support.' (Though the authors do not say so specifically, it may be that such attitudes are most likely to be voiced when the patient is no longer able to state a preference. In this situation, if such family wishes are acted on, the dying process would typically be shortened by hours or days rather than by weeks or months.)

It is not clear why the reported changes in the attitude of palliative care teams to VE/MARS have happened mainly in Flanders and the linguistically-mixed area around Brussels but 'probably not yet to the same extent' in French-speaking Wallonia. Religious factors seem an unlikely explanation, since Roman Catholicism is the predominant faith of believers in both areas. However, it seems likely that cooperation between providers of palliative care and providers of VE/MARS and the increasing interchangeability of their roles will continue and will spread to all areas of Belgium.

The importance of this paper is that it provides a likely template and timetable for similar changes in Britain when VE and/or MARS become legal. Many doctors and medical disciplinary bodies were once as antagonistic to contraception and abortion as many now are to VE and MARS. Eventually, the large majority finally accepted them as a normal part of medical practice – as did most patients. At the very least, they agreed to disagree and to co-exist. Unsurprisingly, not all Belgian palliative care physicians agreed with the authors' conclusions but in the course of what is clearly a continuing debate in Belgium, two leading palliative care physicians who support the inclusion of VE/MARS in terminal care noted some interesting additional findings from other Belgian surveys. Firstly, in a survey of Belgian palliative care nurses with a high (70%) response rate, nearly 80% of responders were 'mildly or firmly' in favour of legalized VE. Only 22% were opposed 'and then only mildly.' That suggests that this expected process of gradual acceptance has already occurred in Belgium.

Secondly, 'receiving spiritual care was associated with higher frequencies of [VE] than receiving little spiritual care.' There are several possible explanations for this arguably counter-intuitive finding. One might be that Belgian priests are not particularly antagonistic to VE/MARS. Alternatively, if Belgian patients have the same low prevalence of strong religious beliefs as is typical of many Western European societies, they may feel more inclined to include VE/MARS in their options for terminal care after they have considered and rejected the traditional dogmatic religious objections to them. It might, on the other hand, be simply a selection effect. That is, the sort of people who seek or welcome 'spiritual' advice might be precisely the sort of well-educated, middle-class people who (if Oregon is any guide) are most likely to want to take control of their deaths.

Their third point was a more general one. 'This controversy relates to a larger societal issue: enfranchised individuals, whether patients or caregivers, can reject or accept euthanasia but they must respect each other, and in an advanced society neither stance should remain imposed or become imposed.'[1] That state of mutual tolerance has clearly arrived in Belgium. Furthermore, while clinicians cannot be forced to carry out procedures that they regard as ethically unacceptable, the proportion of clinicians holding such views seems to have declined quite sharply.

Finally, the promised explanation for the use of that rather clumsy double acronym 'VE/MARS' throughout this summary. An earlier Belgian paper[2] describing the classes of drugs prescribed in 2007 for ending life, as well as the status of the people who actually administered them (physician, nurse or patient) showed that the prescribing physician was present in 86.7% of cases. In this apparently representative Belgian patient sample, the physician administered the drugs in 69.6% of cases. In the remainder, they were administered by a nurse (18.9%), nurse and physician combined (8.1%), the patient himself or herself (1%) or the physician and patient combined (2.4%). While it is evident from the nature of the drugs that in many cases, some or all of the lethal medication was given by intravenous or intramuscular injection, some patients apparently swallowed medication handed to them by a nurse or physician in what was clearly an act of medically-assisted suicide rather than VE – as we defined the terms in the Preface. As in other areas of medical practice, we think that patients should be offered a choice in what may be literally as well as figuratively a matter of taste. Some patients may prefer to symbolise their active involvement and agreement by swallowing at least some of the medication. Others may find swallowing difficult but would want to initiate an intravenous infusion themselves for the same symbolic reasons. Some may prefer the relatively slow onset of unconsciousness from oral medication while others may prefer the rapid unconsciousness obtainable only with intravenous medication. Others still may choose injection rather than swallowing because they want their final taste experience to be of something pleasant rather than bitter, as most of the drugs are.

When MARS becomes legalized in Britain, many people will simply be grateful that they have the choice at last and will be relatively unconcerned about how it is done. Once it becomes a routine option, such details will become more important. Henry Ford famously told the buyers of the world's first mass-produced car that they could have any colour they liked, as long as it was black. At first, most customers were probably untroubled by this imposed uniformity but before long, they wanted their cars to reflect their tastes and personalities, as had always been possible for the buyers of luxury, custom-built vehicles. As with giving birth, so it will be in leaving life.

References:

1. Bernheim J, Mulie A. Euthanasia and Palliative Care in Belgium: Legitimate Concerns and Unsubstantiated Grievances. J Pall Med 2010, 13(7) 798-9.

2. Chambaere K, Bilsen J, Cohen J, Onwuteaka-Philipsen BD, Mortier F, Deliens L. . CMAJ. 2010 Jun 15;182(9):895-901.

Putting people to sleep.

Katharine Whitehorn

It has often been said that the British treat their animals better than their people, care more for their pets than their relatives; it's a view that might be endorsed by a recent scuffle between the RSPCA and the Crown Prosecution Service, who had to intervene to stop the RSPCA persecuting one Julia Nadian for *failing* to put her ailing cats to sleep. They even launched a two day operation involving the police, to seize the cats and give them their quietus, though Nadian said they were old and sick and suffering a bit but not that bad. It's accepted everywhere that it is cruel to keep a very sick and suffering animal alive, but the same, understandably doesn't seem to go for sick and suffering people. The controversy about assisted suicide goes on, and some of us hope we're getting nearer to being let off the worst last days, but most of the versions of assisted suicide being discussed limit it to people who are pretty certain to die in a short time anyway; but if it was me I would dread far more than suffering just weeks before the end the prospect of being incapacitated, blind and paralysed for years, like the wretched Tony Nicklinson who could only communicate via his eyelids. Nobody insists a cat has to be within weeks of death before we let it go; surely we should not deny release to humans with nothing but wretchedness ahead.

Originally published in the Observer, 30th March 2014.

Appendix

Assisted dying – the current situation in Flanders: euthanasia embedded in palliative care

Paul Vanden Berghe, Arsène Mullie, Marc Desmet and Gert Huysmans.
European Journal of Palliative Care. December 2013. 20(6) pp 266-272

I n 2002, three laws concerning the end of life were almost simultaneously passed by the Belgian parliament: a law decriminalising euthanasia, a law affirming the right to palliative care for all and a law concerning the rights of patients in general. At that time, a substantial part of the Belgian palliative care community, like the Belgian healthcare community in general, was very reluctant to become involved in euthanasia, for different reasons. One of them was the radical nature of the act of euthanasia (defined in Belgian law as 'the intentional termination of the life of another person at his/her request'[1]), which is completely at odds with everything healthcare professionals are usually taught. Another reason was the widespread opinion that optimal palliative care, starting with a thorough clarification of the patient's request for help to end their life, would eliminate the need for euthanasia.

Ten years later, in Flanders (the northern, Dutch-speaking part of Belgium), and to a lesser extent in the rest of the country, the caring practice of 'euthanasia accompaniment' (*euthanasiabegeleiding*) is part of the daily work of palliative care professionals, who support the treating doctor and team in all aspects of the patient's request, while only very occasionally carrying out euthanasia themselves. This 'euthanasia accompaniment' includes clarification of the request, communication with the family, consideration of other possibilities, medical and other assistance if euthanasia is performed, and support of the team afterwards. It takes place with full respect for each professional's personal choice regarding their involvement. How did this major shift happen and what questions does it raise?

This shift in mindsets and attitudes was induced by different experiences. In some cases, palliative care professionals were finding that patients' responses to palliative care interventions were poor and that euthanasia effectively appeared to bring a 'good death.' In other cases, palliative care professionals were declining patients' requests for euthanasia and subsequently finding themselves confronted with a situation where patients nevertheless received euthanasia, but from an external medical practitioner. Even if this was done following state-of-the-art guidelines and good practice, the fact that it happened outside the context of the regular and familiar care team (treating physician, family nurse ...) sometimes without the knowledge of the family, made those palliative care professionals realise that it was not optimal care. For them, the change to a more positive engagement, first as witnesses only, was clearly a 'lesser evil.' In a large number of cases, they witnessed euthanasia that was being correctly administrated from a medical point of view, after thorough clarification of the patient's request and adequate communication, and that had good results. Whether or not all palliative possibilities had been exhausted, the patient was relieved and grateful that their final days did not have to last any longer. This convinced those professionals that euthanasia could be part of genuinely good care. Moreover, since the key reasons for euthanasia requests appeared to be a desire to be in control, fear of dependency and existential despair, euthanasia no longer seemed a failure of, or antagonistic to, palliative care, but something that could be served by it. These different experiences led to the growing involvement of palliative care professionals and teams in the accompaniment of euthanasia. In the name of continuity of care, they chose not to abandon patients asking for euthanasia by referring them to external practitioners, outside the familiar care environment, but to continue to provide them with all the necessary support.

Through this growing involvement, what is and should be the natural stance gradually became clearer: for the sake of good care, transferring a palliative patient requesting euthanasia outside their familiar care environment is never the best option. This stance was actively supported from the beginning by the Federatie Palliatieve Zorg Vlaanderen (Federation of Palliative Care Flanders [FPCF]) in numerous ways: through team consultation, guided group supervision of the different professionals involved in palliative care (doctors, nurses, psychologists, social workers) and education on how palliative care could open up to euthanasia. This happened at all levels, within care organisations but also within regional networks members of the FPCF. In 2003, under the direction of its Steering Group for Ethics (with Professor Bert Broeckaert from the University of Leuven as ethical advisor), the FPCF published a reference text on how to deal with euthanasia and other forms of medically assisted dying.[2] In 2006, it published a framework document on treatment decisions in advanced disease.[3] In 2011, a reference document on palliative care and euthanasia[4] was unanimously accepted by the Federation's Board of Directors. It both confirmed and supported the evolution of the past decade. This document states that the complexity of a number of difficult-to-treat symptoms and end-of-life issues often exceeds the competence of primary caregivers. In such cases, the advice of the palliative team, which is particularly knowledgeable in crucial domains (physical suffering that is difficult to relieve, unrecognised depression, guilt issues, pressure from the family, loss of meaning, and so on) has an important added value. Specialist palliative care advice is particularly recommended when it comes to inform patients who ask for euthanasia about the palliative possibilities, as required by the Belgian law on euthanasia. In this way, both patient and physician can be sure that there is really 'no other reasonable solution' to relieve the intolerable suffering – which again is a requirement of the law (see Box).

This reference document further states that palliative care teams, with their multidisciplinary character, possess the highest standards of palliative care skills (including communication skills) and thus are well qualified to practice end-of-life care and also provide euthanasia accompaniment both in a careful (regarding the legal conditions) and caring way. These palliative care teams act as secondary teams: they do not take over the patient's care but support the familiar primary healthcare professionals, who are thus trained, looked after and strengthened.

Where are we today?

Today, one in two non-sudden deaths in Flanders occurs with the support of specialist palliative care professionals,[5] whether within mobile homecare teams, hospital support teams (which are available in every hospital), hospital palliative care units (there are 29 in the region totalling 209 beds) or through 'reference persons for palliative care' in homes for the elderly. In 2011, 1,133 cases of euthanasia were reported to the Belgian Federal Euthanasia Control and Evaluation Committee. Unofficial figures show 1,430 cases in 2012 and 445 in the first quarter of 2013. In 2011, 918 of the 1,133 cases were registered in Dutch, which amounts to about 1% of all deaths in Flanders.[6] If the 2007 estimated number of unreported cases is taken into account,[7] this figure comes to 1.9%. No data are yet available on the provision and extent of specialist palliative support in the reported – and unreported – cases of euthanasia. However, we can safely say that, during the past few years, all palliative care teams in home care and hospital settings in Flanders have been providing support in the care of people requesting euthanasia. Some hospitals are more restrictive than others, imposing additional conditions on the practice of euthanasia, such as obligatory intervention by the palliative care team. According to the WHO definition of palliative care,[8] palliative care should not intend to hasten death. Therefore, euthanasia cannot be part of palliative care. However, we think that euthanasia and palliative care can occasionally be considered together when caring for one and the same patient. This does not necessarily mean that we systematically perform euthanasia when a patient requests it. Only a small number of requests eventually lead to actual euthanasia.

Palliative care not harmed but strengthened

Euthanasia was introduced in Belgium in a generally cautious way, and this certainly has something to do with the fact that palliative care, initiated in the 1980s by volunteers, was already well developed before 2002.[910] Belgian palliative care had had a head start over euthanasia practice, which remained exceptional in the country (by contrast, in the Netherlands, the law authorising physician-assisted dying and euthanasia that came into effect in 2002[11] decriminalised an already existing euthanasia practice). In 2010, Belgium took joint fourth place worldwide on the quality of death index of the Economist Intelligence Unit.[12]

This provided a favourable context for palliative care professionals to support patients asking for euthanasia in the most careful and caring way. After ten years of experience, an intermediate conclusion is that some of the consequences of the introduction of euthanasia initially feared by its advocates or opponents did not materialise. Palliative care did not obstruct or delay the performance of euthanasia. Conversely, it can also be safely stated that palliative care was not harmed by the introduction of euthanasia, but on the contrary was forced to develop further. The overall feeling is that end-of-life care in general has substantially improved. Healthcare professionals and patients alike are more knowledgeable on end-of-life care; they are better able to distinguish between the six or seven broad choices that can be made regarding end-of-life care; the demands of patients are better acknowledged; and professionals are more aware of what they are doing. It is the experience of many of us that the developments seen in the last ten years have resulted in more professional end-of-life care that better responds to patients' wishes. End-of-life care is certainly not perfect yet, but this has more to do with the huge workload and lack of staff (notably nurses) to cope with increasing demand. Standards of care are rising – obviously a good thing – partly because of the influence of palliative care, which in a way has become a victim of its own success (professionals caregivers are significantly overburdened). There is no indication of an alarming increase in the number of euthanasia cases or of significant misuse of any medically assisted end-of-life decision (such as alleviation of pain, palliative sedation, assisted dying without request, and so on). On the contrary, the decriminalisation of euthanasia has stimulated more thorough communication around end-of-life care, starting with advance care planning, between patients and their close relatives, but also between patients/relatives and professional caregivers. This communication is happening at the micro level of the individual, the intermediate level of institutions and organisations, and the macro level of public policy (including around financial and ethical issues). Patients have the right to consent to or refuse a treatment, at any moment, including at the end of life, as well as the right to request euthanasia (which is not the same thing as the right to euthanasia, which does not exist in Belgium). Our experience indicates that the provision of care at the end of life results in the greatest satisfaction when patients' families, proxies and informal caregivers are involved as partners in the process. In Flanders this is commonly called 'autonomy in relationship' (*autonomie in verbondenheid*): close relatives do not obstruct the expression of the patient's autonomy, but their involvement can help the patient clarify his/her own wishes and achieve their realisation in the most comprehensive way.

According to the Belgian law on euthanasia passed on 28 May 2002, the major legal requirements for performing euthanasia are:

- Repeated and consistent request from an adult patient who is competent (that is, who has full mental capacity), made under no external pressure and in writing (or expressed in a written

- Advance directive in the case of a patient in an irreversible state of unconsciousness)

- Persistent and intolerable suffering, physical and/or mental

- Caused by an irreversible medical condition (accident or disease)

- If patient not expected to die within foreseeable future, two independent colleagues must be consulted and a moratorium of one month must be respected between the patient's written request and the administration of euthanasia

- Patient duly informed of their condition, life expectancy and other therapeutic options, including those offered by palliative care

- Patient and doctor reaching the conclusion that there is no other reasonable solution

- Discussion of the request by the doctor with significant others, if patient wishes so

- Euthanasia carried out by a doctor after consultation with the nursing team and one competent and independent colleague; the doctor has to be present until the patient's death

- Case reported to the Belgian Federal Euthanasia Control and Evaluation Committee

A true ethical labour

This article should not suggest that any of these matters are taken lightly, let alone trivialised. In all communication, special attention is given not to convey the implicit message that a palliative care professional is only a true professional if they can 'go the full way' in matters of euthanasia, whether as a physician, nurse, psychologist, social worker, spiritual caregiver or any other member of the palliative care team. The law states that no healthcare professional can be forced to be involved in the act of euthanasia. Every professional has the right to set their own ethical limits. What is expected of them is that they indicate these limits clearly, forthrightly and, above all, in a timely manner. From our experience, it is actually recommended that critical voices remain present in the team as it advances in the decision-making process. It must be stressed that, in the course of these recent evolutions, the palliative care community of Belgium has been – and still is – carrying out a profound ethical labour. The situation described and views expressed in this article are the result of an intensive reflection, not only by ethicists, but first and most importantly by every single professional in Belgian palliative care, including on personal presuppositions, convictions, pace and outcomes, carried out at the level of the individual, teams and organisations involved.

Issues and concerns

Yet, despite the favourable context and the constant engagement of numerous healthcare professionals and organisations, there are issues and concerns, which can be described as insidious side-effects of the introduction of euthanasia in the general landscape of care in Belgium. There are three major threats – that of legalism and proceduralism, of euthanasia following its own course and of instrumentalisation – all of which are at odds with the spirit of (palliative) care.

Legalism and proceduralism

All (medical) care practice occurs against a general legal background, but the fact that there is a law for that one single intervention, euthanasia, has undoubtedly increased the trend towards proceduralism and legalism in end-of-life care. The regulation of euthanasia by a law articulating precise conditions and procedures provides not only society, but also healthcare professionals, with some reassurance that it is correctly performed. When (and only when) all legal conditions are met, euthanasia does not equate to murder, but to a legal life-ending act. The danger of legalism emerges when people think that meeting those legal conditions is in itself a sufficient condition for good care. This problem does not only occur with legal requirements, or in end-of-life care, but also with all kinds of tools (for example, guidelines and care pathways), and in all healthcare domains. What is specific in the case of euthanasia is that some professionals start perceiving all other end-of-life interventions, which are not specifically subject to a legal framework, as not being legal. This erroneous view can be more or less explicit, but when it affects end-of-life care practice, it raises the threshold for interventions other than euthanasia – such as withdrawing or withholding treatment, refusal of treatment, intensification of symptom control or palliative sedation – which are no less necessary, have their own indications and occur far more often.

Conversely, some professionals may be tempted to avoid euthanasia and steer care towards other end-of-life interventions precisely because there is no specific legal framework regulating them (no formal procedure, no legal conditions, no obligation to declare them), and therefore no risk of questions being raised, or even prosecution being conducted by a body such as the Federal Euthanasia Control and Evaluation Committee. It should be clear to professionals that all end-of-life interventions have their own indications and are not interchangeable. This trend has given rise to repeated calls for legislating and/or introducing the compulsory registration of end-of-life interventions that, unlike euthanasia, are strictly medical acts: first palliative sedation, but by extension all types of end-of-life interventions. The assumption is that this would directly improve the quality of care. This is peculiar compared with other fields of healthcare, where it is commonly accepted that quality is not enhanced by legislation, which entails major risks such as loss of flexibility, inaccessibility of certain interventions and an overload of resource-consuming administrative work.

Euthanasia following its own course

Beyond this tendency to want to regulate a broader range of end-of-life interventions, there are also loud calls for an extension of the law on euthanasia to cover other population groups, such as minors, people with advanced dementia and those who are 'tired of living.' There may well be good reasons, and possibly sometimes even majority support among the general public, for such an extension – including among palliative care professionals themselves. There is no indication of an increase in the number of reported cases of euthanasia performed for indications other than those legally accepted. However, these loud calls cannot be missed. Since 2002, over 20 proposals to change the law and extend the conditions under which euthanasia can be performed have been introduced – so far none have brought about a change in the law. The rationale behind such an extension follows a certain logic. Pointing to forms of suffering other than those covered by the current law that could be terminated by euthanasia, those advocating its extension denounce the existing criteria as arbitrary.

- Age – why euthanasia only from the age of 18, and not 17½ or 15?

- Full mental competence at the moment of the request – what about patients who made a written advance directive for euthanasia when they still had full mental capacity (for example, in the event of dementia), no longer have it, but are not irreversibly unconscious (an irreversibly unconscious patient being the only case in which an advance directive is considered valid)?

- Disease or accident – what about those who are simply 'tired of living'?

- Irreversibility – what about patients who may have a chance of cure if they accept further treatment, but decline it?

- Intolerable suffering – how can you distinguish between present suffering, which might be tolerable, and expected suffering, the expectation in itself becoming a source of intolerable suffering?

Relieving suffering at the end of life being one of the primary concerns of palliative care, these questions must be taken seriously and debated in a society that is in constant evolution. However, for the FPCF – an organisation that believes palliative care should be part of regular healthcare provision – the medical grounds of suffering should be paramount. Given the radical nature of euthanasia – where suffering is 'solved' by terminating the life of the sufferer – it can never be a first resort. To avoid the risk of euthanasia being administered for improper reasons, extending it to further populations groups should only be considered if basic palliative care is fully provided to these groups. The force with which its advocates demand an extension of the law provides, in practice, a good incentive for improving the care given to these groups, which is a positive side-effect – just as greater interest in end-of-life care was a positive side-effect of legalising euthanasia. However, there is an indication that euthanasia, once the barrier of legalisation is passed, tends to develop a dynamic of its own and extend beyond the agreed restrictions, in spite of earlier explicit reassurances that this would not happen – in Belgium, such reassurances were given when the 2002 law was being debated. The effort to extend the law on euthanasia, like the effort to legalise euthanasia in the first place, is not exclusive to Belgium but is on the agenda of many movements worldwide, which often enjoy strong public support. In Flanders, one such organisation, LEIF (LevensEindeInformatieForum – a Forum for End-of-Life Information), was set up in 2003 to provide information and training to physicians who give advice in case of euthanasia. An equivalent, Forum EOL (Forum End Of Life), was later created in Wallonia, the southern, French-speaking part of Belgium. It should be stressed that LEIF has played a major role in favour of patient emancipation and empowerment, which is resulting in better end-of-life care. However, the organisation's outspoken promotion of the autonomy of the individual person – expressed, for example, by its claim to the right of radical self-determination – has made its philosophical viewpoint far removed from mainstream health- and end-of-life care. This restricts collaboration with the established representative organisations of healthcare professionals, in particular palliative care ones. This in turn leads to the risk of a 'twin-track policy' in end-of-life care, characterised by little genuine dialogue between each side and a separation between euthanasia and regular care, in spite of what is often good bedside collaboration between the professionals belonging to organisations supporting euthanasia and those working in organised, regular palliative care (several of whom belong to both groups).[13]

Instrumentalisation

Often, the endeavour to extend the law on euthanasia is not only an expression of genuine concern about suffering, but also a manifestation of the tendency to deal instrumentally with death. End-of-life interventions such as euthanasia are seen as an instrument to end a process of disease (or old age) that is demanding and difficult to bear, instead of letting it follow its course.

Although euthanasia can make a good death possible under certain conditions, its legal introduction has set, or at least amplified, this trend towards instrumentalisation. Healthcare professionals note that family members and proxies tend, much more than before, to consider the dying process as undignified, useless and meaningless, even if it happens peacefully, comfortably and with professional support. Requests made by family members for fast and active interventions from healthcare professionals regarding elderly parents are often very coercive, with little nuance or subtlety. While the mediatisation of end-of-life issues has had many positive side-effects, including the growing awareness that one can express one's own end-of-life care preferences, this trend is without doubt a negative one.

The three major concerns described above tend to disconnect euthanasia from (palliative) care and thus threaten optimal end-of-life care. The problem is not euthanasia as such, but rather its dissociation from the context of (palliative) care. The antagonism is no longer between euthanasia on one hand and palliative care on the other, but between euthanasia outside and euthanasia inside the realm of (palliative) care. Every patient at the end of life has the freedom to call on palliative care or not. In a common position paper, the three Belgian palliative care federations (the FPCF, the Fédération Wallonne des Soins Palliatifs and the Fédération Pluraliste Bruxelloise de Soins Palliatifs et Continus) insisted that they 'respect the choice of patients who want euthanasia' and 'place them in the centre of the process.' They further stated that 'patients must be able to freely and autonomously call upon one or more practitioners of their choice. For one patient, this will be their GP or the specialist in charge of their incurable disease. A second patient will also have recourse to the palliative team that has supported them since they learned about the incurable nature of their disease. A third patient will prefer to call upon a practitioner who is a member of an association such as LEIF or EOL.'[14] This implies a clear rejection of the so-called 'palliative filter'; that is, the obligation that all palliative care possibilities have been examined and exhausted before a patient can receive euthanasia – which is not a requirement of the current Belgian law on euthanasia.

While sharing this point of view, the FPCF also affirms its own vision that high-quality palliative care must offer continuity of care, up to and including euthanasia accompaniment, and at the same time respect the freedom of conscience of each individual professional. In our view, palliative care can guarantee that euthanasia requests will be dealt with in a careful and caring way. The above-mentioned threats do not change the fundamental commitment of the FPCF to participate in the debate and work towards solutions in the face of new medical or societal challenges. The FPCF does not claim to have a monopoly on good care, but affirms its preference for a model of care where euthanasia requests are addressed with an offer – not an obligation – of expert palliative care by the multidisciplinary team. We have learned through experience, including mistakes, that this is in the best interest of patients as well as their families and friends.

> Paul Vanden Berghe, Doctor in Philosophy and Director, Federation of Palliative Care Flanders(FPCF), Belgium;
>
> Arsène Mullie, former anaesthesiologist in palliative home and hospital care, AZ St Jan Hospital, Bruges and FPCF Honorary President;
>
> Marc Desmet, Jesuit and Physician, Hospital Palliative Care Unit, Jessa Hospital, Hasselt and Chairman, FPCF Steering Group for Ethics;
>
> Gert Huysmans, GP and Physician, palliative home and hospice care, Netwerk Palliatieve Zorg Noorderkempen, Wuustwezel and FPCF President

References:

1. Full text of the 2002 Belgian law on euthanasia (in Dutch and in French). www.health.belgium.be/internet2Prd/groups/public/@public/@dg1/@acutecare/documents/ie2law/14888537.pdf (last accessed 13/09/2013)

2. Palliative Care Federation of Flanders. Omgaan met euthanasie en andere vormen van medisch begeleid sterven [Dealing with euthanasia and other forms of medically assisted dying], 2003 (in Dutch).

3. Palliative Care Federation of Flanders. Treatment decisions in advanced disease – A conceptual framework, 2006 (in English). www.palliatief.be/accounts/143/attachments/Research/conceptual__frame work_bb.pdf (last accessed 13/09/2013)

4. Palliative Care Federation of Flanders. Over palliatieve zorg en euthanasia [On palliative care and euthanasia], 2011 (in Dutch). www.palliatief.be/accounts/143/attachments/Standpunten/visietekst_palliatievezorgeuthanasie_def_26092011.pdf (last accessed 13/09/2013)

5. Palliative Care Federation of Flanders. Overlijdens met palliatieve zorg in Vlaanderen 2008–2012 [Reported deaths with specialised palliative care in Flanders 2008–2012]. Data collected under supervision of the Flemish government (in Dutch). www.palliatief.be/template.asp?f=k_en_e_meetinstr_regist_richtl.htm (last accessed 13/09/2013)

6. 5th Report of the Belgian Federal Euthanasia Control and Evaluation Committee (2010–2011) (in Dutch; also available in French). www.health.belgium.be/internet2Prd/groups/public/@public/@dg1/@acutecare/documents/ie2divers/19078961.pdf (last accessed 13/09/2013)

7. Smets T, Bilsen J, Cohen J et al. Reporting of euthanasia in medical practice in Flanders, Belgium: cross sectional analysis of reported and unreported cases. BMJ 2010; 341: c5174.

8. WHO definition of palliative care. www.who.int/cancer/palliative/definition/en/ (last accessed 13/09/2013)

9. Chambaere K, Centeno C, Hernández EA et al. Palliative Care Development in Countries with a Euthanasia Law. Briefing paper for the Commission on Assisted Dying

of the European Association for Palliative Care, 2011.
www.commissiononassisteddying.co.uk/wp-content/
uploads/2011/10/ EAPC-Briefing-Paper-Palliative-Care-in-
Countries-with-a-Euthanasia-Law.pdf (last accessed 13/09/2013)

10. Belgian Health Care Knowledge Centre. Organisation of
palliative care in Belgium, 2009 (in English). https://kce.fgov.
be/publication/report/organisation-of-palliative-care-in-
belgium (last accessed 13/09/2013)

11. Leget C. Assisted dying – the current debate in the
Netherlands. *European Journal of Palliative Care* 2013; 20:
168–171.

12. Latest report of the Belgian Federal Palliative Care Evaluation
Committee, 2008 (in Dutch; also available in French). www.
health.fgov.be/eportal/Healthcare/Specialisedcare/
Chronic,geriatricandpalliative/Palliativecare/index.
htm?fodnlang=nl (last accessed 13/09/2013)

13. Palliative Care Federation of Flanders. End-of-Life Care:
No Twin-Track Policy, 2008 (in English). www.palliatief.be/
accounts/143/attachments/Publicaties/endoflifecare_no
twintrackpolicy.pdf (last accessed 13/09/2013)

14. Common position paper of the three Belgian palliative care
federations, 2010 (unpublished).

Acknowledgments

The editors are most grateful to all the contributors who have written original essays for *"I'll See Myself Out, Thank You"*.

In addition, they would like to thank the following for giving permission to reproduce copyright material:

Associated Newspapers: For the articles by Ann McPherson (*Daily Mail* - November 23, 2010), by Klim McPherson (*Daily Mail* - June 14, 2011), and by Brian Sewell (*Mail on Sunday* - July 14, 2013)

Guardian News & Media: For the article by Katharine Whitehorn (*The Observer* - March 30, 2014)

Hayward Medical Communications: For the article by Paul Vanden Berghe, Arsene Mullie, Marc Desmet and Gert Huysmans, which appeared in the November-December 2013 issue of the European Journal of Palliative Care.

News International: For the article by Melanie Reid (*The Times* - March 27, 2012)

Oxford University Press: For the short extract from "Easeful Death - Is there a case for Assisted Dying?", by Mary Warnock and Elisabeth Macdonald, published in 2008.

Telegraph Media Group: For the article by Minette Marrin (*Sunday Telegraph* - March 19, 1995)

Mary Snowden and Adam Bakker

Useful Contact Details

Some of the following organizations may be of particular interest to those who have read "I'll See Myself Out, Thank You":

Alzheimer's Society

The leading UK care and research charity for individuals with dementia.

Devon House, 58 St. Katharine's Way,
London, E1W 1LB

020 7423 3500

E-mail: enquiries@alzheimers.org.uk

Care Not Killing

Campaigning group opposing voluntary euthanasia and doctor-assisted suicide.

6 Marshalsea Road,
London, SE1 1HL

020 7234 9680

E-mail: info@carenotkilling.org.uk

Compassion in Dying

A charity which is the leading provider of free Advance Decision forms in the UK.

181 Oxford Street, London, W1D 2JT

0800 999 2434

E-mail: info@compassionindying .org.uk

Dignitas

Located near Zurich, this global organization can provide a "doctor-supported accompanied suicide" for seriously-ill foreigners.

P.O. Box 17, CH-8127, Forch, Switzerland

0041 43 366 1070

E-mail: dignitas@dignitas.ch

Dignity in Dying

(formerly the Voluntary Euthanasia Society)

Main campaigning organization in England and Wales to legalize "assisted dying" for terminally-ill, competent adults.

181 Oxford Street, London, W1D 2JT

020 7479 7730

E-mail: info@dignityindying.org.uk

EX International

Based in Berne, this organization provides a doctor-assisted suicide for seriously-ill foreigners.

P.O. Box 1042, CH-3023, Berne, Switzerland

0041 31 311 7123

E-mail: info@exinternational.ch

EXIT

(formerly the Scottish Voluntary Euthanasia Society)

This organization's main activity is researching and promoting methods of self-deliverance through publications (such as "Five Last Acts - The Exit Path") and workshops.

17 Hart Street, Edinburgh, EH1 3RN

0131 556 4404

E-mail: exit@euthanasia.cc

Friends At The End

Main campaigning organization in Scotland to legalize "assisted suicide" for terminally-ill, competent adults and also for those with a progressive, life-shortening condition. It provides Advance Dicision forms specifically for use in Scotland.

11 Westbourne Gardens, Glasgow, G12 9XD

0141 334 4222

E-mail: info@friends-at-the-end.org.uk

Healthcare Professionals for Assisted Dying

Campaigning body for medical, nursing and other healthcare personnel who support changing the law to permit "assisted dying" for terminally-ill, competent adults.

181 Oxford Street, London, W1D 2JT

020 7479 7107

E-mail: office@hpad.org.uk

Huntington's Disease Association

A charity which supports people affected by this disease.

Suite 24, Liverpool Science Park, 131 Mount Pleasant, Liverpool, L3 5TF

0151 331 5444

E-mail: info@hda.org.uk

Lifecircle

Located near Basle, this organization provides a doctor-assisted suicide for seriously-ill foreigners.

P.O. Box 29, CH-4105, Biel-Benken, Switzerland

0041 61 401 1031

E-mail: mail@lifecircle.ch

MedicAlert

This foundation provides ID emblems and keeps detailed medical records on its members - its emergency line is always in operation.

MedicAlert House, 327-329 Witan Court, Upper Fourth Street, Milton Keynes, MK9 1EH

01908 951045

E-mail: info@medicalert.org.uk

Marie Curie Cancer Care, and Macmillan Nurses

Provide nurses for people with terminal illnesses who wish to die at home.

89 Albert Embankment, London, SE1 7TP

0800 716 146, and 020 7840 7840

E-mail: supporter.relations@mariecurie.org.uk, and webmaster@macmillan.org.uk

MIND

The main UK mental health charity which ensures that no one, facing a mental health problem, needs to feel alone.

15-19 Broadway, Stratford, London, E15 4BQ

020 8519 2122

E-mail: contact@mind.org.uk

Motor Neurone Disease Association

Promotes research into MND, and provides support to those affected by this disease.

David Niven House, 10-15 Notre Dame Mews, Northampton, NN1 2BG

01604 250505

E-mail: enquiries@mndassociation.org

Multiple Sclerosis Society

Supporting research into MS, and helping those with this disease.

372 Edgware Road, London, NW2 6ND

020 8438 0700

E-mail: helpline@mssociety.org.uk

National Council for Palliative Care

The umbrella charity for all those involved in palliative and hospice care in the UK.

The Fitzpatrick Building, 188-194 York Way, London, N7 9AS

020 7697 1520

E-mail: enquiries@ncpc.org.uk

Society for Old Age Rational Suicide

Developing discussion on a possible law
to provide elderly, competent individuals, who
are suffering from various illnesses, with the
option of a doctor-assisted suicide.

9 Waverleigh Road, Cranleigh, Surrey GU6 8BZ

01483 273700

E-mail: michael@soars.org.uk

The Samaritans

Provides 24-hour confidential telephone support
for those who are experiencing feelings of
distress, despair or suicidal thoughts.

The Upper Mill, Kingston Road, Ewell,
Surrey KT17 2AF

020 8394 8300, and 08457 90 9090

E-mail: admin@samaritans.org

Index

A

Aberdare, Lord   178

Advance Decisions, *also* Advance Directives   6, 28, 129, 131, 132, 170, 187

Ahmedzai, Prof. Sam   255

Aikenhead, Thomas   188

Alvarez A.   186

Alzheimer's disease   87, 88, 89, 116, 129, 162–166, 168, 173, 190, 220

American Express   235

Arran, Earl of   182

Assisted Dying Bill   112, 174

Assisted Suicide (Scotland) Bill   18, 66

Avebury, Lord   6, 106, 176

B

Bach, J. S.   114

Badham, Rev. Prof. Dr. Paul   4, 81, 135, 185

Baker, Lord, of Dorking   177

Barnard, Dr. Christiaan   210

Bayer, pharmaceutical company   221

Bayles, Michael   158

Beecham, Lord   182

Benelux   3, 8, 257

Berkeley of Knighton, Lord 181

Birt, Lord   176

Blackstone, Baroness   176

Blair of Boughton, Lord 176

Bland, Tony   26, 171

Bogarde, Dirk   212

Bradshaw, John   116

Brewer, Colin   1, 9, 78, 119, 161, 185, 249, 258

British Medical Journal   19, 34, 38, 255

Broeckaert, Prof. Bert   270

Brooke, Lord, of Alverthorpe 177

Browne-Wilkinson, Lord   27

Brown of Eaton-under-Heywood, Lord, 179

Brown, Wilfred   15

Buchan, John   120

Buddhism   74, 187

C

Calvin, John   189

CARE   188, 190

Care Not Killing   188, 191

Carey of Clifton, Lord, 179

Catholic Church   81

Chabot, Dr. Boudewijn   212

Christian attitudes to suicide   5, 81, 185

Christianity   4, 7, 109, 139, 185, 186, 187, 188

Christians   135, 136, 185, 190

Code of Justinian   191

Commission on Assisted Dying   65, 67, 283

Confucianism   187

Council of Braga   187

Council of Toledo   187

Cox, Dr. Nigel   30

Craigavon, Viscount   177

Crisp, Lord   180

Crisp, Quentin   3

D

Darwin, Charles   218

Davies, Jean   5, 209

Davies of Stamford, Lord 179

Dawson of Penn, Lord   10, 45, 86

Democritus of Abdera   183

Denning, Lord Justice   186

Desmet, Marc   267

Dignitas   4, 9, 37, 63, 64, 65, 66, 67, 68, 69, 70, 71, 72, 73, 74, 85, 88, 92, 95, 97, 98, 105, 137, 156, 160, 167, 199, 213, 288

Dignity in Dying   123, 124, 125, 138, 209

Donatist sect   186

Donne, John   18

Downes, Sir Edward   67

Down's syndrome   164

DSM (the Diagnostic and Statistical Manual of the American Psychiatric Association)   80

Dying Process, The (book)   251

E

Economist Intelligence Unit   259, 272

Eidinow, Hannah   96

Elder, Lord   180

Epictetus   18

European Association of Palliative Care   147, 250

European Convention on Human Rights   65, 178, 182, 193

European Court of Human Rights   65, 102

Evening Standard   207

EX International   69, 76, 77, 105, 288

EXIT   18, 206, 255, 289

F

Falconer, Lord   19, 39, 65, 93, 126, 174, 175

Farmer, Angela   102

Farmer, Prof. Richard   19

Federatie Palliatieve Zorg Vlaanderen   269

Final Exit 22

Finkelstein, Lord 181

Forsyte, Mary 232, 240

Forum End Of Life 279

Friends At The End (FATE) 18, 70, 214, 249, 289

G .

Gay Times 75

Gemmel, Nikki 119

General Medical Council (GMC) 144

George V, King 9, 10, 45, 86

Glasgow, Earl of 176

Gordon, Dr. Richard 46

Grayling, Prof. Anthony 6, 192

Guardian (newspaper) 74, 75

Guide to Self-Deliverance 17, 211

H

Hackney Gazette 75

Haneke, Michael 128

Harding, Annette 206

Harries of Pentregarth, Lord 177

Harrison, Lord 181

Harris, Prof. John 6, 139

Haskel, Lord 181

Hawking, Prof. Stephen 55, 230

Healthcare Professionals for Assisted Dying 35, 40, 256, 289

Heidegger, Martin 217

Hill, Geoffrey 61

Hillsborough football crowd disaster 26

Hinduism 187

Hollick, Lord 181

Hosking, Janine 158

Hough, Charlotte 206

Humane Vitae 189

Humphry, Derek 22, 210

Huntington's Disease 72, 164, 290

Hunt, Roger 117

Huxley, Julian 211

Huysmans, Gert 267

I

Ibsen, Henrik 166

ICM poll 103

Illman, John 24

Ironside, Virginia 5, 197

Irwin, Michael 1, 69, 99, 119, 174, 249

J

James, Daniel 67, 156

Jehovah's Witnesses 153, 154

Joad, C.E.M. 186

Joffe, Lord 65, 142, 149, 174, 176

John Paul II, pope 136

Jones, Prof. Steve 7, 217

Justinian, Code of 188

K

Kant, Immanuel 217

Kennedy, Ludovic 15, 22

Kennedy, Ludovic 15, 22, 210

Kevorkian, Dr. Jack 244

Koestler, Arthur 16, 19, 124

Koestler, Cynthia 21

L

Lancet 19, 186, 191
Larner, Chris 4, 95
Lawton, Julia 251
Layard, Lord 182
Leach, Nola 188
Lee, Stewart 7, 224
Lemme, Giuliano 242, 243
Lempert, Dr. Antony 5, 144
Lester of Herne Hill, Lord 175
LevensEindeInformatieForum 279
Leviticus Lobby 29
Lifecircle 69, 105, 290
Liverpool Care Pathway 30, 182
Lloyd-Williams, Dr. Mari 119
Lou Gehrig's disease 85
Low of Dalston, Lord 181
Luley, Silvan 63

M

Macdonald, Elisabeth 133
MacDonald, Margo 18, 66
Maitland, Nan 102
Mallalieu, Baroness 182
Manoir des Quatre Saisons 234
Margolyes, Miriam 229, 242
Marrin, Minette 6, 72, 120
MARS (Medically Assisted Rational Suicide) 1, 2, 5, 7, 19, 23, 26, 29, 31, 33, 78, 82, 83, 84, 86, 88, 89, 92, 101, 103, 152, 154, 161, 164, 167, 168, 185, 190, 249, 250, 254, 255, 256, 257, 259, 260, 261, 262, 263, 264, 265

Martino, Sandra 63

McCallum, Prof. John 117
McDonald's 241, 242
McPherson Dr. Ann 4, 35
McPherson, Klim 4, 39
Meacher, Baroness 177
Mead, Margaret 252
Medical Defence Union 14
Medically-Assisted Rational Suicide *see* MARS
mental capacity 80, 84, 87, 274, 278
Miller, Marion 119
Mill, J. S. 107, 151, 152
Minelli, Ludwig A. 63, 105
Minois, Georges 82
Moggach, Deborah 7, 206
motor neurone disease 5, 7, 54, 85, 169, 230, 254, 291
Moynihan, Lord 10
Mullie, Arsène 267
Munglani, Dr. Rajesh 179
Murphy, Baroness 180
Mustill, Lord 27, 144

N

Neuberger, Baroness 180
Neuberger, Lord 180
Neustatter, Angela 5, 202
Nichols, Liz 102
Nicklinson, Tony 68, 102, 141, 149, 192, 213, 254, 266
Nietzsche, Frederick 18
Nigot, Lisette 157
Nitschke, Philip 157, 255

O

Observer (newspaper) 24, 266

O'Donnell, Dr. Michael 4, 44

Oregon 7, 29, 33, 38, 103, 138, 147, 149, 174, 176, 182, 247, 250, 256, 257, 259, 264

Ottaway, Richard, M.P. 50

P

Parkinson's Disease 20

Paul VI, pope 189

Pearson of Rannock, Lord 182

Pratchett, Terry 98, 133

Procol Harum 246

Purdy, Debbie 37, 146

R

Rée, Prof. Harry 125, 130

Reid, Melanie 5, 49

Richardson of Calow, Baroness 178

Roman Catholic 32, 154, 187, 198

Royall of Blaisdon, Baroness 178

S

Sabbagh, Karl 7, 229

Samaritan 63, 206

Sandwich, Earl of 178

Saunders, Dame Cicely 30, 187

Savulescu, Prof. Julian 6, 150

Scott, Glenn 7, 229-247

Seabright, James 95

Self, Will 7, 220

Sewell, Brian 6, 108

Shakespeare, William 82, 116, 166, 218

Sherbourne of Didsbury, Lord 179

Shipley, Lord 180

Shipman, Harold 36, 60, 171, 205

Sir Charles Gairdner, teaching hospital 255

slippery slope 38, 47, 103, 125, 142, 175, 176, 180, 197

SOARS *see* Society of Old Age Rational Suicide

Society of Old Age Rational Suicide (SOARS) 4, 6, 102, 103, 105, 133

St Augustine 5, 186, 217

St John of the Cross 112

Stocks, Mary 129

Stone of Blackheath, Lord 177

Suicide Act 70, 182, 185, 193

Sunday Times 22, 72, 75

Sydney Morning Herald 157

Syme, Rodney 4, 113, 166

T

Tallis, Prof. Ray 126

Tatchell, Peter 5, 183

Templeton, Sarah-Kate 72

Tindall, Gillian 15

Tindall, Gillian 6, 122

Tonge, Baroness 178

Torquemada 189

Turner, Matthew 190

U

University of Leuven 270

V

Vanden Berghe, Dr. Paul   7, 267

VES *see* Voluntary Euthanasia
    Society

Voltaire, pen-name of François-
    Marie Arouet 217

Voluntary Euthanasia Society 6, 10,
    15, 16, 17, 18, 23, 25, 101, 123,
    124, 209, 210, 211, 288, 289

W

Warnock, Baroness Mary 5, 6, 133,
    161, 167, 178

Warnock, Baroness Mary   130, 133

Warwick, Baroness, of Undercliffe
    176

Wells, H.G.   211

Wheatcroft, Baroness   178

Whitehorn, Katharine   8, 266

Wigley, Lord   176

Wilson, Dr. Libby 5, 214

Woodhead, Chris 5, 53

Wootton, Baroness   185, 186

World Federation of Right to Die
    Societies (WFRTDS) 210

World Medicine 13, 19, 44